Dog Love Stories

Dog Love Stories

The Canines Who Changed Me

a memoir

Patricia Eagle

SHE WRITES PRESS

Copyright © 2025 Patricia Eagle

All rights reserved. No part of this publication may be reproduced, distributed, or transmitted in any form or by any means, including photocopying, recording, digital scanning, or other electronic or mechanical methods, without the prior written permission of the publisher, except in the case of brief quotations embodied in critical reviews and certain other noncommercial uses permitted by copyright law. For permission requests, please address She Writes Press.

Published 2025

Printed in the United States of America

Print ISBN: 978-1-64742-852-5

E-ISBN: 978-1-64742-853-2

Library of Congress Control Number: 2024923007

For information, address:
She Writes Press
1569 Solano Ave #546
Berkeley, CA 94707

Interior sketches by Tom Laetz
Interior design and typeset by Katherine Lloyd, The DESK

She Writes Press is a division of SparkPoint Studio, LLC.

Company and/or product names that are trade names, logos, trademarks, and/or registered trademarks of third parties are the property of their respective owners and are used in this book for purposes of identification and information only under the Fair Use Doctrine.

NO AI TRAINING: Without in any way limiting the author's [and publisher's] exclusive rights under copyright, any use of this publication to "train" generative artificial intelligence (AI) technologies to generate text is expressly prohibited. The author reserves all rights to license uses of this work for generative AI training and development of machine learning language models.

Names and identifying characteristics have been changed
to protect the privacy of certain individuals.

for Bill
wherever you're traveling in the cosmos
may our pack of pups be with you

Contents

	Introduction	1
One	Dabb	5
Two	Bandi-Lune	17
Three	Dancer	45
Four	Bebe	83
Five	Pookie	93
Six	Zorro	129
Seven	Gavroche Napoléon	137
Eight	Amber Grace	173
Nine	Mercy Mercy Me	199
Ten	Goodness Gracious	229
	Epilogue	245
	Notes	247
	Gratitudes	249
	About the Author	251

Introduction

Gavroche Napoléon died before the ground froze, something that happens here in the San Luis Valley when these South-Central Colorado temperatures dip to forty degrees below zero. My spouse, Bill, and I buried our twenty-pound terrier mix under the sweep and shade of a large piñon tree situated in a prime spot on our six-acre tract of land near Mount Blanca. From this spot we can sit close to him when we visit our acreage, glasses of wine illuminated by the autumn sun slipping toward the stretch of the western horizon. We call this sacred ground Graceland.

After the coronavirus was underway in 2020, this shady oasis became the choice place to gather when friends came to camp, spacious enough to allow for the pandemic's recommended social distancing. The trouble was that Gavroche's remains were smack in the middle of our gathering area and its vista. We centered a table over his grave and propped our feet up on his headstone. Having evolved from a mean shelter dog quick to bite to a popular homeboy with a hospitable grin, I suspected this thrilled our little dude who was fond of being the center of attention.

One day while struggling to arrange chairs the advised six feet apart under that sweeping ole piñon, I got exasperated and hollered, "Damn, Gavy, you gotta move!"

I straightened up. In my line of vision was an area of soft soil where the prairie dogs had been busy digging. I walked over to the spot and kicked the soil around. *This is doable. I could even*

Dog Love Stories

move Amber Grace to this spot. What about the two dogs I have right now? How comforting to imagine burying them here someday. I stepped back to get a clearer perspective, and it hit me with a jolt: *Why not build a dog cemetery?*

My mind raced. First, level the plot. Then, we could make use of the leftover ancient wire fencing from our century-old home thirty minutes away in Alamosa, supporting it with the leftover trimmed tree trunks we had harvested to make walking staffs. Surely Bill and I could figure out how to construct a gate. Everything sounded workable. However, moving my dogs' bodies did not. But why go to the trouble? I would leave their remains buried where they were and only move their gravestones to the cemetery. I imagined Gavroche wagging his tail at that decision and with a bit of sass adding, *Yeah, Mama, let me stay in the center of things here under the piñon!*

Within days, I started gathering headstones for this array of mutts—terrier mixes, a beagle mix, two Labradors, a blue heeler, a red heeler mix, a husky mix, and a pug mix. Six of my dogs came from shelters, one from a neighbor, another appeared on my porch, one was a rejected runt, and another purchased. The litany of names read: Dabb, Bandi-Lune, Dancer, Bebe, Pookie, Zorro, Gavroche, and Amber Grace—their lifespans ranging from eighteen months to seventeen years. At this point, two were still romping through life with me, Mercy and Goodness, their gravestones set aside until needed. Although the Rocky Mountains are indeed full of rocks, headstones big enough for every member of this motley crew could not be carried far. Instead, I lugged or rolled selected rocks to a place on the road leading to Graceland where I could heft them up into our trusty old Chevy Blazer.

As I expected, Bill was on board for the project. He was not someone I ever described as "born into the world of dogs," but instead was the type of person I would call a "dog tolerator." Over

Introduction

our decades of being married, however, Bill had become a verifiable dog lover. When Gavroche died, he cried so hard I had to direct his arms as he gently lowered our little guy into the freshly dug grave that Bill had painstakingly prepared amidst rocks and roots.

Bill and I measured that ten-by-fifteen-foot space, approximately the footprint of a one-car garage, where the prairie dogs once burrowed. After digging the four-by-four postholes, we hauled water up the mountain to mix concrete and set posts. Soon we were wrapping fencing around them, with just enough to cover three sides of the cemetery. For the final stretch, trimmed tree trunks were set vertically side by side to make a southwestern-style coyote fence. Last, we created a functional gate that fit with a push and a tug. We then slapped the dirt off our work gloves and leaned into a side hug, proud of ourselves for collaborating on our dog-loving project. Within a couple of fall weekends, Bill and I had managed to fashion this sacred container based on a vision. I thought of the generations of my ancestors buried in a remote North Texas cemetery with little fenced graveyards that look just like our new dog cemetery.

By the time I sat down ready to write names, years, and epitaphs on the brown, tan, and gray stones of different shapes and sizes, memories of my dogs flooded my mind and heart. The southern view from Graceland stretches beyond sixty miles into New Mexico, the direction I was facing as I sat gazing across the valley. I meditated on my ten dogs' lives, alternately laughing and crying. Dogs have been with me for most of my life journey, our lives braided together, each dog becoming ingrained at a cellular level with who I have become and who I am becoming still.

My dogs have also helped carry me through the trauma and harmful repercussions of childhood sexual abuse. I move through life differently because of the dogs I've had, coming to understand myself more fully and learning to pay closer attention moment to

Dog Love Stories

moment. I have never known what each dog would bring into my life. Mine have taught me—and continue to show me—how to love more and better, how to trust and be trusted, how to be willing to listen and learn, and how to nurture another species.

Stepping through the cemetery gate, I gaze at this collection of gravestones perched on the slope of a mountain. The air swishes as though tails are wagging as the valley wind carries whines of gratitude for the creation of this special place. I blink, and a gravestone becomes that dog. I kneel to nuzzle my face close to hers or his, blink, and the dog is again a name on a stone. I breathe deeply into that place in my heart reserved especially for them, mindful of how every single dog I have had continues to help me better understand how I want to live.

NOTE: Although each of my dogs has her or his own story, because I often had two dogs at the same time, parts of their stories overlap. Also, I have chosen to use the relative pronoun "who" rather than "that" in the title and when referring to my dogs throughout the book because my dogs are beings, not things.

One

Dabb

(met him in 1961)

"Is he ours?" I squealed. A small brown puppy squeaked from inside a floppy cardboard box on the front passenger-side floor. My older sister Pam and I had just gotten out of Vacation Bible School, and I was bursting from the boredom of keeping my bottom in a chair for two straight hours. I scooped up the little guy and pushed him to my face, inhaling his puppiness. His next squeak brought another squeal out of me and a laugh from Momma. She looked excited. Momma missed her dachshund Dinah who died when we lived in Japan where Dad had been stationed with the Air Force.

Cupped in my palms, the curious pup looked me in the eyes and nibbled my fingers with tiny teeth as sharp as miniature daggers. "Where'd you get him?"

Dog Love Stories

"Someone was giving a litter away outside the base commissary. Part Manchester terrier and part Chihuahua, they told me, but mostly mutt. I was thinking we could call him Dab, short for A Lil' Dab'll Do Ya. How does that sound?" Momma probably swiped the jingle from the 1950s commercial for Brylcreem, a men's hair-styling product.

"Dabb. D-a-Ba-Ba. D-a-Ba-Ba." I imagined two *b*'s and kept saying his name with the sound of the *D* on the tip of my tongue and the pop of *Ba-Ba* at the end pouncing off my lips. "D-a-Ba-Ba. Yeah, I like it!" Pam agreed, though she was not as enthusiastic about the dog as I was. By the time we got home, I was tipsy with puppy love; he was a little more than nine weeks old to my eight years.

Dabb with two *b*'s and I flopped down in the freshly cut backyard, and he started scouting around. Occasionally, he'd run back to me, stumbling over his little feet. I laughed and brought him to my face, feeling his softness against my cheek until he wiggled free and bounced off.

My first toy had been a hand-stitched stuffed dog named Lullaby. The insides of his copper-colored ears were satin, his eyes yellow glass with black pupils, and his nose and mouth sewn of thick black thread. Inside him was a music box that played the lullaby song. Holding Lullaby and rocking were the two things that had quelled my incessant crying as a colicky infant and disgruntled toddler. I still slept with Lullaby, my face pressed against his soft sides. Now I could push my face against a real dog.

When Daddy got home that first evening, he grimaced, then issued sharp directives. "That dog better stay outside, and somebody better pick up his poop." Our house and yard were to stay military standard tip-top clean.

"He will! I will!" I blurted out.

Dabb

"Of course," Momma chimed in right after me, giving me a conspiratorial look.

My teachers and Momma had labeled me a hyperactive kid, and that fit Dabb just fine. He filled out to twenty pounds within his first year and gained enough endurance to run alongside me as I pedaled around the blocks of our dreary subdivision. The development, Wynrock, was one of the first of its kind in Abilene, Texas. When we moved there from Japan, colorful flags billowed outside the spiffed-up office at the entrance, and a freshly painted sign announced homes for sale. That fanfare soon faded; prickly West Texas weeds took over and the flags flapped to shreds.

Five blocks of cookie-cutter homes surrounded a concrete recreation center and a small pool. Lucky for me, our house sat right across the street from the few amenities. Before Dabb, my summer schedule consisted of: wake up, swim, come home, eat a peanut butter sandwich, rest—per Momma's demands—swim till dinner, rest, then swim until the pool closed and the evening neighborhood games began. Dabb changed all of that.

There was a creek behind our house, past the empty fields where new homes were going up before the subdivision went kaput. I found some bushes where I could hide my bike so Momma wouldn't know when I rode past the boundaries she set for me. Sloshing down the middle of the cool creek bed, I felt mud ooze up between my toes while Dabb splashed alongside me. I discovered the world of nature: trees filled with birdsong and water teeming with life, from frogs to snakes. Dabb pounced on the frogs, and I watched out for snakes.

Soon, Momma saw an ad in the paper offering money for horny toads: five cents for big ones and two cents for babies. "We take 'em up east to put in shows," the guy who posted the ad growled as he counted our toads and slid them into his cages. We

Dog Love Stories

never asked what kind of shows. Pam and I just wanted to clink coins in our piggy banks, our sole focus being how many Popsicles we could buy from the ice cream truck with our loot. Dabb's reward was licking our Popsicle sticks.

Toads scampered all over the field behind our house, and though fast, we were faster.

"Go get 'em, Dabb!" and my little scout would take off, alerting us to where the critters were when he crouched and yapped. "Good boy!" Horny toads didn't hurt anyone; they just looked scary with their scales, horned heads, and their tendency to puff themselves up to twice their size and eject blood from their eyes when threatened. That always got a yelp from Dabb—precisely what the toads wanted. It never occurred to us that we might be contributing to a creature's extinction. Catching them was like rattlesnake roundups: clearing out critters to make life safer for people.

Dabb wasn't our family's first dog. In Japan, I had watched Momma laugh and play with her dog Dinah, behavior I did not observe otherwise, particularly when Daddy was around. At the time, my four-year-old brain surmised: dogs make you happy. Dinah lasted about a year before she strayed into the rice field behind our house and died from eating rat poison. Momma cried all day, and I observed how losing a dog can be very sad. After Dinah was gone, we were discouraged from talking about what had happened, though Momma still spoke about the good memories. Despite the silence around her dog's death, it seemed that, for Momma, having a dog was worth the sadness of losing a dog.

Not long after Dinah's death, I was playing at a friend's house and stepped on her sleeping dog's tail. The German shepherd, more than twice my weight, bit me on the face above my right upper lip and slightly below my nose. I could stick the tip of my tongue through the hole before it was stitched. Despite crying

Dabb

and sucking up plenty of blood, it was a miracle I did not become afraid of dogs.

"You've got to pay careful attention, especially to big dogs!" Momma shrieked while driving me to the hospital. Despite this happening at a neighbor's house, later that evening Daddy proclaimed: No more dogs in our house.

That lasted five years before Momma went against Daddy's ultimatum and got Dabb. Maybe seeing me play with Granddaddy's dog changed her mind. After we returned to the States and started visiting my maternal grandparents at their run-down country home west of Fort Worth, I got to know their medium-sized bushy dog named Tippy. He was a mellow creature who was even allowed in the chicken coop when Granddaddy gathered eggs. Tip lumbered after Granddaddy as he gardened and curled up beside him on the porch while Granddaddy slurped a huge glass of iced tea. From watching the two of them, I observed how dogs can be loyal companions. Over time, Tip came to trust me enough to let me pick cockleburs out of his matted, bushy hair, teaching me that showing patience and care helps build a trusting relationship with a dog.

Dabb and I became almost inseparable, which proved to be a liability when playing my favorite neighborhood game. While counting to twenty-five, all the players scurried to hiding places, then the person who was it—the pig—would open her eyes and call out, "Piggy wants a signal!" When the pig asked for that signal, you had to make some kind of sound so that the piggy would have a clue where you were hiding, and if caught, into her pen you would go! Dabb loved the game, even though he never got the gist of hiding, only playfully bowing outside wherever I hid, wagging his tail, and giving me away.

Dabb provided the most constant love I had experienced in my nine years. He didn't get mad at me like my mom, irritated

Dog Love Stories

with me like my older sisters, or ignore me like my dad. I kept a "Doggies Book" [sic] for Dabb where I listed his friends, toys, and trips and wrote stories about him. I described how he walked me to the bus stop in the morning and was there in the afternoon when the school bus pulled up.

We lived across the street from where the bus stopped, and Dabb was there waiting for me daily. Perhaps he was demonstrating a grasp of timing—aware of the day's changing light and temperature—or he was hearing the bus pull into the entrance of the housing development three blocks away. "There's Dabb!" would resound through the bus, and I would look out, so proud of my little buddy, waiting for me and wagging his tail. One fourth-grade friend who rode the bus wrote a poem about how Dabb came to meet me at the bus stop every day. After my friend read it to our class, our teacher posted it on the board, and Dabb and I became famous.

Dabb had his friends in the neighborhood, too, which I recorded in his Doggies Book: Foxie, Fluffy, Dooley, Puddles, Lucky, Gigit, and Woody. Foxie was his best friend. At age ten, with incorrect word usage and punctuation, with my child's heart I wrote about watching what Dabb did after Foxie died and how that convinced me that dogs feel loss too:

> I could just see the smile on Dabb's face when they played together. Then one day a car ran over Foxie. They had watched the street to get the blood out of the street and it went in the gutter. (Dabb didn't know Foxie had died.) That night Dabb was going down there and he smelt Foxie's blood. He stood there crying out loud it was very sad. Now he has other friend's but he hasn't forgot Foxie because one day he went to Foxie's house and whined outside of Foxie's dog house.

Dabb

Taking the time to observe my dog's behavior was teaching me to be a better dog companion.

Dabb became my solace amidst a befuddling home life where my parents fought often. Daddy came into my bedroom while my sister was out and during Momma's late shifts at the department store where she sold lingerie. He touched my body under my pajamas in ways that felt both good and scary, leaving me confused and ashamed.

When Daddy was at home, Dabb had to stay outside. But when Daddy was at work, Dabb came into my room. I breathed more deeply. I experienced how a dog can provide safety when others do not. My child's heart was not concerned about how much time Dabb and I spent together or what others thought about our companionship. Already in our three years together, Dabb had taught me that a dog can be your best friend. The way he looked at me, I knew I was as important to him as he was to me. I was learning how good it feels to love a dog and be loved by a dog.

At eleven years old I asked for a new bike for Christmas. My old one was too small and falling apart. Daddy put a small but heavy present under the tree and announced I would like it more than a new bike.

"Maybe it's a radio. You'll love it!" Daddy joked. "What I should get you is a new dog, one that stays clean. Get rid of that stinky mutt you hang out with all the time. Let me do that and then you can have the bike you want."

"I don't want a different dog. And I don't want a radio." My old bike was too short for my long legs, but I would keep it before ever giving up Dabb.

On Christmas morning I picked up the heavy gift and peeled off the Santa wrapping paper. It was a brick labeled with directions to a place in the garage. I raced through the back door,

Dog Love Stories

found the spot, and yanked an old blanket off a shiny silver-and-gold Huffy bike. Daddy had given me what I wanted after all! I opened the garage door and took off, Dabb skipping alongside me with a smile on his face.

By late spring, I was sneaking out to ride on a dirt road that was even farther than the boundaries Momma had set. To get there, I had to ride along a highway for a short while, and I couldn't take a chance on Dabb getting hit by a car like the dogs and other animals I frequently saw dead on the road. Usually, Dabb ran free, but I made him stay in the backyard on these occasions so he wouldn't follow me.

One day when I came home from an out-of-bounds ride, Dabb was not in the yard. "Where's Dabb?" I asked, looking around. Daddy was home early, cleaning tools in his garage.

"He must have gotten out somehow," Daddy said without looking up.

Had Dabb tried to follow me on my ride? I hopped back on my Huffy and took off on a search, calling and whistling, confident I would find my little dog. But no Dabb. I checked with neighbors and playmates all around Wynrock. No one had seen him. I rode until I could not see any more, then dragged myself home well after dusk. Momma stayed quiet, her eyes downcast, while Daddy determined, "He probably just ran off."

"He wouldn't run away. He'd never do that." I felt a hitch in my breath as my chest tightened. Something did not feel right, but I could not name what that was.

For weeks I continued to ride my bike around Wynrock's boring blocks, searching and calling for my little brown dog. At home, I stared out my bedroom window for hours, wondering how Dabb could just disappear. *Maybe he had followed me out to the highway and been hit by a car?* But I had searched that stretch of road and had not found him. A piercing soreness spread across my chest, my heart aching in a way I had not experienced before.

Dabb

I didn't know how much love could hurt. *How long will a hurt like this last?* I thought I was taking care of Dabb by leaving him in the yard, and yet he disappeared. It didn't make sense. After weeks, Daddy tossed out Dabb's bed from the garage and filled the holes Dabb had dug in the yard.

One afternoon, Momma called me outside, "Patty Beth, come here quick!"

"Dabb! Is that you? Where have you been?" He was skin and bones, filthy, and covered with ticks. I fell to my knees, kissing and hugging him with tears of joy. Though barely able to stand, he wagged his tail. I had never given up hope that he might come back. And here he was right in front of me, looking at me in a way that made my heart gush love.

"Someone probably carted him off and dumped him somewhere in the country," Momma guessed, "but his big heart led him back home to you." We filled a washtub outside to bathe him, picking off dozens of big fat ticks. After he ate, I carried my pint-sized wonder into my bedroom. Lying with him in my arms, it was not difficult at all for me to believe a dog's heart could lead him back home to the person who cares for and loves him.

When Daddy got home, he was surprised to see Dabb. "Well," he grumbled, slapping the sides of his legs, "that little dog knows how to find his way home." Dabb had never liked Daddy and now seemed afraid of him. It occurred to me that some people don't like dogs, and dogs often know who those people are. I wondered, *Did something happen between Dabb and Daddy that I don't know about, besides Daddy complaining about Dabb being dirty, stinking, and digging holes?*

"Who would steal a dog and throw him out?" I questioned Momma in front of Daddy. She shook her head and avoided looking at me. Daddy harrumphed out of the room.

"Just be happy he's back," Momma mumbled quickly once Daddy was gone. "It's a miracle."

Dog Love Stories

My love for Dabb knew no bounds after that, even as I matured and entered junior high at twelve years old. Daddy, retired from the military, drove a truck for a moving van line and was often away, so Dabb could spend ample time in my bedroom. Once I arrived home from school, we would be off on a ride or a hike down at the creek. When we were together and alone, it was like there was no division between us; we were the same creature. When Daddy came home, Dabb seemed to know better than to come inside.

Almost a year later, while Daddy was out of state on a job, Dabb began having trouble standing and started throwing up. "He's just getting old," Momma assumed, "and he has never been like he was before his long journey home."

"But he's barely five!" I was not sure how long dogs lived. Tippy seemed old at six, but maybe that was because Granddaddy was old, and Tip acted like him.

"Dog years aren't like human years," Momma explained.

Dabb soon became gravely ill, and I spent one night cleaning up his vomit and diarrhea. "Come on, buddy, please get well," I whispered in his ears as I nuzzled his face. He stared back at me with a look of tender resignation. "No, no, don't give up," I begged, wanting to clutch him to my heart but aware he felt too badly for that.

The next morning, I begged to stay home, but Momma would not let me. Rushing into the house after a miserably long day at school, I found his bed in my room empty. "Where'd you move him? Where is he?" I shouted, frantic, running from room to room, my heart pounding in my ears.

Momma called me to the kitchen. She stood there with hands on hips and legs spread, her soldier-like image mirrored on the linoleum floor. "I took Dabb to the vet, and the vet and I decided to put him down, put him to sleep. There was nothing else we could do."

Dabb

"Put him down? I don't understand." I had not heard those words before. They didn't make sense. "Put him to sleep? Like he won't ever wake up?"

Momma sighed and nodded, her lips in a tight line.

"No! No!" I screamed, stomping, sobbing, and walking in tight circles. "He would have gotten better if I had stayed with him! I *should* have been with him! He just needed some kind of medicine! He died while I was at stupid school?" I clenched my fists so I would not throw something. "I didn't even get to say goodbye!" I shut my eyes tight and bit clear through my bottom lip, despair and anger surging through my body like a tidal wave finally hitting home shore.

Momma turned to empty a bucket of dirty mop water, the floor now clean of Dabb's vomit and poop. "It was Dabb's time to go. You'll have other dogs in your life. You know your dad would not have us paying a vet bill to try to save Dabb. I couldn't wait for you to come home from school and then go back to the vet. I was already there." She did not turn around as she waited for the sink to drain, not meeting my eyes or offering a tender touch.

Wailing, I ran to my room and slammed the door. A framed picture in the hallway crashed to the floor. *We couldn't pay for Dabb to get well? Didn't Momma care?* I grabbed Lullaby off my closet shelf and curled up in bed, sobbing into the fur of my old stuffed dog. I pressed the heel of a palm into my heart, but the pain of Dabb's death cut straight through me.

My best friend was dead.

No one talked about Dabb, and his bed and bowl disappeared. But I had the "Doggies Book," a little container with his baby teeth, and a Christmas stocking I had sewn him. These comforted me. For months I chewed the insides of my cheeks bloody. They never had a break to heal while I experienced how a dog's death means different things for different people.

Dog Love Stories

In less than a year, Daddy took a new job in Dallas; we were leaving Abilene. After we moved to Dallas, on my walks home from school, I cried out my loneliness from missing Dabb and not having any friends. One afternoon, I sucked in some deep breaths to help me stop crying before I arrived at our house. When I walked through the door, Momma and Daddy were shouting at each other again. Daddy worked the night shift and woke up about the time I arrived home from school. I closed my bedroom door, turned on my record player, and grabbed fistfuls of Kleenex for another predictable nosebleed that happened during these fights. I settled into a rocking chair—my substitute for Dabb and the soothing comfort his presence used to give me. I was glad Dabb was not living with us there, confined to a small, prissy backyard where Daddy planted and pruned. Dabb would have been miserable. He needed to be free to wander, to ride with me, to play in the fields and creek. Every direction I rode now—*when* I rode, since thirteen-year-old girls did not ride bikes in this big city—there were houses, houses, and more houses.

I turned up my music and rocked harder, cringing each time Momma and Daddy raised their voices or threw something. Inside, I felt raw and torn, but besides missing my little brown dog, I couldn't understand why I felt so bad. At least my memories of Dabb offered comfort. I had thought I needed Dabb to survive, but I was starting to realize, *I can be strong enough on my own.*

Dabb
My First Love
1961–1966

Two
Bandi-Lune

(met her in 1976)

Talking in a soft voice—different from the firm, loud voice I used in the gym all day as a physical education teacher—I crept toward the terrified dog and sat about three feet in front of her, careful to avoid eye contact.

"Hello, love. Who are you?" I continued with a soft babble. After fifteen minutes, she inched toward me. I looked up, reached out, and gently stroked her with utmost care. She flinched while shivering in the warm Texas afternoon. "See, that's not so bad, is it? Don't be afraid." We both let out an audible sigh, holding one another's gaze and essence in silence.

I first heard about this dog at my night job waiting tables at an upscale restaurant. My new husband, Dave (who also worked at the restaurant), had met a well-known Austin television personality who raised purebred Labs for hunting. In the banter between waiter and customer, Dave shared how he wanted a good hunting dog—even though we could not afford one. The popular broadcaster slipped Dave his card, claiming he had a "runt who could hunt."

Dave had gone out to pick up his hunting dog while I was teaching, and when I came home, I found Dave ranting and flapping his hands in the air, frustrated the Lab was afraid of him. The jovial broadcaster, apparently not worried about how isolation could affect a dog's well-being, told Dave he kept runts separate from the rest of the litter. This dog had spent her first year alone in his large backyard.

"She won't even come near me! I'd rather buy a puppy than get a damaged dog!" Dave shouted.

I stepped out back, leaving him to his rant as I wondered why he had ever married me. Depression—in part from Dave's incessant overt attractions to other women—often rendered me over-the-top emotional. In other words: damaged.

After spending time with the shy, skinny runt of a Lab in our backyard, I offered to keep the "damaged" dog. Perhaps in coaxing her to feel whole, it would help me do the same for myself, finally, at twenty-three years old.

Picturing the masked cowboy in dark clothes from old westerns, I told my new dog, "You look like a bandit." I tried calling her "Bandit," but that didn't evoke a reaction. When I tried "Bandi," however, she perked up. "Oh, that's your name, is it?"

Bandi was sleek but too thin. Her black-as-the-night coat contrasted with my light blonde mane. Her right front leg was noticeably crooked, making her walk with a limp and probably landing her in the runt category. Nevertheless, after I sat and talked quietly with her, she began looking at my face with

Bandi-Lune

eagerness, a yearning to trust and connect. By week's end, I had received a few nose nudges. No licks yet.

Giveaway dogs can be a mystery. A dog like Bandi, fed but never given a name, had been deprived of human contact for her first year of life. Such neglect can affect a dog's behavior, as Bandi was demonstrating. I had read about babies left alone and rarely touched in orphanage cribs: damaged. How could Bandi know that this backyard, although much smaller, would not be like her last one? How could I know if she would ever break out of her shy and fearful reticence? We were puzzles to each other, both using our pack-like instincts for safety and to explore possibilities, hoping for trust to be established, for something lasting.

Bandi was an alert, quick learner who adapted with ease to a leash. While I played tennis, she focused on the ball lobbing back and forth across the net, taking off after any that sailed over the fence. I loved this version of fetch and convinced my tennis partner it was fun playing with slimy, slobbery balls. Before long, with loving companionship, consistent feeding, and daily runs together, she became an attractive and healthy Lab of fifty-five pounds, her awkward leg barely noticeable. Even she seemed no longer aware of it.

Bandi hung out in the backyard during my workday, with access to the garage for shelter. Whenever I was home, she stayed close to me indoors. It could have been the water, food, and protection that kept her from jumping over the wobbly chain-link fence, or it could have been the mutual tug on her heart and mine where a bond was solidifying while the one with my philandering husband was disintegrating.

Partying at home on the night of my twenty-fourth birthday, Dave and I passed joints with a group of college friends. "Let's go to the lake and take a swim," I suggested, wishing to take a dip under the light of July's full moon. We all squeezed into Dave's

Dog Love Stories

Malibu, with Bandi between the window and me, both our heads hanging out the window drinking in Austin's hot, humid night air. This would be her first time at the lake since she had been secluded in the previous owner's backyard, which bordered Lake Travis. I wondered if she had ever swum there.

"Do you like to swim, girl? There's a big bowl of water just waitin' for us." She turned her dark eyes on me and flopped her tail. "I bet you love water. After eight months together, I think I already know that about you." After all, she was a Lab.

We arrived at Lake Travis, scrambled down the rocky path to a good sitting area, and stripped. The summer sun had left the lake feeling like warm bathwater. I slipped in, and Bandi jumped after me. I could see her paddling beside me each time I lifted my arm while doing the crawl. She was indeed a strong swimmer. My sure strokes, the warm water, the moon dipping in and out from behind clouds, my pot high, my incredible dog, and a sense of possibility for my life hypnotized me. I had been teaching PE for two years now and was considering graduate school. I wanted to focus on those things that gave me hope, since my marriage did not. Finally, in a daze, I swam back to join the others who were already passing another joint. We were buzzed.

"Where's Bandi?" I asked, looking around. No one had seen her since she jumped into the water with me. "I thought she was following me back!" I snapped, jumping up, anxiety rising from my gut to my voice. Bandi had proven to be a fine swimmer, so I had not continued watching her closely while lost in my stoned reverie.

We all started a search, calling her name as my level of panic rose to a hysterical pitch. "Bandi! Bandi!" I shrieked, scanning the rocks, the shore, the lake. The moon made the landscape more visible, but Bandi was impossible to see since she was as black as the darkest part of the night when the moon slipped behind the clouds. "Bandi!"

Bandi-Lune

After fifteen minutes, Dave and the others started growing restless. It was one in the morning. "We have to go," they insisted. People had to work the next day. We still had an hour's drive home.

I looked at them like they were crazy. "I'm not going anywhere without my dog!" I had only had Bandi eight short months, but our heart connection was already strong. "Y'all go on. Dave, come back and get me." I dared him with a threatening look, and he nodded. He often stayed out later than this partying during the week, and he could damn well stay out all night for me. I didn't care if it was an hour each way; there was no way I was leaving. I turned to look at the expanse of water in front of us all, and my heart squeezed. *Maybe she was out beyond the cove where we had been swimming?*

"Bandi!" I shouted, my voice straining and my heart breaking with my carelessness and the thought of losing her. I started yanking my clothes off, readying myself to swim farther than I could see from the shore. Before diving in, I stared out one last time and discerned a tiny dot in the water far far out in the lake. "Bandi!" I screamed louder, hushing the others so she would only hear my voice.

The dot began moving toward us. *My God, was she that far out?* The moon moved out from behind the clouds, making Bandi more visible. I dove in and began swimming hard in her direction, stopping periodically to call her name. We were swimming toward each other, the distance closing between us.

Finally, she was directly ahead of me, exhausted, barely able to keep her head above water. I had been a lifeguard for years and was ready for a fight, but she didn't resist as I flipped her limp body over, then put an arm around her chest so that her droopy head rested on my shoulder above water. Although I had never had to save anyone before, this someone was one of the most important beings in my life. I pulled with my free arm and kicked with purpose. I felt her heart beating rapidly, or was that mine?

My impatient but relieved companions met us on the shore and helped lift her onto the ground. She was unable to walk. She must have swum out so far, she could not find her way back, but she kept swimming, perhaps in circles. I jumped into my clothes without drying off. Dave and a friend carried Bandi up the rocky slope to the car. "Put her in my lap," I insisted. I laid dry towels on top of her shaking body while cradling and stroking her precious head. "It's okay, girl. I wasn't gonna leave without you."

Driving away from the lake, the moonlight shimmering on the water caught my eye. "Thank God for the moon—la lune—she helped me find you, girl. Let's add 'lune' to your name, Bandi-Lune." She turned and looked deeply into my eyes, reflecting the love, gratitude, and relief pouring out of mine.

My willingness to go along with Dave's idea of an open marriage soon fizzled. Even when we first started dating in high school, Dave often broke up with me to go out with others. I would feel an intense jealousy toward the women he attracted so easily with his humor and charisma. Now, my insecurities continued to muddle my attempts to date others. If it were not for Bandi-Lune and how I loved teaching, I might have ambled straight into oncoming cars one night when crying and walking too close to traffic. Bandi and I soon left Dave and found a little rental house on a dead-end road that backed up to a florist shop.

The shop threw out days-old flowers in their back bin that I gathered and spread throughout my new home. I furnished the living room with four frayed rocking chairs I alternated rocking in—the preferred pastime of my childhood and teen years—and I rocked and cried and rocked and sang and rocked and thought and rocked and prayed and rocked and dreamed. It was my first time living solo—with Bandi-Lune along, of course—and I felt

Bandi-Lune

relief from the confusion and loneliness I had experienced in my marriage and also with my parents after Dabb died. Bandi and I were not alone; we had each other.

Although Bandi liked our little cottage, her sense of security came more from my presence. She would sit and press her head into my palm that was resting on her head as I rocked. Having a dog encouraged a schedule of care, giving me someone else to nurture, and in so doing, I became stronger. When I took care of myself, I was able to take better care of my dog.

During the open marriage fiasco, I received guidance on applying for a graduate studies grant. My background as a PE teacher with a particular interest in disabled students had me leaning toward a program in recreational therapy in Northridge, California. I was offered the grant and accepted into graduate school starting that fall. Bandi-Lune and I were eager for new horizons. On the way to LA, we would attend my high school and college friend Carolyn's wedding in Colorado. But the first stop was at a friend's house in Amarillo.

Bandi got out of my twelve-year-old Toyota Corolla to drink, eat, and pee, then hopped right back in while I was getting my bag out. "What's up, Lune?" She wouldn't budge. "Come on inside with me," I coaxed. She looked away. I rolled the windows down so I could leave her in the car overnight. "Okay. Hop out and do your business if you need to." She had never run off. I was loath to force her to come inside; she had her reasons. Bandi had watched me pack up and move from our first home together, then get rid of furniture until our next home was empty. This trip was the farthest Bandi had traveled in her entire life. She was making decisions as she was able, and I wanted her to feel as secure as possible. If staying in the car with our possessions was what did that for her, then fine. Who can say what is going through a dog's head, but when a dog has fears of abandonment, she will do whatever feels best for her survival. Dogs, as with people, want to feel safe. I found her curled up in the back seat in the morning.

The following night we camped in a Colorado state park. I pitched my tent, made a sandwich, then watched Bandi run down a slope into a creek and reliably find the same thrown rock and bring it back to me, over and over. The stream was full of stones. How did she know which rock was hers? I had found one with a shape and some dings to identify it, so I knew she was retrieving the same stone. When I got tired of tossing the rock, she resorted to pushing it down toward the creek with her nose, finding it, returning, and starting over. She entertained herself until her nose was raw from this obsessive rock retrieval game. "Let's go to bed, girl," I said, drying her off with a towel before we crawled into my tent.

An hour past dusk, Bandi started growling. Footsteps crunched on the gravel outside my tent. I grabbed my flashlight and unzipped the tent to see who was out there. In the dark, I could barely see a man nosing around my site. "What are you doing?" I demanded, right before Bandi slipped out of the tent, charging at the intruder and barking in a way I had never before witnessed. "Come here, girl," I called, placing my shaking hand on her head.

"You w-want some company?" the guy stuttered, rattled by my dog, who sounded ferocious and twice her size in the dark.

Other campers were within earshot. I saw a light come on in a tent near ours and heard voices. "Get out!" I yelled in my loudest PE teacher voice. When someone directed a light our way, the intruder spun around and walked off. Soon after, a truck started and pulled out of the park. I had noticed the guy earlier and wondered why he didn't set up camp.

Back in the tent, I drew Bandi to me. She was still damp, and I urged her to crawl under the covers. I was trembling as if I had been the one retrieving rocks from the creek all evening.

Bandi-Lune

Bandi comforted me, licking my face and pressing into me until I quit shaking. "Thank you, girl," I whispered. "What a good dog you are." She sat up several times during the night, maintaining her vigilance. Although her protection comforted me, I never fell asleep.

The following day, the Lune and I hightailed it out of there and on to the mountain wedding venue in Evergreen. On the drive, I continued to thank Bandi. I remembered feeling safer from my dad with my dog Dabb by my side as a child. Once again, I was experiencing how a dog can be protective and help me feel in less danger. Bandi's fearful, shy, and reticent traits had morphed into loving, playful, and now, protective ones.

In my yellow ruffled bridesmaid sundress and clashing brown leather platform shoes, I played my flute, then sang, a cappella, "Give Me Love That's Soft." Carolyn's wedding guests were polite afterward about my earnest musical offering. Bandi watched from inside my car, glad, I am pretty sure, that she was not close to where I was playing my flute, which always made her whimper and burst into yowls. She might have given my performance the lift it needed. Instead, during the two nights there, she entertained guests by hopping in and out of the car's open window at will, feeling safe and secure in her "mobile home."

While still at the wedding venue, I had noticed my spare was under a mountain of belongings in the trunk. Not a wise place if I needed it. One evening I was parked in front of the porch where the bride's parents and their friends were lounging with wine and martinis, and they were thoroughly entertained when I unpacked everything onto the grass. It looked like I was having a yard sale of clothes, books, pillows, blankets, camping gear, and kitchen items—all the stuff I could fit into my little Toyota for my big move. Bandi-Lune, however, was not entertained. She looked on with nervousness and jumped through her window with a look

Dog Love Stories

that said, *I'm not leaving this car even if you take everything out.* I repacked it all with the spare on top. Lucky me, since a day later a tire went flat on the first mountain pass as I was leaving Colorado. I was able to get that tire out and onto my wheel right before a high-altitude afternoon rainstorm unleashed.

After changing the flat, I realized I would not be able to clock the ten hours I had calculated to get to the Grand Canyon, but I could make it to Monument Valley on the Utah/Arizona border. Despite this detour, I still hoped to make it to the Grand Canyon the next day, my twenty-sixth birthday.

Bandi and I arrived at the Monument Valley Tribal Park and scouted for a safe-looking site, somewhere close to a family and away from single male campers. The cinnamon-colored rock monuments were breathtaking, the stillness snaking around them pierced by an occasional raven's call. I pitched our tent, and my girl and I curled up together, snug, safe, and sound. The following day, we took off in search of a grocery store for final birthday dinner purchases and to get the flat repaired before heading to the Grand Canyon.

The line to the park entrance station was long. My faded red Corolla that now looked pink puttered as we inched along, no AC, all windows down so that Bandi-Lune and I could catch any breeze that came along. I had a battery-operated boom box on the passenger seat that I popped cassettes into, and I was singing along to Joni Mitchell's *Ladies of the Canyon* album. I observed how the ranger kept shaking his head, and I watched car after car make a U-turn and drive away. Finally, I was eye to eye with the guy in a weird hat. "Ma'am, our campgrounds and lodging are full. You can take a short drive and see some of the canyon from viewpoints, but right now"—he glanced at his watch—"you barely have two hours before you'll have to leave the park."

I could tell he was tired of repeating the same thing over and over. "Well," I hedged, not wanting to miss my birthday at the canyon, "I'm meeting some friends who arrived a few days ago, and they already have a camping space." I kept a straight, no-nonsense face. He reached out and patted the Lune on her head while she leaned into his hand and gave him a lick. The perfect distraction. I paid the entrance fee and drove on through, with Bandi hanging her head out the window like the champ she was. Twice now she had helped me out of fixes!

I drove around the Grand Canyon camping area, glad for a chance to stay there for my birthday and hoping to find a camping area with a spot for my tent where the people looked safe and friendly. At last, I saw a campsite with no car, two tents, and three people—two guys and a girl—who looked around my age. I pulled in and told Bandi to stay.

"Hey!" I offered in my friendliest voice. "I was wonderin' if I might share this campsite with y'all since the campground is full. Maybe I could pitch my tent right over there." I pointed to an empty area that was still part of their site.

I saw them all look at each other and mumble quietly. Then, finally, the girl nodded at me and said, "Yes, yes."

"Thanks so much! Do y'all have a car or shall I park right here?" I wanted to be considerate and not just because I needed a place to camp.

Again, low murmurings and a pause before she answered, "No, no car. Park there."

It occurred to me that maybe they were foreigners. Had they hitchhiked? I noticed their big backpacks with patches of places they had been and brands of shoes that did not look familiar. Typically, people would be asking who I was, where I was going, something.

"Do y'all live in the States?"

Again, they all looked at each other and mumbled some more until the girl looked up and replied, "No. We are . . . Français."

"Oh, you're French! C'est incroyable! Parce que je parle

français. Vous êtes tous Français?" I could not believe my luck. I had lived in France as a foreign exchange student during college, and now I rarely had the opportunity to speak French. A place to camp with French people was even better than having my spare handy when I had a flat! I introduced Bandi-Lune, who had already jumped out of her window to play fetch with these dog lovers while I pitched my tent. She was tired of being cooped up in the car. Within minutes she turned these strangers into friends.

As these travelers were pulling out their pitiful supply of dried food, I invited them to join me for the birthday dinner I had on hand. Not having had much acknowledgment of my birthday growing up, I had learned to be in charge of my own celebrations. Since I was moving, I had dishes and silverware and even wineglasses. My companions' eyes grew bigger and bigger as I set out the food and wine. We ate and drank and talked and laughed until the moon was out, and the stars twinkled. I felt the lure of my adventurous move west to the Pacific, to Los Angeles, divorced, with my incredible dog companion, ready to expand and explore the world! I had a grant and a job at the university! I felt like I had something of value to offer, that my life was finally coming together.

The next day, driving into Los Angeles, a glob of black gunk splattered down from an overpass onto my windshield. I could barely see to find my way to the Venice address where a friend of a friend had offered me a place to stay until I found an apartment. Per my host, Thea, we unloaded everything visible in my car out of precaution so stuff would not be stolen. Then I scrubbed the stubborn black tar-like substance off my windshield while Bandi sniffed around.

After two nights on Thea's floor, I found a side apartment in a large old home with a private fenced side yard outside my door. Again, Bandi-Lune sat and watched me lug one box after the

Bandi-Lune

other inside, this time not as skeptical as when I pulled everything out of my trunk at the wedding. Did she grasp this was more permanent?

Weeks after that twenty-sixth birthday celebration, I started grad school while also working as a teaching assistant at the university. I left the Lune in the side yard with plenty of water and chew toys while I made the thirty-minute commute—in good traffic—to and from Northridge. Once home, we would head to Venice Beach for a run, a skate, or to play fetch in the waves. We were now California girls, a sunny blonde skating the boardwalk with her smiling black dog running beside her.

There was one other recipient of the grant I had received, Darrin, a wheelchair athlete paralyzed from the waist down from a motorcycle accident. Darrin needed somewhere to stay while scouting out a place to rent, so I offered him my spare bedroom. We drove together in the mornings to our campus office and rolled and ran together in the evenings. Darrin, a dog lover, enjoyed holding Bandi-Lune on her leash on these excursions since she was closer to his eye level.

I had never been around anyone in a wheelchair, so Darrin kindly pointed out what would help him be comfortable in my home. I moved what he needed in the kitchen to the bottom cabinets and rearranged the furniture so he could maneuver with ease. Bandi followed Darrin around the house, along with his girlfriend, who wore a prosthesis on one leg. "Jill and I can do more in bed with only one good leg between us than most couples can do with their cumbersome four!" They laughed hard while Bandi thumped her tail, and I chuckled. We were delighted to have Darrin and Jill in our home.

One morning I waited for Darrin to shift into my car, fold up his wheelchair, and hand it to me to load in the trunk before I could walk around, get in, and take off.

I sighed heavily. Darrin noticed my impatience.

Dog Love Stories

"Why don't you spend a day in a wheelchair?" he responded. "After all, you're studying to be a recreational therapist. Time in a wheelchair could help you understand your wheelchair clients better."

"Sure," I answered glibly. I didn't see how it would be a problem, and I was game to learn. *What a good sport I am*, I thought quietly, congratulating myself on my willingness.

Later in the week, we borrowed a chair from the university, and I plopped down in it, enthusiastic for the challenge. From the get-go, I was baffled. *Where are my arm muscles?* By the time we got across campus, blisters were forming on my hands. Darrin hung back so I could experience how others treated me. Before the Americans with Disabilities Act, those in wheelchairs were pretty much on their own. I waited at doors until kind people opened them for me, but some students were in too much of a hurry to be helpful. I felt invisible and like a beggar. I had to find driveways to use since it was impossible to get over curbs. There were no direct routes. Finding a bathroom I could navigate was practically impossible. Paper towels and sinks were out of reach. I considered dropping my ruse, standing up, getting behind that damn wheelchair, and pushing it wherever I wanted to go.

By the time I got back to our office, I was a physical and emotional wreck. My hands were bleeding and my arms screaming. Still in the wheelchair, I maneuvered myself to face Darrin. "I'm sorry for my impatience and ignorance." Looking at Darrin, I was struck by the kindhearted face Bandi often gazed into and recognized again why she had bonded with him.

Darrin and Jill soon found their own place and moved out. Our apartment felt empty and quiet with only Bandi-Lune and me. Even though the Lune had been alone during the days, having two or three peeps around in the evening made up for the lonely daytimes. She loved me, but I was learning that, just like with

Bandi-Lune

humans, the more love and attention dogs get, the happier they are.

I should have known she was getting bored hanging out in the side yard all day. One Saturday morning while out running on the ocean walk, we passed a group of middle-aged Black men. One of them called out, "Hey, Bandi-Lune! How ya' doin' today?"

I stopped, perplexed. "How do you know my dog?"

"Oh, she down here ever' mornin' keepin' us company. We seen her name on the tag. She's a nice dog. Black like us!" They burst out laughing at this. "We rope her up when the 'catcher comes so he thinks she's our dog!" He showed me the rope and then they chuckled about out-trickin' the dogcatcher.

Well, well, well. We all introduced ourselves. The men explained they hung out there often. I thanked them for caring for my dog. When I turned to leave, they hooted and slapped their legs about how Bandi had outsmarted me. I felt damn lucky that Bandi had found kind men rather than people who could have stolen her, hurt her, or taken her to the pound.

I had already encountered the dogcatcher once before at the beach when he almost ticketed me for having Bandi off-leash. How do you play fetch in the waves with a dog on a leash? I feigned not speaking English, responding in French. Exasperated, he moved on. He had plenty of other opportunities for dispensing tickets. After that, I kept my eyes peeled. Tickets in LA were *steep*, and I could not afford one.

When I got home, I discovered her escape route. Bandi-Lune had been hopping onto my trash can near a corner fence and climbing over. One of my neighbors confessed to watching her do so many mornings and remarked how she managed to always be back by my return. She had to cross a busy street to get to the ocean walk! I remembered how Dabb had been at my bus stop after school every day. Dogs are so much more intelligent than we often give them credit for. Clever girl, but I could not take any more chances. Bandi was going to have to stay inside my apartment from now on.

We started doing short early morning runs and longer afternoon runs. But after clocking under forty-five minutes in a weekend 10K, I was approached by the Santa Monica Track Club and invited to train with them. They worked out two hours every evening except weekends, demoting Bandi's long afternoon runs into late short evening walks.

I tried to reserve most of my weekends for the Lune. Sometimes we would spend a whole day on the beach, with Bandi plunking wet, sandy balls in front of anyone close by after wearing my arm out. People would toss her some balls for a while and then, annoyed, start looking around for her owner. My girl would move on to the next unsuspecting person, always keeping her eye on me.

One of her favorite pastimes came after a storm when a gazillion tennis balls would wash up on the beach from who knows where. I purchased a bat for just such occasions, and we would stroll along the water's edge as I batted one ball after another into the waves. Bandi never tired from chasing them, but my arms turned floppy from fatigue.

One very windy day with the howling Santa Ana winds snaking through the nearby mountain passes, I returned home from the university and gasped. The inside of my apartment was an absolute mess. Curtains were down, clothes pulled out of my closet, and the carpet was ripped away from the front door. At first, I thought someone had broken into my apartment, and I panicked, thinking my girl was gone. I rushed through the apartment, finally spying her trembling, tucked in a tight ball behind the closet door in my bedroom.

"Girl, what is it? Are you hurt?" I kneeled and gave her the once-over but only found some threads and splinters around her mouth. Meanwhile, every time the wind wailed, she cowered more. Suddenly, it dawned on me that this whole fiasco resulted from her being afraid of the whining, nerve-racking, hair-curling wind. I took her in my arms and held her close. "Oh, Bandi-Lune, I'm so sorry those awful winds scared you."

After telling friends what had happened, I heard stories of other dogs having anxiety attacks that resulted from the "devil's winds." Apparently, these relentless, yowling winds—more audible to a dog's ears—can provoke some anxious behavior in both dogs and humans. I got some calming homeopathic medicine from a vet, who also confirmed that this behavior often resulted from the winds. A willing neighbor friend agreed to check on Bandi during long afternoons. Still, it was not as stimulating as her forays to the boardwalk and spending time with her friends there. And what was worse, she was no longer getting the daily exercise she loved.

Upon settling in LA, my dreams of finishing grad school and running achievements soon began dissolving. The commute to Northridge was getting to me, but now that I was running with the track team, I needed to be close to them, and that meant living near Santa Monica and not moving near the university. The team's coach kept yelling at me to "slow the fuck down!" He recognized that my musculoskeletal system needed to strengthen to run the miles I was now covering at the speeds I was clocking, but I thought he just didn't realize how fast I was. My knees began buckling when I stepped off curbs. Soon, I started missing workouts and even skipping the Lune's walks and runs.

Then, I commenced tumbling down the proverbial rabbit hole, propelled by a nagging depression and lack of confidence I'd experienced since childhood. I got pregnant by one of my teammates, who immediately disappeared when I told him, leaving me to make choices alone. I ended the pregnancy. The

Dog Love Stories

undergraduate students I was teaching were brutal in their comments about my Texas accent, laughing at and mimicking me while I lectured, further zapping my confidence. I began squeezing in appointments with a speech therapist to eliminate my twang and drawn-out vowels. I was barely making enough to cover rent, bills, and fuel costs. My diet shifted to the comfort of milk and ice cream almost exclusively. I wondered if I could get a job teaching physical education in the Los Angeles school district, for a bigger salary and more time with the Lune. After interviewing, I accepted the only available position in the middle of the school year: a job teaching PE at a public school for pregnant girls.

I said goodbye to my grant, grad school, Darrin, the long commute, and the track team, and started teaching five classes of approximately twenty pregnant girls, ten years old and up. About half were from LA, and the rest shipped from across the states to live in the Catholic home associated with this school. Hearing the stories of how the girls had become pregnant was heartbreaking: by fathers, brothers, uncles, neighbors, clergy, teachers, and in the best of situations, a boyfriend. The girls were shamed and blamed. The men and boy-fathers went scot-free.

Apart from the emotional demands of this new work, I did enjoy the schedule, more time with Bandi, and increased financial ease. But about four months into the new job, I ran into a fetching dude—whom I'd met months ago at a friend's—while skating on the Venice boardwalk with Bandi. Dude had a glitzy apartment in Hollywood, drove a little red Triumph convertible, and had just broken up with the latest *Playboy* cover girl. Although I was athletic, I was no cover girl.

Dude barely noticed Bandi-Lune, although I believed this would change after he got to know her. Instead, after dating several months, he remained jealous of the time I gave my dog. I resumed an old familiar chomping habit on the inside of my cheeks. I frequently felt my chest tighten. But at the expense of my dog, I continued to crave proximity to this guy's penchant for reckless adventure. Sadly, I had not recognized that the way someone treats your dog says a lot about the way they will treat you. It seemed he controlled how deep I was falling down that rabbit hole: he, the manic puppeteer, and me, the broken, dangling puppet. I was reminded of how I had felt as a kid with my dad, wanting to feel stronger and braver when I didn't believe there was anything I could do to change the things that happened with him.

At Dude's insistence, Bandi and I moved out of our comfy side apartment and into a larger place where he was living with friends. My self-confidence was at rock bottom, and risk-taking was an easy out. I could barely make it to work, then struggled to get through a day of teaching. Coming home to Bandi was the best part of my day—as she alone embodied home for me—but I sensed how powerless I was becoming. I was unable to extricate myself from my current situation, and I was painfully aware of my dog's vulnerability to the choices I was making.

Jeff, a guy in our apartment, had been spending time with Bandi while I was at work, and they were becoming fond of each other. As a camera person on movie sets, Jeff would have long periods off and then be on a work schedule for a week or two. At the end of the semester, when Dude wanted us to take off for a trip up the coast to Seattle so he could "do some business," which involved brokering large gems that came from who knows where to wealthy Saudi clients, I left my teaching position, entrusted Bandi's care to Jeff, and took off in Dude's little red Triumph convertible, my long blonde hair blowing into tight knots. I was leaving Bandi, something I had vowed to never do, although I was convinced it was temporary.

A deep, nagging depression became the most predictable part of my days for the next four months. I yearned for Bandi's head pressing into my palm. My once-flying runner's feet turned to lead, and I dragged through the days, noticing I was gaining weight and puffing out, which totally turned off Dude. Since I had not been consistent with anything in my life, not using my diaphragm fit neatly into that pattern. I was three months pregnant when I finally made it to a Planned Parenthood in San Luis Obispo and learned that the latest they could do an abortion was the next day. I decided to do it, then take a bus to LA to get Bandi and return to Texas. I could not connect the dots yet on how that would all happen since I had sold my car and was now broke. I only knew I wanted my dog again, more than I wanted to be with this guy. Clearly, I was not yet facing the fact that what I was doing today would not change the impact of what I did yesterday, to my dog or myself.

Dude happily bought my bus ticket. Gazing out the bus window, I was trying to sort out what to do next in my life when I started having severe cramps. After my friend picked me up in LA, my pain became so intense we rushed to the emergency room. I explained I'd had an abortion the day before.

"It looks like you're having a miscarriage, ma'am," the doc informed me.

"That's impossible. I had an abortion yesterday. The clinic called later and told me a tissue check showed I completely aborted the fetus." I was matter-of-fact, like this was some kind of business deal.

"Did anyone check to see if you were carrying twins?" the young resident queried. His eyes were kind and his voice soft. He seemed like the kind of guy who would honestly care if he got a girl pregnant. But what did I know? I sure hadn't been a good judge of men thus far.

Twins? I clutched my stomach, groaning, and my body began shaking uncontrollably. Someone pulled a blanket over me. Then another contraction came, and a clump of bloody tissue slid out,

Bandi-Lune

plopping in a metal container. I began crying about getting pregnant, having an abortion, and for all the ways I had fucked up my life in the last year. I sobbed for leaving Bandi, losing my grant, and quitting grad school. I hated that I had injured my knees, dropped off the track team, and left my job. *What is wrong with me?*

I left the hospital numb and silent. My friend's apartment where I was staying was cluttered, loud, and next door to Bandi's and my old apartment, which reminded me of all I had given up for my irresponsible and rash decision to take off with Dude. I called Jeff to say I would be coming over the following day to get Bandi, and I gave him a synopsis of what had happened since I left. He was not surprised; apparently, Dude's patterns were consistent. Jeff never cared much for him. After a long hesitation, Jeff answered, "See you tomorrow."

I had made promises to Bandi-Lune that I would take care of her, that she could trust me. But I had broken those vows and, despite feeling helpless, desperately wanted my dog and my life back.

When I got to Jeff's, I wanted to throw up. Was it the miscarriage, this apartment, or remembering how I had abandoned Bandi four months prior? She lifted her head and wagged her tail but did not stand when I walked into Jeff's apartment. He was sitting beside her, talking to her in a soft voice. I walked over and kneeled beside my girl, burying my head in her fur. What a relief to be touching her. She let me but didn't press into me like before.

"Is she okay, Jeff? Is something wrong with her?" My voice was thin and wavering.

Jeff said her name. She perked up and turned to him, licking his face and wagging her tail.

"She's been great," Jeff answered, tears on his face. "We've become quite close." Bandi edged closer to him and laid her head on his lap. I was now kneeling beside an empty space.

Dog Love Stories

"Bandi-Lune, I sure have missed you," I sputtered. She cocked her head and looked at me but stayed right where she was. This did not feel right. My gut lurched.

"Jeff, I'd like to take her on a walk." Maybe she would warm up to me if he were not close by. Once leashed up, she was reluctant to leave him and kept looking back, like I was dognapping her. "C'mon, Lune, let's take a stroll around the block," I said in a fake cheery voice.

The Lune and I descended the long steps to the sidewalk. Insecurity, confusion, and anxiety were muddling my perspective: *What am I going to do with Bandi? I don't have a car. I have enough money for a bus ticket, and I could probably borrow for a plane ticket, but how will I get Bandi to Texas? I don't even have a home!* I could not fathom how to get a job, an apartment, a life again in LA or Austin. I had burned bridges. I wanted Bandi for *me*. I needed her to help *me* crawl out of my depression. But what did *she* need? How could I take care of her when I was doing such a shitty job of caring for myself? On some level, I knew there are times when a responsible owner puts her dog's needs ahead of her own, but I could not get my heart on board with my head.

Bandi-Lune kept hesitating and looking back at Jeff's apartment. I tugged her leash and beseeched her to look at me. "C'mon, girl. We'll figure it out. I was wrong to leave you. Please, just give me another chance." Bandi glanced at me, then turned and marched ahead. "I'm sorry, Bandi. I'm so sorry. I love you, girl. *Please* love me." As soon as I said those three words, something snapped inside me. Memories pushed up: How as a little girl I wanted so badly for my dad to tell me he loved me, especially after our alone times together. How desperate I felt when Dave was dating other women during our marriage, and I would beg him to love only me. Me! Please love *me!*

I was sobbing and stopped to sit on a ledge. *What am I doing? What's best for my Lune? What does she want?* It sure didn't seem like she wanted me, and I could not blame her. I did not want me either.

Bandi was keeping a safe distance, looking at me uneasily. She made it clear she did not want to dive back into my indecisiveness and histrionics. I felt immense shame and regret for so many poor decisions in the last year. Now I could not think of reasons for staying alive, especially without my dog.

Bandi was like a horse heading for the barn when we turned around. I unleashed her, and she bounded up the stairs to Jeff's apartment. When I came inside, she was standing with her front paws on his lap, and he was stroking her as he wept.

"I'm going to let you keep her, Jeff," I blurted. Again, I was numb and matter-of-fact, like with the ER doc the day before, only this time tears and snot were streaming down my face. Jeff looked at me in silence for a long minute, surprised, then leaned his head against the Lune's and took a deep, rattling breath.

"I'll love and take good care of her, Patricia, just like you have." His voice was shaking, likely from combined relief and disbelief.

"Well, I haven't done such a good job of caring for her in the last five months, except for leaving her here with you. I don't know what I'm doing in my life right now, Jeff, and I want what's best for her." I stood there and watched him calm down as my body tensed up and resisted everything I was saying. *Am I giving up my dog?* "Would you please stay in touch with me? Let me know how she's doing?" *Am I really doing this?* "I'm going back to Texas. I'll call you when I have a phone number to give you."

"Of course." Jeff was noticeably reassured, yet still being the thoughtful and sensitive man I had known him to be.

"Thank you, Jeff." I walked over, and we hugged quickly, then I kneeled to give Bandi-Lune a gentle embrace, closing my eyes and placing my face against hers. She let me, even softened a bit as if relieved, like she understood she would be staying and was thanking me for that decision, like it was all mine to make. She had been as clear as she could be about what she wanted. With respect, I was putting her needs first. She gave me a slight nudge and lick, then sat down beside Jeff, leaning against him. A searing ache ripped across my chest.

I stood and backed off, still watching her, but she turned to look up at Jeff. Once at the door, I paused and looked back once again. Bandi watched me, sitting squarely beside her new owner, looking almost regal in her secure posture. I slumped away, still crying, wondering what I was going to do next, where I would go, how I would get there. Somehow, somewhere, I knew what I was doing was right, was best for Bandi-Lune, and probably for me. It just hurt so damn much.

A friend flew me back to Austin and encouraged me to stay with his family while I regained a sense of well-being. I stayed in bed for days: aching breasts, a hollow belly, no schedule, no work, no dog. I could not take a walk without a profound sense of emptiness. I called Jeff as I had while traveling with Dude, only then I was checking on *my* girl, and now I was checking on *Jeff's* girl. He was taking her on film sets now and said she was a star with cast and crew alike.

I moved from one friend's house to another, able to pay at the second place because of a job I had gotten with the Governor's Commission on Physical Fitness, leading in-service trainings for PE teachers across the state. It was a decent position, although I despised the lecherous advances of my much older boss. I started looking for something else.

I was surviving on the edge of a precipice, taking in the view or contemplating jumping off, depending on the day, unaware I had constructed a facade that allowed me to function in the world. Something felt terribly wrong within me, like a deep wound manifesting as a heavy bag of shame I dragged around no

Bandi-Lune

matter where I went. At the time, I was barely able to recognize I was suppressing childhood memories of sexual abuse.

Soon I landed a position as fitness editor and advertising salesperson with a small newspaper. Life got better when I met the publication's printer, Bill—a gentle and caring man—and we started dating. Two years later, we married. Marriage isn't the best arrangement to enter having not addressed significant personal issues, but from what I could tell, most people do exactly that. Bill and I managed to navigate each other's imperfections and were doing our best to make a successful go of our marriage.

Two years into the marriage, I began feeling the urge for a dog, but my sense of failure with Bandi-Lune still loomed. *Can I be trusted with another creature's care?* One painful experience should not keep me from sharing my life with another dog, especially if my life was feeling more stable. While in town one day, I turned into an Austin shelter's parking lot and came out with a miniature pinscher/terrier mix whom I named Dancer, who was much like my very first dog, Dabb.

After having our new dog, Dancer, for a year, I interviewed for a temporary job gathering information on women's history of sexuality with a research university out of Philadelphia. Job training would happen in Los Angeles. I got the job and immediately contacted Jeff, who told me I was more than welcome to come visit Bandi. "She hasn't been feeling well, I'll warn you," he mumbled. I heard a catch in his voice.

I was anxious to see the Lune. After all, that was my real reason for being in LA. Five years had passed since I had seen Bandi, who was now ten. About one year old when she became my dog, she had spent four years with me and now five with Jeff.

The stairs to Jeff's apartment looked like a climb up Mount Everest. I began to wonder if I was making a colossal mistake: *Will seeing me make Bandi feel worse? What if she doesn't even know*

Dog Love Stories

who I am? What if Jeff hasn't taken care of her as he promised? The heels of my leather boots clicked on the old wooden steps as I slowly mounted the stairs.

When I knocked softly on Jeff's door, it opened on its own. He was expecting me. "Patricia," he said, his tone welcoming. Jeff stood and walked toward me. After a quick but warm hug, he stepped away so I could see Bandi. She lay curled up on a comfy sofa under dim light. "She hasn't heard you come in. Her hearing isn't very good anymore. She may not last much longer," he said, his voice quavering. The room was inviting, simple, and cozy, obviously a place where Jeff often sat to read with his dog. *His* dog. A dog he loved dearly.

I walked over and lowered myself onto the couch. The slight movement caused Bandi to open her eyes. They were cloudy, and the end of her snout was snow-white. As I reached over to stroke her head, she focused on me, and I felt there was a glimmer of recognition, or was that just my heart yearning for such a thing?

"Hello, girl. It's so good to see you again." Jeff slipped out of the room, giving us time alone. "God, I've missed you, Bandi." I spoke softly, my heart aching with tenderness. Tears began. "How have you been here with Jeff? I'm a dog mom again, Bandi. I think I will be a lot better at it after all you taught me." I was trying to get an even breath but could barely talk. Bandi kept her eyes on me. One of my hands was on her bony hip; the other rested palm open on my lap until I felt she was ready. "Dancer is my dog's name now. She's about a third your size, and we live in the country." I was rambling, wanting to share something of my life with the Lune, oddly desperate to convince her I was more responsible now, more stable. My regret and shame about my failures in LA—especially leaving her—were still fresh and painful.

Then I got a lick, just one little flick of her tongue. I took in a short breath. She lifted her head and with utmost gentleness

Bandi-Lune

placed it in the outstretched palm in my lap, letting out a long and loud sigh, as if saying, *You did come back to see me again.*

My God, I thought, *can dogs remember and forgive us despite the mistakes we've made with them?* Then it occurred to me: *Maybe I can now forgive myself.* Tears covered my face, and all I could manage to do was sit still as I cradled that beautiful black-and-white head, thanking her over and over for the years she had been my patient, loving, and faithful companion.

Bandi-Lune died six months later while still in Jeff's care.

Bandi-Lune
Traveling Companion
1975–1985

Three

Dancer

(met her in 1984)

I clapped my hands over my ears to tone down the barking. The noise and chaos of dogs jumping on metal cages helped me understand why I had never visited a shelter before. Finally, I stopped walking, closed my eyes, and stood still until the din quieted. When I opened my eyes, the prettiest little dog stood alone and subdued in a cage in front of me. She looked like a tiny deer. ONE-YEAR-OLD MINIATURE PINSCHER/TERRIER MIX, the sign read. She stared, wearing a confused and hopeless expression, and made a weak attempt at wagging a bobbed tail.

Moments before, I had turned, on impulse, into the Austin Animal Shelter parking lot. Bill and I, married for two years, had bought a house with a screened-in back porch and painted concrete floors on a quarter acre in Spicewood, Texas. It was all perfect for my eight-year-old stepson, who spent most weekends with us. The stability I was feeling in my life, along with my desire for dog companionship, had me thinking it could be perfect for a dog as well. Bill listened to my talk about wanting another dog, nodding, and encouraged me to visit the shelter soon.

I looked at this small, deerlike creature. "How about a walk, little one?"

She reminded me of my first dog, Dabb, also about twenty pounds and a terrier mix. Out of the cage, she showed more energy and seemed comfortable, both on the leash and in my presence. I had told myself I was only visiting the shelter to look around, but why not get a dog now? I had not had a dog since leaving Bandi-Lune in Los Angeles four years earlier, and I still grieved leaving her. Now thirty-two, could I trust myself to be the responsible dog guardian I aspired to be? When I'd had the opportunity with Bandi, I had blown it. But I knew I was a better person for what my first two dogs, Dabb and Bandi-Lune, had taught me. It was time to prove that to a new dog and myself. I adopted the small black-and-brown terrier mix.

With my new girl in tow, I stopped at the nearby athletic fields of Austin High School for some one-on-one time before driving home. All I had was the funky make-do leash/collar from the shelter, but my new companion was compliant and did not resist. We walked to the grassy area in the middle of the track, and I lay down on my back, turning my head to be on eye level with her. Immediately, she crawled up on my belly and settled down, resting her chin on my heart and making eye contact. "Oh!" I gasped, feeling her heartbeat.

I stroked her coat and asked about her past. "How did you arrive at a shelter? Someone took the trouble to dock your tail. Did you get lost? Your owner die? Did you run away for a reason?" My new companion was not showing any signs of abuse. Her coat had a sheen indicating good health, and she did not

Dancer

appear particularly anxious. She did have one little raw sore on her hind leg, about the size of a dime. The way she crawled up and lay on my belly and chest indicated she seemed to feel at home with me.

"May I be your human?" I asked. When she lifted her head and looked into my eyes, I took it as a resounding, *Yes*.

"You resemble a little reindeer. What if we call you Dancer?" Again, another tender look. "Okay, Dancer, it's settled."

Bill and I ended up in Spicewood when he took a job in Marble Falls managing the printing plant there. Spicewood was conveniently located twenty minutes east of Marble Falls and forty-five minutes west of Austin. The quaint little town had a type of wood that smelled spicy, and this spicebush grew along the nearby creek that fed into a sublime swimming hole called Krause Springs, located not a half mile from our house. The two hundred or so people who lived in Spicewood were scattered beside the Pedernales River and on farms and ranches along the rural roads.

Dancer rarely needed to be leashed, trotting along and staying within reach as though we had been walking together for years. Our home was on Double Horn Road, one of the more scenic roads to bike or walk in the Texas Hill Country. A rare truck or car drove by on the road's two lanes. An assortment of wildflowers danced in the side fields while a vast blue sky dipped down on all horizons. We would head off from our home at the intersection of Spur 191 and Double Horn Road and mosey west, past the raucous brays of Jericho the donkey, until we reached an abandoned farmhouse, sometimes walking up to the old home for a hefty dose of sublime yellow if the daffodils were in bloom. Spending time outdoors with Dancer, she continued to remind me of Dabb, not just because of her size and colors but also because of how well we explored together.

Dog Love Stories

On our walks, we traveled through the "town proper": the worn-down and empty former convenience store and service station, the ancient but operational post office with the original brass post boxes, the community center, and the old-fashioned country Baptist church where our friend Doug preached. Bill and I were not members of Doug's congregation, but we were friends, nonetheless. After we had gone in together to buy a small sailboat, Doug asked if we could name the boat *Visitation*. If anyone asked, he explained, they would be told, "He's out on visitation." Dancer and I frequently saw Doug on our walks, and she counted him as one of her first friends in Spicewood.

Next stop was Ben and Inez's run-down farmhouse. They were brother and sister, both in their late eighties. Inez had a hunched-over back that could not keep you from spying her warm smile. She and Ben liked to rock on their rickety front porch, just waiting for us to walk by so she could ask with sincere interest how we were every time. Dancer always looked for them since they occasionally saved scraps for her.

Near our basic but new three-bedroom, one-bath house were several trailers where tenants came and went. There was a new baby at one, and the parents tossed plastic bags with used diapers outside the door. Dancer's schnozzle led her right there, and *bingo*, she discovered her favorite snack! I remembered how Bandi-Lune had jumped a fence to wander while left alone during my workdays, and now I was finding how my new dog had her own penchant for self-amusement. I had strayed from graduate studies in recreational therapy to an ambitious plan to become a doctor—an endeavor that required time in Austin to complete necessary courses. Dancer stayed in the house or on the screened-in porch during those days. If Bill or I were home, we let her out front where she stayed close to the house, except when the wind carried the whiff of a diaper. Opening our front door to a splayed-out dirty baby diaper was not a sight we relished, so

48

Dancer

we decided to fence the backyard to break this disgusting habit, vowing to tackle the project as soon as I finished my current semester of premed studies.

One day while I was in Austin near the end of that semester, a car hit Dancer when she was on her way home with a diaper treat. Bill later told me he heard the driver holler and, looking out, saw Dancer limp off the road to hide under one of the sheds behind the funky old farmhouse next door. Whispering to her, Bill gently pulled her out, then rushed to the vet. With her broken leg in a splint, she limped around with a hangdog look for weeks and licked and gnawed on a dime-sized red spot on her hind leg until it turned raw. I sat with her as often as possible, gently stroking her banged-up leg and dabbing her worry spot with ointment from the vet. We built that backyard fence before she was out of the splint.

Like Dancer, in attempts to self-soothe and calm down, I had a habit, started after Dabb's death, of chewing the insides of my mouth raw. Discouraged with headaches and my doctor dreams, I soon dropped out of the premed program. Migraines had become an excruciating part of my life, my head often feeling too heavy to carry. My eyes would become extremely sensitive to light, and soreness at my temples throbbed with such insistence that only ice packs provided relief. I self-soothed with my chewing habit. Apparently, Dancer and I were both doing what we could to handle our anxiety.

The following year, my therapist suggested I use his cabin in Cripple Creek, Colorado, for a getaway to provide relief from headaches and perhaps gain insight into why I had them. Although the month of solitude was rejuvenating and replete with dreams, the headaches persisted.

I missed Bill and Dancer while gone for the month and on my return was glad to see the two had bonded. This was Bill's first time being responsible for a dog, not having ever had one in his life. He had fed and walked Dancer and been her companion for a month. By sharing the joy and responsibility of having a dog with my significant other, Bill and I became a part of *her* pack. She was now *our* dog.

Bill and I decided to take a family trip with Dancer to Port Aransas, four hours south of Spicewood. Dancer chased crabs, so close to invisible with their color and speed that I wondered if their movement was only the air shifting. She tried to catch them, flinging one after the other up in the air as they clamped onto her little paws until she shook them loose. She loved the ocean and the dead fish, not to eat but to roll in. Bathing helped, but the problem was we had to put her in the car to get back to the motel where we cleaned her. The lingering stench of stinky fish on Dancer and in the car was overpowering. Our entire trip home had Dancer smug with her foul smell while Bill and I hung our heads out the windows like dogs gasping for fresh air.

"Are we going to take her on our trip to Louisiana at the end of the summer?" Bill's question carried a tinge of worry, knowing we would be visiting coastal areas there too.

"Lemme check with someone I know who has a goat farm here in Spicewood. She sometimes keeps her herding dogs in some outdoor kennels. She offered to keep Dancer there for our last trip. Mighta been a good idea, eh?" Bill laughed and held his nose for an answer.

Weeks later, I took a cursory look at the kennels and found them shady, cool, and safe, so I accepted the farmer's offer to board Dancer.

"Here's the plan, little fish wallower. You're going to stay at the goat farm until we come home. We won't be gone long, and everything's gonna be okay. You'll see." I was trying hard to convince her and myself. Looking into her trusting eyes, I prayed my good intentions somehow crossed human/dog boundaries. But

Dancer

the day I left her with her bed, chew toys, and bowls, the sight of my little black-and-brown dog in those isolated outdoor kennels presented a much scarier picture than I imagined on my initial check.

Dancer stood on her hind legs, front paws on the fence, frantically barking and whining as I drove off. *Where are you going? Why am I here? Is this another shelter? Are you coming back? I thought you loved me!*

Memories of leaving Bandi-Lune in LA flashed across my mind. *Is this a good idea? What am I doing?* My doubts made the situation almost unbearable, but I willed myself to drive away and not look in the rearview mirror.

Does a dog understand separation to the extent that humans do? We usually know if a person is coming back when they leave, and dogs seem to understand when we head to work in the morning that we will habitually return in the evening. After all, many dogs spend much of their lives waiting for someone to come home. But when they watch us scurry about packing and getting everything taken care of before a trip, they sense our anxiety. Then, when they are loaded in the car and taken someplace unfamiliar where other dogs are barking, they feel both their anxiety and ours, plus the panic of separation, particularly if they have been taken to a shelter before or abandoned at some point in their lives. These thoughts cycled through my mind during our entire trip.

Within five minutes of arriving home and unpacking the car, I zipped over to the goat farm. The raunchy smell of billy goats hit my nasal passages as soon as I drove over the rattle of the cattle guard. The owner met me at the out-of-the-way kennel where Dancer was already hopping around, having recognized the sound of my old Volvo. "She's been just fine. Didn't eat much. Got a little lonely out here. Somehow got a sore there on her hind leg." Hearing her bullet monotone sentences, I wondered if the

Dog Love Stories

goat farm owner had even touched or stayed to talk to Dancer when feeding her.

As I swept Dancer into my arms, my desperate dog began wildly licking my face. She went into a full-body tremble and whined like she was injured. Then I noticed her eyes were starting to swell. Her muzzle puffed up, and circular lumps began spreading throughout. Hives. "I've got to get her home right now," I cried out as I whisked her to the car, trying to calm her down. No longer paying attention to us, the goat farmer closed up the kennel as we zipped off. As soon as we arrived home, I called Dancer's vet, who recommended a dose of Benadryl, moving a cold cloth over her body, and close observation.

After the Benadryl, I placed Dancer on the floor between my legs and stroked her bumpy body with the cold cloth. Her worry spot was chewed bloody. "I'm so sorry, girl. That didn't work so well, did it?" My guilt was palpable. Regret surged through me, and I vowed to be more selective about where I would leave her next time.

Perhaps the hives had been a culmination of separation anxiety and Dancer's relief of finally seeing me again. In an hour, the hives began to recede. How could I know what went on at the goat farm other than Dancer feeling abandoned, a lack of concern from her caretaker, dreadful loneliness, and the fear of sleeping in a kennel amidst coyotes howling and owls hooting?

I vowed to never forget how emotions can impact a dog's physical health.

After Dancer's last bout of chewing that little spot raw on her hind leg, it occurred to me that she might be lonesome. Soon a neighbor asked if we wanted a puppy their male dog—a Lab/beagle mix—had sired on one of his forays into town. Bill and I got one. The daddy dog, Boomer, was the town favorite, and we

Dancer

had come to know him well. Bebe plopped into all our lives like a burst of joy, and Dancer was exhilarated from the get-go.

"Oh, you love having a sister, eh? You must have had a sibling earlier in your life." Dancer stuck close to her puppy/sis as they played, explored, and slept together. Over the next year and a half, the two sisters became inseparable, and that raw spot on Dancer's leg completely disappeared.

Sometimes I let the dogs hang out with me as I weeded and pruned my flower beds out front. They slipped off one morning, and Dancer showed her sister the diaper stash, both indulging in this disgusting dog's delight. From then on, during gardening time, they were leashed.

One Saturday, I was tending to the wide assortment of red, orange, and yellow zinnias and an array of lavender and white irises along our front walk. Passing through these colors and fragrances several times a day was a healing journey all its own. Dancer moved with me as I scooted down the sidewalk on my little garden stool with a hand shovel filling a bucket with weeds. We were chatting each other up, or so I acted, as I spoke and answered for Dancer.

"You're happy to have Bebe with us, aren't you? And you are such a good older sister!"

Yes, I love playing with my sister. Now I'm not as lonesome when you're gone all day.

She would cock her head to the side and fix her brown eyes on mine, giving me an occasional wag of her nub as if in agreement with whatever words I was putting in her muzzle. Bebe was lying unleashed on the porch sleeping in the sun . . . or so I thought. The whiff of a diaper must have reached her beagle nose, and she had stealthily crept past us. The screech of tires and a horrible, loud thump interrupted our conversation. Bebe, whose full story is in the next chapter, had not made it back safely across the road.

Dog Love Stories

I locked Dancer inside and rushed Bebe to the vet. Later that morning I brought Bebe home from the vet and took her body—now in a bag—up to the porch to give Dancer a chance to see and smell her. Dancer sniffed for a long time before making little whimpers as she hesitantly circled Bebe's body. I kept pressing the heel of my hand into my heart like that would stop the pain.

Later, Dancer sat and watched me bury Bebe not far from a Hill Country stream in a grassy field. That evening, she ignored her dinner and got up numerous times to look throughout the house for her sister, then returned to her little green bed and plopped down wearing a look of despair. "I'm so sorry, sweet one. It's hard, isn't it? I miss her, too, but not anything like you must feel." I crawled onto the spacious blue dog pillow, bigger because of Bebe's absence, and curled up with my grieving dog. Dancer laid her head on my outstretched arm, and I stroked her slowly while my heart ached for the both of us.

My soul felt as raw as the little sore on Dancer's leg that, in Bebe's absence, was again requiring care and medication. Dancer chewed her leg as vigorously as I chewed the insides of my cheeks. We both needed help.

About five months after Bebe's death, while on a trip to Houston to visit a close friend, I unexpectedly ended up with a new sibling for Dancer, Pookie. "You didn't want to be an only-child-kind-of-creature, did you?" Dancer's nub was moving fast when she saw Pookie, and she began nuzzling, guiding, and playing with the pup. Letting out a long exhale, a smile spread across my face.

At first, Dancer and Pookie fit together on Dancer's little green pillow. But hungry Lab puppies grow fast, and it was soon necessary to move Bebe's blue bed out of storage so the dogs could lie together on a bigger cushion. As Pookie learned the leash, Dancer pranced beside her as if showing how a dog

Dancer

should behave on a walk. She mothered by prodding Pookie's soft clumsy body, encouraging her to get up when Pook would roll over impulsively onto her back, all four feet sticking in the air with that round pink belly in full view. Then Dancer would give her a push and a snarl as if saying, *Enough of this silliness!* I stayed out of these interactions and let the two sisters gradually establish their pack patterns and communications.

Soon, Pookie was three times Dancer's size. Dancer's motherly instincts were replaced with sibling-like behaviors: squabbles over toys, food, or my attention. But rather than getting carried away with her irritations, Dancer frequently gave in to Pookie while still showing her who was boss. She made up for her age and small size with a fierce, loud bark that let Pook know she was dead serious, especially when Pookie got the toy socky—a sock stuffed with the other sock of the pair then tied in a knot—and poked it repeatedly in Dancer's face to try to get her to play. Dancer remained tolerant and good-natured to the core. Watching them, I vowed to always do my best to have two dogs, realizing how important it can be for dogs to have other canines around.

Dancer was almost six and Pookie an adolescent when Bill and I made the abrupt decision to move to Jackson, Mississippi. Bored with his Marble Falls job, Bill decided to make a change. He had been wooed to Louisiana, then Washington State for temporary positions that allowed him to learn other printing operations. When a plant in Jackson heard about Bill, they offered him a permanent manager position. My stepson, Shawn, who had been living with me in Spicewood the last six months while his dad worked out of state, had just finished a tenth-grade report on the book *Mississippi Burning*. The two of us were dismayed. Jackson, Mississippi?

The thought of leaving Spicewood hurt. I loved our simple manufactured home, my garden with the big white house for the martin birds who returned every year, the splash of zinnias and irises down our front walk, Double Horn Road, Krause Springs, and our community there. I had been working as an environmental recruiter in Austin for the past two years. My job was going well, and working in Austin allowed me to see friends there frequently. I was relieved to have Shawn with me in Spicewood and was not sure what it would be like to live in a place with Jackson's history and politics. We both liked the idea of being around more people of color, but being in a state and around white people with a strong racist history made us uncomfortable. Bill, tired from traveling, was more focused on the job and the opportunity for the three of us to live together.

Our house sold, and movers came and packed us up, a perk of Bill's job offer. Dancer and Pookie watched, neither having any experience with us moving. Our home slowly emptied until it was nothing but a hollow shell. When I called my dogs to me, the echoes from my voice ricocheted off the empty space and concrete floors. I was glad it was December, the dormant roots in my garden and front flower beds not pulling at my heart.

We had three cars to drive—Shawn having received the gift of an old car from us on his sixteenth birthday—along with two dogs and two crated outdoor cats. My vet had given me some medicine to calm the animals, which soon had them snoozing, except for Dancer. Although she was drowsy, she refused to give in to sleep, sitting beside me with her eyes fixed straight ahead for two entire days of driving. She would nod and slip, then come straight back to attention.

"You're not gonna give up, are you, Dance? Wanna see where you're going, eh?" Did she have a memory of being driven to the Austin shelter and left there? "We're all in this together, sweet one." I had no sense if this Mississippi move was a good or bad idea and wished I had some medication to calm my anxious

Dancer

nerves. Instead, I chewed the insides of my mouth to bits. I knew Dancer would be gnawing on her back leg soon.

We landed at our new place at the end of December. I settled the pets, then Shawn, Bill, and me. Because a realtor had helped us find a rental here while we were still in Texas, I had no idea our new home was on a busy road, which was horrible for animals and humans alike. I checked the periphery of the fence and the gates to make sure there were no escape routes before the dogs could be free to explore their new backyard.

Owls and coyotes were the night sounds in Spicewood, but here the loud whir of traffic was not twenty feet from our windows. The saving grace was that Dancer and Pook had a large backyard, now carefully vetted, where they could run and romp. I experimented with placing dog beds where they could have the best vantage points of their humans and be warm. Dancer would lie with Pookie on the big blue bed, grooming herself or, prompted by our latest life change, chewing her little worry spot.

I struggled to find a comfortable place anywhere in that house. Jackson was cold, snowy, damp, and lonely. I knew no one. Bill was working long hours at his new job; Shawn was finding his way in a new school and making friends. I unpacked boxes in the sprawling, spiritless house we hoped would be temporary while looking for one to buy.

Depression socked me. A doc friend mailed me some Prozac, which helped, but I continued to struggle with why I felt so bad and what I could do about it. *What am I going to do for work? How does one live without any friends close by?* I searched for answers to give me comfort while chomping on the insides of my mouth, tasting blood, and wondering if there would soon be a gaping hole in my face. The dogs were good company, but despite their best efforts, even they could not do enough to buoy me.

Dog Love Stories

At the end of our bustling, busy road, I discovered LeFleur's Bluff State Park, and we started going there daily for long walks. It was hard to leash up the dogs and get them into my car, something that had never been a concern on Double Horn Road. I would often plop into the front seat and burst into tears after the tangle of leashes, human legs, and dog legs in my efforts to get the dogs loaded. Already I hated Jackson, and we had only been there a month. But the park was a boon, helping me to quit moping around and the dogs to feel more secure as they felt my spirits lift.

The herons, geese, and ducks honked or cranked and flapped away as we walked through the park, intruders to their homes. Even though I valued birdlife, at this point I was sloppy, letting my dogs crash through their habitat. Hopelessness and despair clung to me as I meandered aimlessly, numb to my world and its creatures. There was a time in my life when I wanted to slow down to "see" as I walked along, noticing what my busy eye missed. But at that point, I simply wanted the entire Mississippi experience to be over.

There is no doubt in my mind that dogs can read a human's face just like a baby does. Smile, and dogs will wag their tails. Cry, and many will seek to console. Dancer certainly did. She would move softly around me, tuck her head under my arm, or lay it in my lap. I did my best to reassure her, as I had during other times of depression, that I was going to be okay. Often, she would let out a big sigh that could break my heart, aware as I was that I had no idea how to slip as easily out of depression as I slipped into it. I thought I was doing a pretty good job of hiding my sadness from Shawn, and sometimes with Bill, but I never even tried with my dogs. I could be who I was with them and might elicit some concern, but they never got impatient, exasperated, or judgmental with me for being down. Still, I remembered when I

Dancer

was a depressed mess in Los Angeles and how Bandi-Lune had finally turned away from me. I did not want these dogs to give up on me, and I sure didn't need Dancer to chew a hole in her leg.

After two full months of misery, I mentioned my isolation and depression during a phone conversation with my former boss at Management Recruiters in Austin. She suggested continuing to work for them in a home office. I waffled, thinking how working from home, I would still feel alone. Finally, she blurted out, "You have a teaching license. Go apply for a teaching job and get out of that house!"

Fine, I thought after hanging up. I looked up the address for the Jackson Public Schools administration offices, grabbed my purse, and took off. I didn't even change out of my sweatpants and old sweater covered in dog hair. Once at the office, I received an application and filled it out.

"University of Texas, eh? Great school!" the administrator interviewing me repeated several times before mentioning an unexpected job vacancy at a high school teaching French, one of my majors. "Would you like this position, starting next week?"

I took the job. It would mean long, lonely days for the dogs, but hopefully, the result would be a happier dog parent, stepparent, and spouse. Soon I was coming home every afternoon, loading the dogs in the car, and taking off to the park. Although the lake in the middle added to the park's beauty, we stuck to the wooded areas since, as multiple signs warned, the lake was also home to alligators. Mississippi by itself was enough of a bigmouth predator to me, and I was only beginning to figure out how not to get swallowed up by it.

Although Dancer was glad to have Pookie's company, she was always looking for her humans. Pookie, however, wanted to be with Dancer more than anyone. I learned that Pookie did better in our backyard during long days, but only if Dancer was with her, and Dancer was never a problem if there were no used diapers around. That did not appear to be a problem in our new, very suburban neighborhood. Both dogs' behavior reflected my improved well-being, with the best gauge being Dancer's worry spot clearing up.

Because of a strange practice within the Jackson school district and other districts across the nation, I was soon required to move to a school that was being "restructured" due to poor testing scores. Restructuring meant a principal could let go of any staff he wanted and handpick whomever he wished moved to his school. My spirits had just begun to feel some balance and uplift in the position I had initially fallen into, and boom, I was handpicked for an enforced change. Maybe this was how Bandi, Dancer, and Pookie felt when forced to move. Not all the new locations I had plopped them into were ideal. Dogs, after all, do not have a choice when they are moved. I packed up my classroom and accepted I would now be driving across town to teach in a different school.

Shawn adjusted well in his new school and was soon on his school's basketball team. He made friends quickly and was busy, even getting a job at a nearby pizza joint. Bill was tethered to the printing plant, working long hours, with one demanding printing deadline after another. We rarely enjoyed the fireplace together in our new den, and I became increasingly lonely in our marriage.

I dragged through the summer while settling into our new home. I especially liked our big outdoor deck that made soaking up sunshine convenient and provided a spacious doggy playground. Inside, Dancer had taken to an ottoman that went with an overstuffed chair. She would curl up in a cozy little ball on the ottoman and doze in the sunlight streaming through windows that bookended the wide fireplace. Windows framed a backyard that held magnolia, red maple, and pine trees. Beautiful trees were something this state did have going for it.

Dancer

Dancer was content with life wherever she lived if she had a sibling to play with and look after and a family who loved her. When I arrived home, every cell in her body would vibrate. She would wait patiently for Pookie to finish her buoyant dance before softly nuzzling me, trusting we would be off on a walk soon.

Although we had been in Mississippi for two years, I still didn't like it any more than I had at first. I missed walking down Double Horn Road in Spicewood, the empty gazes of cows, horses neighing in the fields, and the playful colt who ran after the big horses with its tail lifted high. I wanted the gnarly oaks, the ornery mesquites, the giant cottonwood in front of the old Baptist church, its leaves rattling like delicate chimes in the breeze. Vines and dark forest blocked views on my Mississippi walks, unlike the expanse of land and sky in the Texas Hill Country where I could see as far as my eyes wanted. I missed my Texas friends and the ease of community in Spicewood and Austin.

Thankfully, Dancer and Pookie filled much of this big empty hole created by all my longings.

Bill and I finally took off for a much-needed trip together to Texas—our first in over two years—but on our first night away, the printing plant called, and Bill flew back. As I drove on alone, I decided to separate from Bill and move back to Texas. My decision to leave was difficult, but I was tired of guessing what Bill's feelings were since he rarely opened up with me. For the past two and a half years, I had given Mississippi and our marriage my best shot. Shawn was about to graduate from high school, and I felt confident he would do well. Perhaps it would even be a good bonding time for Bill and Shawn to live together without me. Life has a way of twirling us around like a lasso, and then on a toss, who knows where we'll land or how tight the noose will be.

By the end of my trip, I had a plan: make a résumé, check on schools in Houston where I had friends, send out inquiries, and

Dog Love Stories

explore places to live that took dogs. The hardest part was letting Bill and Shawn know my decision. Shawn took it in stride and seemed to understand my decision. Bill was sad, but he had been unhappy since we landed in Jackson. His go-to was work, then more work. Loneliness had taken a toll on our marriage.

Who owns whom in dog–human relationships, especially when multiple creatures are involved? Sometimes I felt like my dogs owned me, then at other times, I owned them as a parent, guardian, and companion. In the case of Dancer and Pookie, they were unquestionably my dogs within the context of our family. Bill and Shawn cared about the dogs, but they did not possess the vigilance needed for having dogs: making their home safe and comfortable or feeding, exercising, and taking them to the vet. Leaving one or both dogs never came up for discussion.

After accepting a teaching job in Houston and finding an apartment near my new school, I returned to Mississippi to finish the school year, then began packing. Oddly, both Dancer and Pookie seemed energized by my stuffing boxes. Perhaps they picked up on my energy, and it affected their behavior. I, too, was excited as I pondered dreams put on hold for years: return to graduate school, start writing again, spend time close to my mentor (who was one reason I had decided to move to Houston), and find a therapist who could help me mull through the sexual abuse trauma that continued to fester. I yearned for a sense of place, at least within myself. As the photographer of my life, I was unsure where to snap the next image, but the camera panned while looking for the best frames. I had not lived alone for fourteen years, and since marrying Bill, every move had been for his work or his children. Right now, I didn't know what the rest of my life would look like.

My new apartment was a simple one-bedroom with a small living room that opened into a tiny courtyard. A dingy bar separated the dining area from a dark kitchen where I battled Texas roaches,

Dancer

never winning the war. At least the dogs could find a patch of afternoon sunshine on the living room floor while lying in front of the west-facing glass doors. They were both about to become indoor creatures for eight to nine hours a day, and I hoped to God they could handle it. After settling, Dancer huddled on my lap, tucking herself into a tight little ball, perhaps seeking security amidst all the change. I stroked her, needing her as much as she needed me and not wanting the move to precipitate her chewing.

I walked them on the apartment grounds before work and immediately on my return. Then, after a short rest, I would load them into the car for a drive to a nearby levee that bordered an open area with wetland views and birdlife. A barred owl regularly graced our stroll. It was cool there in the evenings, constantly humid, but with the breeze I could feel refreshed, and when I felt refreshed, so did my dogs. A symphony of descending dusk sounds calmed me, and the setting sun, due west behind the landscape, cast a beautiful reflection of the trees in patches of water and ponds. All this, combined with the pinks and blues of an open Texas sunset, was like a STOP road sign. *Look,* this is the noose loosened. *This* is your soul thriving. *This* is how to nurture yourself.

Oddly, I never saw but one other resident at my complex with a dog—a stuffy, fluffy poodle. But I soon became familiar with several of my friendly neighbors who loved getting to know Dancer and Pookie. I noticed the women were usually dressed somewhat provocatively and in high heels. They would arrive home in the mornings when I was about to take off for work, then leave in the evenings when the dogs were having their before-bed walks.

"Oooo, that little guy is so handsome!" someone often commented. I don't know why people frequently think of all dogs as male. "Those two seem to be best of friends!" was an exclamation I often heard.

Most of the women said they had never had a dog, but they sure seemed like they had been born into the world of dogs with how they gushed over my two and scratched them with their long, brightly painted nails. The dogs relished the attentiveness of their neighbors. Even the men were polite and eager to pet Dancer and Pookie. Pretty soon, I think the entire complex knew their names, though not my own. I remembered how Bandi-Lune had helped make strangers into friends at the Grand Canyon, and these two were now doing the same.

"Do you live on Forum Park Drive?" one of my colleagues asked me several months later. When I told him I did, he mentioned that it was an area known for prostitution and encouraged me to be careful. Ohhhhh, that explained my neighbors' schedule and dress, but "Be careful"? My apartment community was so friendly and welcoming. I felt quite safe. I had never walked outside the surrounding metal fence that opened and closed with a code for the residents. I felt naive for misunderstanding my neighborhood, and realized I needed to put on my big city shoes and pay closer attention.

"I know a guy who rents a roomy upstairs garage apartment with big windows in every direction. Plus, you'd be much closer to me there," Sidney encouraged. He had been the life partner of my beloved friend John before he died of AIDS the previous spring.

When my six-month lease was up, I exchanged friendly farewells and well-wishes with my neighbors and prepared to move on. Moving again certainly prompted reflection: *Where am I going? Do the geese wonder that? Innately they fly on each year. Are my instincts moving me forward?* Surely there were plenty of reasons to keep on keeping on even though I was not feeling the grace of flight with this fourth move in three years.

The two-bedroom upstairs garage apartment had a room for a guest and my desk, a big sunny kitchen with space for a table and chairs plus a small sofa, and a living area that looked out onto backyards, trees, and the street just past the driveway. A fantasy

Dancer

of having a couch in a kitchen had been stuck in my head for years. "Look, girls, sitting here, you can see out the window and look at squirrels in that tree!"

In the living room, Pookie was big enough to sit on the floor and look out that window, and Dancer could see out when perched on her ottoman. "You two deserve to have views, too, and you have plenty in our new home!" Pookie's tail thumped as they both stared out the front window.

We strolled in our neighborhood that held old homes with front gardens boasting a variety of warm weather plants. A high school with a track where the dogs and I could run was only a block away. And best of all, we were only blocks from Sidney and a long park with a walking path that ran alongside one of Houston's numerous bayous. I knew time outdoors and exercise were necessary for my health and vital for dogs.

Dancer was becoming an elder and Pookie an adult. Even I was feeling my age as the early forties set in. Dancer still pranced like a little reindeer; however, she displayed more grumpiness with Pook's insistence to play tug-of-war. We walked to the high school track several times a week so that I could run, and the dogs could romp.

It is no secret that dogs smile. I noticed that little upturn in my dogs' mouths, a curl of their lips, when they were particularly happy. I was seeing it frequently during those days when they were tussling at the track while I ran, or when friends came for a visit, or at the mere mention of a walk. And just like with humans, dogs' smiles can be contagious. Dancer and Pookie smiling more had me smiling more and had them smiling more in a continuous cycle.

Dancer and I quit chewing on ourselves.

As summer approached, I pondered affordable things I could do that could include my girls. I was barely making enough salary as

Dog Love Stories

a teacher to cover rent, food, fuel, and other necessities. Houston was feeling good, but it was still a mammoth city. I missed our country days in Spicewood, and I thought the dogs did too.

Years earlier, Sidney had inherited his grandma's old farmhouse and ranch on several hundred acres just outside the little town of Goliad eighty miles north of Corpus Christi, and he had taken us all there. I loved it and noticed that not much had changed from when his grandma had lived there until she left unexpectedly after a fall in her elder years and never returned. Her closets were full, and the dresser top still had some jewelry and church gloves on it. All kinds of dated tins, jars, and utensils packed the kitchen. The entire house was cluttered. I asked Sidney if it would help him if I sorted through it all so that he could pick what to keep and what to give away. Perhaps the old place would take on a new shine. He agreed.

I learned of the ranch through my junior-high, high-school, college, and after-college friend, John, Sidney's former partner. John taught me at crucial times in my life that male energy could bring trust, love, laughter, and sensitivity, unlike what I had experienced with my dad. John loved going to the ranch, and I understood why as I sifted through the layers of living from the people who had spent time there.

Dancer, Pookie, and I took off just days after school was out. They hung their heads out the truck window, reminding me of Bandi-Lune years before when we hit the Grand Canyon—dogs ready for an adventure! Driving onto the land, I breathed in scents of cow manure and grasses like an Eau de Country cologne. After unpacking, we all settled onto the old wooden front porch, managing to fit on the porch swing with Dancer in my lap and Pookie as my armrest. A peeling white fence surrounded the house, with a crooked front gate creaking just right. The sun was setting, and all manner of pinks, yellows, and blues splashed across my view. White-winged doves cooed their refrain that some have said sounds like, *Who cooks for you? Who cooks for you?* The visual and auditory tableau had us all feeling right at home.

The next day, I woke up just as the sun was coming over the horizon and scurried to the front porch, already illuminated in the early morning light. The sky turned pink to yellow to bright gold. The sun was just rounding above the horizon's clouds. That big ole orange ball steadily floated up, showing why time seems to pass so quickly when we stare at the celestial process. Bobwhite calls pierced the air, cracking the morning in two each time they thrust out a *bob-white!* As the sun popped over the horizon, I could hear birds calling from every direction: mockingbirds monopolized while mourning doves cooed in the background amidst the songs of meadowlarks, martins, and the chirps of sparrows. The more I listened, the more I heard. Cows ambled by, staring at us as if questioning who these new creatures were staring back at them. Both dogs snarled as if trying to remember "cows" from their country days gone by.

Dance and Pook turned their heads to check in with me in sort of an acknowledgment of "home" and echoed my relieved sighs with contented groans of their own. It reminded me that when their humans are feeling at home, dogs feel at home too.

Once the sun heated up the morning, I went in to survey the scope of my work for the next five days. Sidney was coming out at the end of the week, and I hoped to have made a big difference by then. I decided to start with the bedroom where I was staying so I could have a place for my things. I took everything out of packed closets, from under beds, from on top of the vanity, and from chests of drawers, then sorted through the contents, thoughtfully considering what to keep. Some items were simply too precious to throw out or stuff back in a drawer—like the dainty church gloves, a pair of pearl clip-on earrings, an enamel comb, and a hand mirror. I arranged these on top of the vanity to look like Martha, Sidney's grandmother, had left them there, just so. I felt like an archaeologist panning through an ancient site. As I sifted through Martha's belongings in each room, it was as though she was sharing her life with me, gracing my visit with her stories, her dreams, her struggles—all those "daily bread" experiences that both challenge and nurture us. I whistled while working, both because I was enjoying the experience and to dispel any worries for the dogs that I was packing for another move. It worked, judging from the grins on their faces.

The South Texas days were humid and stifling. Each time I stepped through the front door, I felt relief when Gulf breezes blew across my sweaty face and body, blowing away debris and clutter in my mind and spirit. Somehow what I was doing for Martha's home, I was also doing for myself. It was as though I was spreading out my life dreams like the old quilts I found in boxes, noticing the stains, rips, and holes where mice had eaten through. Regardless, patterns persisted in emerging, and it occurred to me how with curiosity, willingness, and hard work, life can still piece itself together into an exquisite work of art.

The back room filled from floor to ceiling with piles of Martha's things for Sidney to look through and decide whether to keep, store, give away, or toss. The kitchen felt ominous with all its cupboards and cabinets. Everything felt like an antique. Finally, I tackled it, setting out tins of Maxwell House Coffee and Hills Bros. Coffee and biscuit tins adorned with pretty little girls in hats decorated with flowers. There were tins for de-mothing crystals, cleaning products, tobacco, you name it. When it came to old kitchen utensils, they ranged from worn wooden spoons to metal ladles and strainers to hand mixers turned by wooden handles.

Dancer and Pookie watched with fascination, thumping tails at my delight and chatter, but by the time shadows were slanting,

Dancer

both dogs edged to the front porch, encouraging me to join them. There we watched the sun set as swallows nesting on the porch fluttered and furled in the eaves, wishing other creatures weren't there regardless of how still we sat.

Sidney arrived as expected on the weekend, and we finished cleaning out his grandma's house of the last forty-five years' worth of her life there. I felt so much closer to this woman whom I'd never known. Little did I know I would be having dinner with her on the last night, or so it felt, when Sidney entered the kitchen in full grandma git-up: an old dress, lace-up pumps, white gloves, clip-on earrings, and, of course, a dressy Sunday hat. I laughed so hard I could barely eat, despite feeling ravenous. John once told me how Sidney was endearing to everyone, and indeed he was with his laugh and sparkle. I bet even Martha got a kick out of the scene.

Before school had let out that spring and the June trip to Goliad, a friend had told me of a guest ranch she had heard about in far West Texas smack on the border of Texas and Mexico. "It sounds like the kind of place where you'd want to spend some time. Take the name and number of the woman proprietor and give her a call." I put in a call the next evening and learned the woman was also a teacher, only she taught in a one-room schoolhouse in the tiny town of Candelaria. The price for a stay at the ranch exceeded my budget. We continued to talk for well over an hour, sharing stories about teaching, our dogs, and our love of the outdoors.

"I've been wanting to travel this summer. What if you stayed here at the ranch and kept an eye on the place along with my dog, horse, and plants?" She said Dancer and Pookie would be welcome. That clinched the deal.

Soon after returning to Houston from Goliad, Dancer, Pookie, and I took off for the wild west for our next summer adventure. My girls settled in the back bed of my Nissan truck that had a topper with a window on each side—the screen knocked out of one so they could hang their smiling heads out. The topper also had a sliding window that fit the cab's window. It allowed Dancer and Pookie to poke their heads up front where I was sitting, so we could chat as I clocked the eleven hours west from Houston to the ranch, another hour past Candelaria.

We were one happy pack. I wanted to hang my smiling head out a window too.

We drove through Alpine, then turned south at Marfa and into the increasingly isolated but scenic Chihuahuan Desert territory where the Rio Grande River divides Texas from Mexico. By now, it was an early July evening, though still plenty hot. Soon we were driving past what had to be the Candelaria schoolhouse, just across from the small Mexican town of San Antonio del Bravo. Theresa, the proprietor, had shared with me that families from Mexico sent their children to school there. (Border security didn't increase until years later, after 9/11.) I wanted to stop and explore, but Theresa had explained to me that the next eighteen miles to the ranch were a long, hard drive and could take well over an hour. Plus, there were some ominous clouds on the horizon threatening a West Texas downpour. I plowed on as the dogs alternately stuck their heads out the side window and then through the cab's window, panting with excitement. Dancer was pacing in the back because of winds that had come up, something she had never liked, just like Bandi-Lune hadn't liked the Santa Ana winds. I had never been anywhere so remote in my life, nor on such a rough road. It was like I had slipped back through time and was driving my two-wheel drive truck on a turn-of-the-century western trail.

After checking Theresa's directions, when I got to a fork in the road, I chose to turn right. The road soon narrowed, and I decided I better turn around. Then I realized I couldn't because,

Dancer

apparently, I was in a creek bed, not on the road. Backing out, I noticed something awry. A flat. *Oh, geez.* I hopped out, surveying the situation, along with the darkening skies, wishing I had practiced changing a flat on my truck before leaving Houston. The thought crossed my mind that I might end up spending the night in the bed of my truck with the dogs. Then I heard thunder roll and remembered I was in a dry creek bed that would soon be full of rushing water. *I can do this,* I thought, and kneeled to check on my spare under the truck bed.

"Looks flat," I heard as I was pushing myself under. Pulling back, I banged my head on the bumper while sitting up. A cowboy was sliding off his horse just on the rise of the creek bank. *Have I dipped into some kind of time travel?* Pookie and Dancer ran toward him with an observable relief that perhaps someone with more experience had arrived to help their distraught mom who was using words and a tone they recognized meant something bad had happened.

"Boyd. Theresa's dad." He stuck out his hand. "She told me to be on the lookout for you. Almost missed you back here in the creek bed." He winced while taking in my dilemma and then eyed the skies. My directions had me passing Boyd's home on about mile three of this precipitous journey. "We better get this fixed before all hell lets loose," and with that, he slid under my truck with the agility of someone much younger, and together we got the flat off and the spare on in no time. I paid close attention in case I had to change a flat again anytime soon. Boyd was kind and efficient, soon dusting off his jeans and donning his hat. "Better get going. I bet Theresa'll be out lookin' for ya. Back up some more, then follow the road." He said this like the road was the most obvious thing around, especially compared to the dry creek bed I had taken for a road. He patted the dogs' heads, tipped his hat, and hauled himself up on his horse in a manner that told me he had done that thousands of times in his day. I

Dog Love Stories

think the dogs were ready to take off after him and become cow dogs right then and there. With my insistence, Pookie hopped back in the truck, and I lifted Dancer in just as some fat drops landed on my head.

Boyd was sure right about all hell breaking loose. Thank God I was on the road and not in that damn creek bed where I would have been floating toward the Rio Grande by then. Instead, I was following Theresa, who had, by the grace of God, come out looking for me. After drying myself and the dogs on the ranch house porch, my heart was still pounding from my close call. Theresa calmly led me to my room, where she lit a candle since the electricity was out. I gasped. The adobe walls absorbed the candlelight with startling beauty in what felt like a golden womb. The dogs were groaning and already lying down. Theresa pointed out the bathroom and a back door in the bedroom that opened to the outdoors. In her soft West Texas twang, she assured me, "We'll have time to get to know one another and tour the ranch tomorrow."

Come morning, I would discover a spectacular view on stepping out that back door. After coffee and a bite to eat, Theresa and I took off on a hike before the day got too hot. It did not take long for Pookie to get cactus stuck in her nose, which was minor compared to the threats of rattlers and desert heat. Her curiosity got the best of her, and she ran like a hyper Lab, soon totally exhausting herself. Dancer watched Hank, Theresa's dog, and learned to go from the shade of one ocotillo to another. Even then, she clearly got too tired, now at ten years old, from the heat and distance walked. From then on, I decided to leave her on the back porch and leash young, rambunctious Pook for her safety.

Theresa took me on a long hike to some Indigenous American paintings on cliff walls—ancient handiwork, she explained, that possibly dated from five hundred to twelve hundred years ago. They had faded considerably but were still evident. This

Dancer

entire twenty-two thousand acres was mind-blowing and so much more than an empty desert: steep canyons, eye-catching crystals, smoothed metates, hidden springs in pockets of trees, and views across the Rio Grande into Mexico. Theresa pointed out three to four hikes she hoped I could remember after she departed so that I could safely explore this magical territory.

Before Theresa left for her travels, Dancer started barking for no reason that I could discern. "What is it, Dance?" I asked. "New territory, sounds, people, critters?" This experience was not like being at Goliad, all safe and cozy feeling.

She looked at me as if asking, *Can we go back to Goliad? What if you don't come back from a hike and I'm left here alone?* We were indeed out in the middle of nowhere, and Dancer was not feeling very comfortable. She was chewing her leg again and now added barking to her repertoire of anxious behaviors. I began taking the time to hold her in my lap, stroke her calmly, and whisper words of courage that might help us both on this adventure.

Spending time alone on this amount of isolated acreage was a stand-alone experience for me. I was always wary of possible dangers. I would write a note saying what direction and trail I was on and leave it on the kitchen counter. All it would take would be one slide on the rocks, one rattlesnake, a mountain lion encounter, or an aggressive javelina. But my due diligence paid off, and although I know all those fears were a possibility, the three of us stayed safe. Dancer eagerly greeted me on my return from these desert forays, gradually ceasing both her barking and leg chewing.

The desert lent itself to my reflections on an impending divorce from Bill, my move to Houston, my plans to start grad school, my loneliness and depression, my headaches and what to do about them, and those nagging memories of sexual abuse that had surfaced six years ago. After a spate of therapy, I had stopped

Dog Love Stories

when we moved to Jackson. The turmoil of those memories had become like chaotic bumper cars in my head. Maybe that was why I was having such painful headaches. All I was doing for therapy was journaling and spending time in nature and with my dogs. I tried prayer, too, which felt more like begging for guidance, signs, anything that might help me move forward.

I took the dogs down to one of the shady, cool springs nearby one afternoon, and we all soaked to relax. Pookie had been limping from cactus spines in her paws, and the healing waters did us all good, even independent Hank who sometimes joined us and snoozed in one of his favorite spots. The wind felt like a presence in the silence, as though combing the desert brush with long fingers. I felt proud of my girls for their trust, whether I deserved it or not, because I knew I was taking a risk just being where we were. When I called them, they came right to me, having developed an awareness that we were in no place for them to mindlessly stray. In the evenings, when the wind slipped noisily down the canyon, the dogs checked my expression nervously, only relaxing when they heard my deep sighs and saw my eyes calmly close.

One early dusk, I decided to walk down to the aboveground water tank for a cool-off swim. The dogs followed along. At this time of day, there was plenty of shade for them. Climbing up one ladder then down another into the circular tank, I spied a swallow, soaked and barely clinging to the side wall. When I put my palm out, she crawled right onto it, trembling. She looked like a cliff swallow, which made sense with the nearby cliffs and canyon. I placed her in the folds of my clothes lying on the platform, hoping this would warm her up. Dancer and Pookie watched from below.

More swallows and even a bat were now flying close, all gracefully dipping into the tank, with their resounding twitter-squeaks filling the air. "Little one, did you fly too close to the water and

Dancer

fall in?" I sat with her until almost dark, humbled, and deeply touched by nature, watching over the tiny winged creature who finally stretched out her dry wings and flew away. From the platform, I looked down at the dogs listening to me talk to another living being, cocking their heads from time to time. Dancer appeared on guard position at the base of the ladder to the tank, looking up at me with concern and then at Pookie, as if warning her. *You better stay close. Mom is doing something important; I can tell.*

Only days later it was time to say goodbye to Rancho Viejo, the desert, the canyon, and Hank. I was packed but had not yet loaded my truck. Watching Hank and Pookie play, I thought how good my dogs had been out in the middle of nowhere, here and in Goliad. It had felt important for us to share these adventures during our first trips as a family of three. God, I was glad nothing had happened to them at either place since I would never have made it to any vet in time. Yes, they had been seasoned travelers, hearty hikers, and always good sisters and friends. As I was surveying the area, Dancer was lying on top of a pile of my stuff, giving me the stink eye that said, *Don't even think about leaving me here!*

"I wouldn't ever leave you, Dance. Never ever!" That familiar grin returned to her face, and I noted that her leg was completely healed.

I never doubted my dogs' wordless love for me. They helped life feel full and rich, filling the days with wags, wiggles, licks, and kisses—*their* ways of communicating. Dancer and Pookie's willingness to connect and their capacity for sensitivity helped me to feel my soul's depth. Humans, I had come to realize, need an equal amount of reciprocity in their relationships. I grieved this had ceased happening in my marriage when Bill worked sixty-plus hours a week and rarely took the time to connect with me.

After our divorce, life opened. I sought how I could offer more to my dogs, my students, my studies, my friends, my dreams, and my growth. I was ready for a hefty dose of hope in my life. I wanted to learn to be alone for an extended time, finish my graduate degree, and understand how I could thrive more in life and not simply survive.

My biggest challenge remained the migraines that plagued me. Sometimes I missed a day of work; sometimes I had to leave work early. At home with ice over my eyes, forehead, and temples, the dogs would tippy-toe around. *Lie down and relax*, twelve-year-old Dancer prodded her younger sister, who was always restless for a walk. They lay on each side of me, and with a hand on each of them, it helped me calm down. "I'll walk you this evening," I promised, and I usually did. I tossed the slimy old socky toy—"Go on, play some tug-of-war"—which seemed to go on longer and be more fun when they had me as an audience.

Soon the combination of working, grad school, navigating migraines, and being a good dog mother became a supreme challenge. On the afternoons of faculty meetings in the school library, I watched the second hand slowly click through the numbers on the clock as someone droned on about something that rarely offered any value to my students or my teaching. I counted the hours my dogs had been indoors since leaving shortly after seven that morning, then cringed upon realizing it had now been over nine hours. I still had the long freeway-drive home, hopefully not to be further delayed by rush-hour traffic. Teachers with children to pick up were allowed to leave at four, and I often thought, *But what about my fur kiddos?*

One afternoon, after a ridiculously long faculty meeting, I arrived home late and anxious. "Hey, doggies, I'm home!" I called on entering my apartment. Pookie came running to me, but no sign of Dancer. "Dancer?" I walked through the living room and kitchen and was heading to the bedroom when I saw her standing in the bathroom with her head pressed into a corner, a fresh pile of poop in front of the toilet. She had never pooped in the house, and Pookie had only when she was a pup. "Oh, girl, you aren't in trouble because I'm so late!" I knew not to scold my dogs for behavior that was my fault. I scooped up the pile, plopped it into the toilet, and then kneeled to hug her. She was unresponsive. I went to get Pook's leash and called to Dancer, but she did not budge from the corner. "Let's go, little one. I'll carry you."

Even in my arms, she was stiff. What was going on? When we descended the stairs, I eased her onto the grass. Pookie was desperate to pee and poop, and as I scooped up her business, Dancer stood there motionless. I sat on the grass and spoke softly to her until she finally peed, then wobbled around with a vacant and expressionless look. "What is it, Dancer? Something is wrong, I can tell." I lifted her gently and rushed upstairs to call the vet. I was able to get a late appointment.

"This isn't going to be the news you want, but all signs point toward complications from a sudden stroke, or a brain tumor. We can run more tests, but if I'm right, cost for treatment could be considerable and might not work for very long or at all with an older dog like Dancer. Instead, I recommend we try some medication that could make her more responsive. It will also make her more comfortable while you think about what you want to do."

Stroke? Tumor? The vet knew from past visits how I barely managed on my teacher's salary. Treatment, he explained, could be in the thousands.

"But it happened so quickly! She's been just fine." Had I not been paying close attention? Too consumed with making lesson plans, my damn headaches, the divorce? He assured me these things could manifest suddenly. I gathered Dancer up in my arms, thanked him, and asked for the medication.

The meds did not help, and every day she got worse, barely eating or drinking, circling around or not moving unless I leashed her and directed her wobbly gait outside or in the house. Going to work during this time was pure torture. I was distracted and wanted to call home and ask Pookie how Dancer was doing. Pookie hung close to her sister, obviously concerned about Dancer's dramatic change in behavior. When I rushed into the apartment at the end of every day, her little nub of a tail moved ever so slightly, even if she could not get up. Sometimes she had peed and pooped on herself. The meds did help her recognize my voice, even though she could not see well. I carried her outside, then back upstairs, and I walked Pookie alone as she still needed her exercise, being a young and energetic dog. On our return home, she pulled at her leash, anxious to get inside so she could check on her sister.

At the end of the week, we returned to the vet. I was prepared for the worst, knowing I could not afford an expensive vet bill to attempt drastic, uncertain measures that had been floated on our last visit. I'd been chewing on the inside of my cheeks all week and wishing I didn't have to be around so many people every day. Tears came up unexpectedly and hefty sighs that had my students asking if I was okay. The vet and I decided it would be best for Dancer to be put to sleep, that anything else would likely not offer the desired outcome. I had rubbed my chest sore all week and was kneading it again while the vet checked out Dancer for the last time. I said I wanted to take her home for a final night together.

The girls and I settled on our couch in the kitchen, our favorite place to cozy up together. Dancer crawled on top of Pookie's back and pressed her head into the corner of the couch. Something about that pressure seemed to relieve her pain. Pookie lay there, eyes half-closed, uncharacteristically still, willing to stay in this uncomfortable position if that was what her big sister needed. It was heart-wrenching to see these sisters like this, one seeking relief and comfort and the other willing to give it. *If Pookie can stay in that position for as long as Dancer wants to lie on top of her, then I can stay on this couch all night,* I thought. I propped my feet

Dancer

on a kitchen chair and placed a hand on Dancer's bony rump, giving Pook a loving rub, too, every so often. Over the years, Dancer had taught me the value of taking quiet time together to calm down, and that was what we were doing there on our last night together. I noticed her chew spot was healed, and I wondered how long it would be before the insides of my cheeks returned to normal.

During the long night hours, I remembered coming home from school as a thirteen-year-old and hearing my mother say she had had my beloved first dog, Dabb, put down. Put him down? Isn't that what you do when you call someone a name or belittle them? How could that describe letting one of my beloved creatures go? It was a phrase I never liked or understood. Imagining Dancer going to sleep felt better, but that did not make the decision easy. I sang to her and hoped she could feel the love and warmth in my voice through the night as she, Pookie, and I rested in our puppy pile.

After Dancer's other sister, Bebe, died at eighteen months, I heard a few off-putting comments like, "Well, at least you didn't have her for that long." Now I worried about hearing, "Well, at least you had her for many years." Although the length of time we have a dog or a person can make a difference in the layers of memories, it is not at all a measure of the intensity or depth of love we experience. Dancer could have lived another half dozen years as a small dog in good health. Just because we have had an animal or a person for a long time, it sure doesn't mean it's easier to let them go. Dog love transcends time, regardless of how long a dog has been with us. I knew I would choose the opportunity of having to say goodbye and hurting like hell over never having dogs at all.

Darkness slowly gave way to morning's light. The heaviness in my chest got heavier as I looked at the clock and realized we had only one more hour together. I looked at sparrows sitting on the telephone wire and some budding spring foliage. We were approaching spring, an excellent time to plant. *Could I bury Dancer in my friend's yard in Austin and plant a tree on top of her?* A call to this friend sealed this idea.

"Pookie, I need you to stay here while I take your sister to the vet again. Letting her lie on your back the entire night was such an act of love and devotion." For four and a half years Pookie had been with Dancer. Now Pook looked at me with the saddest eyes, like she knew this was a goodbye.

Friend Kelly drove me to the vet while I held Dancer. She tucked her head under my arm and kept scooting deeper in my pit until she was pressed against the car seat. I stroked her short hair and sat quietly, trying my best to breathe calmly for us both. I told her how much I loved her and thanked her for what a good dog she had been and for being in our lives: Bebe's, Pookie's, Bill's, Shawn's, and mine.

We were the first appointment. I cradled Dancer as the vet injected the medication, repeating to my little gal—as I had all week and all night—how good she had always been in our lives. Whispering to my beloved dog and holding her close as she died felt like an honor. I felt her small, fragile body go slack as she went out without so much as a sigh.

I carried my beloved girl back home, then Pookie and I sat with her for about an hour. I let Pook smell her sister. I believed from seeing Dancer with Bebe's dead body and from watching my first dog, Dabb, whine after his bud Foxie had died, that dogs grasp this kind of loss. Pookie was quiet, noticeably withdrawn, and lethargic—not begging for a walk or a treat. After all, it had been a long night, and she had let her sister lie on her back the entire night. Dancer still looked alive, more relaxed now, like she was asleep. Her little feet felt soft and pliable, as if she could still prance like a deer. But I could feel the void in her body, as did Pookie.

I moved Dancer's body downstairs, where I had propped open an ice chest in my truck, and gently placed her inside,

Dancer

wrapping her in a colorful woven shawl a friend had once gifted me. Then the three of us took off for our last journey together, a three-hour trip to Austin. Once there, my friend Sharon and I dug a deep, wide hole, and placed Dancer's cold little body in it. I covered her with the shawl, then shoveled some rich soil over her before Sharon and I planted a possumhaw holly in the spot, a small deciduous tree with bright red berries. I hoped birds would come to sit in the little tree, sing, eat the berries, and keep Dancer company. Maybe, like me, she would remember the martins circling us as we gardened in Spicewood, the chorus of songs we heard from so many birds as we sat on the front porch in Goliad, or the twitter of swallows above the water tank at Rancho Viejo. I imagined the tree's roots reaching down to Dancer, seeking nourishment from her body. Surely Bebe, Bandi-Lune, and Dabb were now welcoming her somewhere in some special dog heaven–like place. Sharon went inside and I leaned on my shovel and watched my tears fall onto the fresh grave.

In the days and weeks that followed, I kept putting off vacuuming, not wanting to see Dancer's tufts of hair disappear. I refused to put up her dog bowl. Her collar and leash hung by the door, limp and useless. I needed to have visible memories of her as I went through the grieving process. I also wanted Dancer's smells to stay around for Pookie as she grieved.

Dancer had had two sisters and been through the death of one. She had become Bill's and my dog together, loved Shawn, been my constant comforter when trauma memories surfaced, endured the move to Mississippi with us, then Houston, and seen me through a painful divorce and several jobs. Yet her spirit seemed to steadily get stronger while mine frequently teetered on the brink of despair. It was almost like she'd had my back for twelve years, carrying that will to keep going for me when alone I could barely muster up the strength needed to go on.

Dog Love Stories

I had never written an obit, but it was time to start. I wrote how Dancer had gone from being a country dog in Spicewood to a yard dog in Jackson to an apartment dog in Houston. She taught me that home is more of a feeling shared than a place. I described how stroking her like a worry stone helped calm me and bring me "home." She often reassured and comforted Pookie and me with her mere presence. I mentioned how she was an excellent companion to me and Pook, the most prolonged day-to-day presence either of us had ever experienced. We ran, hiked, and drove thousands of miles together. We slept, meditated, played, and loved together. I described how Dancer reluctantly gave in to her suffering and, with graceful resignation, let go and slipped into death without so much as a sigh of relief.

Pookie was bereft, and neither of us was much use to the other in our grief, although I tried my best to comfort her. She didn't want me to pet her. She turned her head away when I cried, and she would go somewhere to be alone. Relationships were shifting. Dancer and Pookie had been one another's primary focus for over four years, and the combination of the two had been mine. Pookie and I both needed time to muddle through our heartaches. It would take however long it took for us to grieve the loss of Dancer, but grieve we would, and holding on to our memories of her, I trusted that Pookie and I would find our way forward and eventually toward each other.

Dancer
Loving Sister
1983–1995

FOUR

Bebe

(met her in 1988 while I had Dancer
and before I had Pookie)

The Bindseils' old country house had a big front porch that looked out on heaven, as far as I was concerned. Chickens pecked around, a rooster pretended to be territorial, and a cat or two lounged around with no interest in farm life. Their dog, Boomer, if he was at home, was always on the lookout for whoever might be coming down the road. Dancer, who was still alive at this point, and I passed the Bindseils' house daily on our walks, and if we were lucky, Boomer would be there to greet us.

Bill and I liked to say Boomer had a job as mayor of Spicewood. He roamed the town, welcoming people arriving at the old Baptist church on Sunday or stopping by to check their post office box on weekdays. He would wag and greet with the warmth of a practiced politician, only Boomer was 100 percent sincere. He was the size of a Lab and probably had some Lab in his mix, but there was no need to identify him as a particular breed because he was *Boomer*, and that was enough. People overlooked his dusty coat and were compelled to lay a hand on him anyway just 'cause he was so gosh-darn nice, standing there with an easy grin, calmly wagging his tail.

Like many politicians, Boomer apparently did a little cavortin' on the side with the ladies in town. One day, Mrs. Bindseil hollered at Dancer and me from her porch, "Boomer just had some puppies with one of the female dogs in town! They're tryin' to find homes for the pups! Would y'all like one?"

"Absolutely!" I bellowed back, thinking what a fine brood those pups would be with a dad like Boomer.

The idea of having two dogs appealed to me. Dancer seemed lonesome whenever I left her for long periods during the day, especially after we curtailed her sneaking around looking for dirty diapers. I knew that dogs like a pack, so why not give Dancer a friend?

Pretty soon, the puppies were weaned, and it was time to go fetch my choice. I went with a little gal, holding high hopes she would turn out like her dad. Dancer had sniffed that little pup more than the others, sealing the deal.

Momma was a beagle, so the pup was brown, black, and white with floppy ears and a delicate white stripe that ran straight down her forehead to her nose. She had her dad's grin and was already leaning toward looking more like her Lab mix dad than her beagle mom. We started calling her "Baby Boomer," or "B.B." for short. Dancer did not care what we called the pup; she was so excited to have B.B. around—cleaning her, nudging her outside, teaching her to play, and cuddling on Dancer's small dog bed.

In my mid-thirties now, I was teaching yoga and meditation classes in our renovated attached garage. Between that and working as a recruiter forty-five miles east in Austin, I felt busy:

Bebe

doing, doing, doing. I craved more time to just *be*. Coming home from a day of recruiting, I would sit down with Dancer and B.B., and they would pull me into a *be* frame of mind and soon I was thinking of B.B. as "Bebe." It felt like an affirmation to be more fully present every time I said "Bebe," and it was not hard to achieve once I started stroking those soft, floppy beagle ears.

Bebe soon lived up to her beagle breed with her hole digging. Apparently, it was her way of dealing with boredom during my days at work. It did not take long for our quarter-acre backyard to look like an air raid had dropped bombs out there. Thank goodness Bill and I had fenced off my garden to quash Dancer's appetite for used baby diapers at our neighbor's. But sometimes I would let the dogs out front for a change of scenery and, sure enough, Dancer introduced Bebe to diaper dining. Their days of hunting and gathering soon ended, and I kept them exclusively in the back, far from any diapers.

As soon as the Texas summer temperatures dropped to something almost reasonable, off we went on our evening walk. Bebe bounced beside Dancer and me, her ears flopping, and her tail wagging faster than Boomer's ever did. We would pass Boomer making his rounds about town or hanging out on his owners' porch, and he would come out to nuzzle the dogs and place his big ole head right under my hand, grinning the whole time. Boomer was never interested in walking with us. He had the town to keep an eye on, his rounds to make, neighbors to welcome home, and his own furry ladies to check on.

Just past the Bindseils' house on the other side of the road was the property of an older German couple, Ida and Otto Vogel, who were clearing their land to build a house while living in the garage they had finished in the meantime. Whenever the dogs and I walked by, they always waved their arms and, if close to the road, would stop working long enough for a little conversation.

Dog Love Stories

They loved the dogs and enjoyed watching Bebe zip by them after a bunny, baying like she did when hot on the chase. A decade later, Ida would thoughtfully gift me with a sewing basket she had created by stitching a "fluffle" of bunnies together in a circle, the basket topped with a handle, all stuffed lightly with cotton. A basket of bunnies, she explained, to forever remind me of Bebe's favorite pastime.

Bebe tripled the lengths of her walks by slipping under the barbed wire along the road, intent on her chase of rabbits. She also tripled in size as the months went by. Having a big dog and a small dog suited me. Dancer could still jump up in my lap while Bebe curled beside me, acting as an armrest. Soon, we had to get a dog bed big enough for the two.

I never saw Bebe bully Dancer with her size, but she could run faster and farther, and I let her. I would follow her flapping ears and long tail bobbing through a sea of grasses as she loped along, announcing her hunt with yodeling beneath the big blue backdrop of Texas skies. Dancer and I would wait patiently until she would finally materialize ahead of us, looking back with a what-are-y'all-waiting-on look. Then, after a little sticker-pickin' from her paws, we would proceed on, getting lost in another spectacular Texas sunset or enjoying the flowers—zooming in on the cosmos, as I used to think of it. Once, while gazing at the brilliant red-and-yellow trim of the daisy-like Indian blanket flower, the colors suddenly shifted. Looking more closely, I discovered it was a moth with the exact colors and design of the flower! Perfect mimicry. Nature offered such beauty and, along with my pack of two dogs, I was left with a wide grin of gratitude.

Bebe and her sister were rarely apart, and if one dog was inside while the other was out, each began looking for the other. I knew I was important to my dogs, but after spending all their days together, they were more important to each other. They played

Bebe

together, ate together, slept together, walked together, and together vied for Bill's and my attention. Why watch TV when I could come home and watch my dogs play tug-of-war and tease and chase one another around the house or yard, often prompting a good belly laugh. Life was better for me with a dog, and two were double the pleasure. Yes, having two dogs meant double the feeding, walking, and overall responsibility. But it also meant realizing Dancer had a playmate, sister, friend, and company, and that eased my worries and anxieties, especially during the long days when Bill and I were gone. In addition, Dancer now felt no need to perpetuate her nervous habit of chewing on her hind leg, which had completely healed.

Bill wanted to explore possible new directions in his printing work, so he soon left our pack to take a position in Louisiana. I stayed in Spicewood, needing to continue working with a therapist on sexual abuse memories that had surfaced a little over a year before. Our home felt too big and the nights too long with Bill gone. For the dogs, the attention of two humans was better than only one. I began to spend more time with Dancer and Bebe, which helped assuage Bill's absence for us all, and in turn, the dogs provided me great comfort.

As noted in Dancer's story, one Saturday morning when I was out front weeding and pruning the flower beds with Dancer right next to me, brakes screeched, followed by a horrible resounding thud.

A woman jumped out of her car screaming, "I didn't even see him!" I popped up, looking for Bebe, who I thought was on the front porch. I ran over to my girl, who was lying in the road weakly trying to lift her head. I could not see any blood, but obviously, something was terribly wrong.

"Please, wait here with her while I go call a vet and get my keys!" I begged of the babbling woman who was distraught and kept repeating how *he* came out of nowhere.

Dancer followed me inside, and I called the vet and told her the situation. She was about to close early as she did on Saturdays but agreed to stay. With keys and blanket in hand, I left Dancer inside and ran out. Bebe was still conscious but in pain. Spreading the blanket out beside her, I lifted her fifty pounds onto it as she whimpered. My adrenaline was pumping so hard I could have raised a car. The woman helped me carry Bebe to my car where I had opened the passenger door. With great tenderness, I positioned her on the seat, waved the woman away, jumped in, and took off. Before we even got to Highway 71, Bebe flopped her head across the emergency brake and onto my thigh. I had a twenty-minute drive to the vet's office in Marble Falls and knew I had to drive with extreme care for Bebe's comfort and so I wouldn't get stopped for speeding by a state trooper.

"Hang in there, girl. Please hang on. I should have been paying attention, sweetheart." I stroked her soft ears and muzzle and got a lick in response. I refused to let my sobs stop me from talking, attempting to soothe her as I kept my left hand firmly on the wheel while using the other to gently stroke those soft ears, her head, and neck. Everything inside her body had shifted uncomfortably to one side, and she took short, painful breaths.

The vet and her assistant were waiting outside. They hustled Bebe inside with extreme care as I followed on their heels. Laying her out on a table, the vet moved her stethoscope over Bebe, then followed with her hands, searching for a pulse and feeling for injuries. Bebe was silent and still. The vet finally looked up, shaking her head. "She's gone. I'm so sorry. I'm sure she has extensive internal injuries from the impact." She and her assistant told me to take some time with her and crept out of the room.

My tears flowed as I placed my hands on Bebe's warm body, stroking her handsome head and tri-colored body, feeling those ears over and over. I had never even thought about Bebe dying

Bebe

this young. I cried for her, for Bandi-Lune, and for Dabb. I cried for Dancer and the hole Bebe's absence would leave in her life. I cried for Bill and how far away he was right then. I cried that I would no longer see Bebe bounding through the fields in pursuit of bunnies. And most of all, I cried that I had not been paying closer attention while weeding and babbling to Dancer, hence not catching Bebe sneaking to the diaper stash.

After the vet and assistant put Bebe in a black bag and placed her in the back seat, I continued to cry all the way to Spicewood. I stopped to ask the Vogels if I could bury her there, and they said they would begin digging a hole in the rabbit grove where Bebe often hunted. But first, I needed to take Bebe home and find something beautiful to bury her in. Plus, I wanted Dancer to see her sister again.

When I got to the house, I found my nine-year-old friend and neighbor, Jamie, waiting. She had heard the screech and then watched me peel out, taking Bebe to the vet. She handed me a scribbled apology note from the woman who had hit Bebe. Jamie helped me bring Bebe up to the porch. I opened the bag, then let Dancer out of the house as Jamie and I sat silently on the ground beside the dogs. Dancer sniffed for a long time and began making soft little whines as she circled Bebe's body. Looking at Jamie, it hit me that I was around her age when I got my first dog, Dabb.

I found a bedspread embroidered with tiny blue and yellow flowers, then we loaded Bebe in the back seat and headed to the Vogels', Dancer sitting in Jamie's lap. Otto and Ida were waiting beside an open grave, Otto in his dirty overalls and Ida sweating in an old homemade dress with an apron. They helped us take Bebe out of the bag and place her on the bedspread, then we each grabbed an end and lowered her into the hole. Dancer sat still close by and watched. Otto began shoveling dirt into the grave as I kneeled beside Dancer. Jamie went to the car to get flowers she had cut from my front beds to place on Bebe's grave. I was still crying, though not the sobs that had erupted at the vet's, as I felt slightly self-conscious with this kind but pragmatic couple in their seventies whom I suspected had experienced death in myriad ways. Once the grave was filled, they touched me sweetly on the back and walked up to their garage. Jamie and I took the zinnias and irises and laid them on Bebe's grave one by one, then returned quietly to the car hand in hand.

Jamie's mom gave her permission to stay the night, and I was grateful for her company. After calling Bill to share the bad news, Jamie and I made peanut butter sandwiches, poured glasses of milk, then sat in front of the TV with Dancer. I had no awareness of what was on the screen. Instead, I watched Dancer, who had not touched her supper and kept looking around the house for Bebe. She sniffed a few of their toys, would come to sit beside us, then go on another search. The *click, click, click* of only one dog's claws was a lonely sound. The house felt like a gaping hole without Bebe's exuberant energy, and neither Dancer nor I wanted to try to fill that empty space.

This was my first time to be with any creature at their death. When my grandparents died, I didn't live close to them and had not been there. Sadly, I had not been with Dabb either, but his death had made me feel like my heart was being pummeled. Leaving Bandi had been like a death, and I remember thinking I could hear my heart crack as I walked away. Holding Bebe that day as she was dying was an entirely new experience, and I didn't even know where to go with my grief. Watching Dancer pace and Jamie glancing at my face made me feel like I needed to get up and do something, but I could not fathom what that would be. Finally, I lay down and coaxed Dancer onto the now too-big pillow she usually shared with Bebe, and she curled up in my arms. "Things will get better, little one, but it will take time."

Bebe

The sound of those brakes screeching and the thump of Bebe's body on the car resounded in my ears. I tried to calm Dancer when she would allow me, but she remained as restless as I was. She did not want to stay on the pillow but kept going on another search for her sister. With Bebe gone, it was clear something was not right, and although I knew what that was and Dancer didn't, we were both in a place of high anxiety. Despite practicing meditation for years, when I returned to the couch to sit still and breathe deeply, it didn't do a damn thing for me. Jamie reached over and took my hand, and I felt a flush of tears.

I was grateful for my little friend's company that evening. Jamie had proved thoughtful beyond her years on walks with Bebe, Dancer, and me. Once, she had told me how she could sometimes "see things in the air." I was unsure what she meant, so I asked her to explain. "Oh, colors and little things floating around, something like fairies. Do you ever see anything like that?"

I turned and looked at my little blue-eyed wonder of a friend jauntily walking beside me. I remembered confessing something similar at her age and realized how much she was trusting me with her revelation.

"Well, here's something that I once saw," and I began my story. "One Christmas Eve night, I woke up before any presents had arrived and decided to peek out my window, and there was Santa in his sleigh with all his reindeer pawing the ground! I couldn't believe it but also knew I had to get back in bed quickly or he might not leave any presents. So, back in bed, I somehow fell to sleep. The next day, I told my mom and sister what I had seen, and they played along for a while, then suggested I might want to keep such a discovery to myself. But it was too exciting to hold in, and I announced to neighbors and schoolmates what I had seen and got plenty of snickers. Sometimes we must be careful about who we share experiences like this with, even when we believe they are real." I wanted to accept Jamie's experience and tack on a bit of what I hoped was wisdom.

I did not tell her about my fairy godmother, however, who had been more real than Santa and his reindeer. I never told anyone about her. She appeared to me the nights Dad came to my bed. At the urging of my fairy godmother, I would magically slip out of my body while my dad did things to me that I did not understand. Magical thinking became a tool I used to survive. When Jamie saw colors and fairies in the air, was it any different than when I saw Santa or my fairy godmother?

On that walk before Bebe's death when I told Jamie about my Santa sighting, she had listened and nodded most maturely. It was as though we were collaborators in the fairy world, opening ourselves to all kinds of magic. Maybe we were, for Jamie started dancing beside us using an imaginary magic wand to cast spells on us that left me, Bebe, and Dancer feeling lifted and magical indeed.

Having Jamie with me while burying Bebe and then later at home had been most comforting. It was almost like our shared experience of magic placed Bebe not only in the presence of human angels—Jamie, the Vogels, and me—but also with a flock of fairies surely dancing around her. I believed, without a doubt, that the fairy godmother from my childhood was also comforting Bebe. In this good company of angels, fairies, a fairy godmother, and, of course, with Dabb and Bandi-Lune running alongside her, I trusted Bebe was off chasing bunnies across some heavenly field. The sound of her baying lulled me to sleep.

Bebe
Visiting Angel
1988–1990

FIVE

Pookie

(met her in 1991 while I had Dancer)

My friend John's intentions were nothing but good when he encouraged me to go for the little gal running circles around everyone else. "That's your girl. She's got energy, like you!" he announced. Eight white fuzzy fur balls scrabbled and squirmed around the mama's teats, but this one was yanking more than most, then rolling around and pushing on her littermates.

"Yes, she's been the most active in the bunch," the owner commented, "and one of the five not spoken for yet." One more week before the babies could leave their mom, who looked ready for them to be gone, or at least the one we were eyeing.

During my Houston visit that morning, I had shuffled into John's kitchen to find him circling want ads. "Whatcha doing?" I asked, reaching for the coffeepot.

"You said you wanted a Lab again, so I'm lookin' for some!"

Dog Love Stories

He smiled that wily grin of his. John knew my dog Bebe had been hit by a car six months earlier and that my other dog, Dancer (who was still alive at this point), and I were grieving her death. Bebe had been a mutt, but the dog before Dancer and Bebe, Bandi-Lune, had been a Lab and an exquisite companion.

After scanning the possibilities from the want ads, we found ourselves at a home that looked like someplace a dog would want to live: big fenced backyard, trees, kids, and, we soon found out, the whole slam-dam-fam lived there—the owners and their two kiddos and both the mother and father dogs with their eight white pups. The dogs' parents were obliging; the dad greeting us warmly while the mom looked up amidst the bustle of white blobs with a tired but friendly grin.

Coming upon Dancer at the shelter had felt predestined. I had picked Bebe because she looked like her dad, Boomer. Someone else had picked my dogs Bandi and Dabb. This was my first time to buy a dog, and it seemed like such a gamble. How does one choose one fur ball from the next out of a litter? I picked up the busybody John had pointed out and took her to sit with me away from the others. Clearly, this little one was still learning to use her feet, rolling around in the grass, struggling to stand, and practically giggling with joy at being alive. Suddenly, she pounced onto my lap and looked up expectantly as if saying, *Well, wanna team up?*

In a week, the owner was having another pup delivered to the Austin area, and she agreed to deliver my wiggly girl at the same time. The next Saturday, I drove in from our home in Spicewood to retrieve my two-month-old retriever from a guy in a parking lot. My pup seemed happy to see me, or maybe she was reflecting my delight and anticipation.

We had a forty-five-minute drive home, and my new four-hundred-dollar purchase was standing on her hind legs looking at me from inside the box I had brought, whining. I was

Pookie

now thirty-eight, with my fifth dog, and the first I had paid money for, other than a shelter fee.

"What are we gonna call ya, peanut?" I had told John, whose last name was Honeycutt, that I was thinking of naming her "Honey-Pooh" since he had instigated the search for my new dog. When I ran it by her, she grumbled, sounding more like, *Are we home yet?*

The first place I took her on our arrival was into my stepson Shawn's room. I plopped her next to him in bed. "Our new dog," I announced. "Honey-Pooh!"

Shawn opened his sleepy, fifteen-year-old eyes, took her in his arms, and mumbled, "Pookie!"

I grabbed the camera while she nestled there—Shawn stroking her soft puppy ears—and called, "Pookie, look over here," and she turned. Pookie had confirmed her name.

Dancer was elated, although not as much as her new sister. Pookie had been away from her littermates for almost four hours by that point, and she was looking for her pack. After some romping around, Dancer nuzzled her affectionately, and the two cuddled up on Dancer's little green bed. Pookie, about ten pounds smaller than Dancer's twenty, had already found the teddy bear I had given Dancer for comfort after Bebe's death, and the bear was in the tight huddle.

Pookie was a quick learner and Dancer a good teacher. Pook caught on about going outside to poop and pee; watching a house-trained dog is a good way for a new dog to learn desired behaviors. But as the months went by, Pookie's indoor behavior resulted in a few mishaps. These could have been avoided if I had thought to restrict her area while I was away, but I unrealistically counted on Dancer to direct too much of Pook's behavior. Perhaps after tussling around, Dancer wanted to rest, and Pookie needed an outlet for her boundless puppy energy.

Dog Love Stories

Most often, I left the two on our back porch with the screen door propped open. One day it was raining, and I thought Pookie would be okay inside with Dancer for a few hours. Returning home that afternoon, the dogs greeted me, Pookie with some stuffing hanging out the corners of her mouth. "Whatcha got there, girl?"

Pookie was ecstatic to see me, but Dancer had a hangdog look that communicated, *I told her not to do it, but she wouldn't listen.* Then, glancing up, I saw my treasured, retro floral-patterned couch de-stuffed on one end. The frame was exposed, and white fluff was everywhere. "Ohhhhh, I see. You decided to eat the couch!" I sighed and looked at Pookie, who stood there wagging her tail, oblivious to what she had done. "Not your fault, Dancer. Yours either, Pook. Guess I thought you could make better choices."

I was not a knowledgeable dog parent at this point but more of a fly-by-the-seat-of-my-pants kind of owner. I had not considered how every dog should be evaluated individually, with guidance for their temperament and age. After all, my first four dogs had been a breeze: Dabb had grown up mostly outdoors; Bandi was so timid and submissive as a one-year-old that she was never a problem; Dancer, also about one year old, came with good behaviors, perhaps from her previous owner; and Bebe was a hole-digger but not as rambunctious as Pook, plus had stayed outside most often. On the other hand, Pookie was hyper from the get-go, and right now, she was a stuffing-filled ball of energy. I wondered how much fluff was in her belly.

In retrospect, why had I not taken the initiative to read a book or two on dog training? I had consulted books about my other passions: yoga, running, vegetable gardening, growing flowers, and birding. Being a responsible dog parent was important to me. Yet I had not sought knowledge apart from my meager experience. Somehow, my prior dog ownership fooled me into

Pookie

believing I knew enough, when clearly, I did not. I proceeded as though, somehow, I was going to magically stumble upon the best ways to handle my dogs. Perhaps people are more apt to read books on parenting children than dogs, although both situations could use guidance.

I pointed to the couch and said firmly, "Pookie, NO!" Pookie only danced around, still silly with happiness to see me. It was hard to even say a name like Pookie sternly. "Oh, damn, I know it's my fault you had the couch for lunch." I got a bag and scooped up its guts. "Let's go for a walk and see if the movement will help you get rid of your latest meal."

What good does it do to scold a dog if she can't associate the bad behavior, which may have occurred hours earlier, with the consequences? Most importantly, I could have prevented the mishap from happening in the first place. The next time it was too cold and rainy to leave them outside, I put Pook in the laundry room with nothing to tear up in her reach. "C'mon, Dancer, I need you to stay in here with your sister so she has some company." Dancer, of course, complied, lying down next to Pookie on their bed.

For the most part, I had learned my lesson. However, I got sloppy a couple more times, thinking Pookie's size meant her brain had assimilated all desired behaviors. First, the end of an oriental rug was consumed, but unlike with the couch, I could hide the chewed end under a piece of furniture. Then, a leg on my wooden rocker was gnawed. Little did I know that in subsequent decades seeing that rocker leg would tug at my heart whenever I glanced down at that autograph.

With Dancer's constant companionship and my commitment to giving my dogs plenty of exercise, I successfully redirected Pookie's energy. We walked Double Horn Road, Dancer prancing obediently beside me and Pook on a leash. Occasionally she stopped and rolled over on her back, poking her four big paws in the air with that barrel of a pink tummy in the middle. When I saw neighbors at the post office, I heard variations of, "Seen you and your dogs on the road the other day. Looked like that pup had had enough!" I would give Pook a tug on the leash to get her back on her feet and off we would go, with her gradually getting the hang of how a walk meant staying on her feet and heading in one direction for an extended period, then back to where we started. Seeing her crash on her pillow on our return was the desired outcome.

As Pookie added pounds, her tug on the leash got stronger. She wanted to run faster than I walked or ran, and while she gagged at the pressure on her throat, my shoulder would ache from the power of her pull. She was inching closer to half of my weight and big enough to put her front feet on the kitchen counter and drag off a pizza that was cooling. At least we managed to salvage half of it for dinner.

I was teaching yoga classes at the time and mentioned the reason my shoulder was so sore in one class. Unbeknownst to me, one of my students was a former FBI agent who was now raising and training Labs for locating drugs and more. Dan offered to run Pookie through the daylong tests they used to determine which three-to-four-month-old pups would be selected for their training program. They sold the pups that did not pass. Pookie was already five months old but not too old to be trained if she passed the test. "She'll be easier for you to work with and a better-behaved dog if she is trained," Dan insisted.

Pookie was happy to be going anywhere in the car. I left her at Dan's and was back in six hours. "You've got a doozy," he chuckled. "Pretty hyper but plenty smart! We'd pick her in a nanosecond."

"Well, she was the most active out of eight pups," I said, confirming Dan's assessment of her energy.

Pookie

"We enjoyed working with her. Got a great temperament. Affectionate but not needy. If you'd like us to put her through basic training for a week, I'm happy to do so."

Sounded like military school to me. After Dan explained how she would be boarded, taught, and cared for, it seemed like a valuable opportunity for Pookie *and me*, and he insisted on doing it at no expense since she could slip in as part of their upcoming class.

We returned home to pack Pook's military duffel and tell the fam what was in store. Training started in three days. Bill and Shawn thought it was hilarious that she got into "military school," as I kept calling it, and Dancer could not figure out what all the excitement was about. Pookie was just Pookie, happy that everyone around her was happy.

At the end of the week, Dan told me I was the next to be trained. In addition to the FBI, he also sold his dogs to police departments and workers using Labs to detect pipeline leaks. "It's usually harder to train an inexperienced handler than the dog," he explained.

Pookie proved to have much more focus, energy, and memory than I did, looking at me quizzically as I babbled directions with a goofy grin. "Sit, Pookie. C'mon, girl." I gave the command a little too loudly in my frustration as Pookie gave me a confused look.

"Be concise and only use the command," Dan guided.

"Sit, Pookie," I said loudly.

"Don't say her name, just the command," Dan repeated. "It's not necessary to raise your voice," he instructed in his kind but firm voice. Then he turned to Pook and said in the same voice he had used with me, "Come," and she trotted over. "Sit," and she sat.

Watching Dan, I realized how inconsistent I had been in my training efforts. He also pointed out that smiling when I meant business could confuse a dog. I did not have to look mad, just serious. After she responded to my command, I could then smile as I praised her. No wonder my dog had been utterly confused. When we were done, I felt like I had been there all week. But the gist was that she would likely become noncompliant if I did not reinforce what she had been taught.

What a difference! Pookie was still joyful, and her new behaviors seemed to make her even happier. Well, of course! I was not hollering at her, yanking her leash, and displaying exasperated behavior. My shoulder healed. Life was peaceful. Even Dancer was relieved. The training had transformed our walks into meditative outings where I could walk calm prayers instead of uttering desperate pleas for help with my dog.

Within a month, Bill's temporary job in Louisiana finished, and he accepted a job offer in Mississippi. The dogs followed me around the house, perplexed with why I was boxing up belongings and emptying rooms. My spirits were sinking. *Mississippi?* I looked around at our humble home that I treasured and the soothing nature that surrounded us there in the Texas Hill Country, and I could hardly bear the thought of leaving it all. *Mississippi?*

It was December when we arrived at the house we had rented in Jackson. My insides were as cold and dreary as it was outside. Pookie and Dancer roamed their new spacious backyard and, with yearning looks, begged me for walks. I found the state park at the far end of our road, and all our spirits lifted. During the winter days, the park was practically empty, and I began letting Pookie off-leash. I wanted my arms free, my mind blank, my feet moving at a leisurely pace. When I leashed her, my lapse in maintaining her training had her pulling again, and one day her six-month-old fifty pounds injured my right shoulder. I had heard that Labs could be late bloomers, and Pookie was not a year old yet. I could see that for my growing dog to maintain

Pookie

what she had learned in her training, it was up to me to reinforce those behaviors with practice.

"Pook, you gotta help me here, even if this is my fault," I babbled as I held her leash with my uninjured left arm while keeping her on the right side as Dan had taught me. We worked with heel, come, stay, sit, down. Amazingly she acquiesced and returned to being the honor student she had been for Dan during his training. "Good girl!" I praised with a genuine smile on my face, giving that big Lab body of hers a good rubdown.

Not a year into the miserable Mississippi adventure, we purchased a home and moved again. Move number two for the dogs. This backyard provided Pookie with a deck to fly off as she ran in circles, a slobbery ball retrieved in her drooling mouth. In the fall, she created tornadoes of leaves as she cruised through the raked piles, emerging from the flurry with pure delight spread across her face.

By now, I had landed a teaching position within the Jackson Public Schools. Days were long and full; however, I still prioritized dog walks. I knew how important it was for them and me. I tried leaving the dogs out back in the warm months until Pookie learned she could crawl over the chain-link fence. "Hey!" my neighbor hollered at me when I stepped out back on returning home from school one day. "That big white dog knows how to climb fences. Found her nosing around in my backyard today and shooed her home."

"Pook, you're gonna have to stay on a long lead while I'm at work. You'll have water, shelter, and sun. We've got to keep you safe, girl."

Dancer stayed with her sister in the backyard, continuing to be Pook's touchstone in life. Pookie loved us all, but after leaving her litter, she had been with Dancer 24/7. I am not sure Pookie could separate who she was apart from her sister.

Dog Love Stories

A year later, Pookie and I took a trip without Dancer to Gulf Shores, Alabama. She ran in the waves until exhausted, then after a short rest, a wet slimy ball would drop in my lap, and she was ready to go again. This was her first experience of having my undivided attention, and it showed in her exuberant glee. When we arrived home, however, she lunged at Dancer like a football player, tackling her sister with love and affection.

Dancer! I went to the ocean and got to run in the waves and roll in the sand! I missed you, Sissy, but I had so much fun! Dancer licked her sister, probably tasting salt water and possibly remembering her own trip to the ocean years earlier. Dancer and I had had time alone with each other in her life, and now I knew how valuable it was for a new dog to have that experience.

"Houston is a great place to live! I think you'd like it," my friend and Pookie's namesake, John, encouraged. I had begun to consider moving there while talking to John one day on the phone. Shawn was about to finish high school and my marriage with Bill felt dismal. I was desperate to make a change.

"Yeah, Sister Antoinette is there too," I added. She had been my mentor since being my first principal in my teaching career. Houston was indeed a draw for me with both Antoinette and John there.

"Well," John hedged, "this AIDS journey might take me down before you get here." My gut lurched. Without seeing John, it was easier to think he was doing better, his humor and cheerfulness intact during our conversations. Sadly, John turned out to be right, dying several months before I made the move.

Pookie was three when she, Dancer, and I moved into a little ground-floor apartment near the Houston school where I would be teaching. This was their third time moving with me, and it still made them nervous. I remembered how, after moving out to LA with Bandi-Lune, I gradually became sloppy in my

Pookie

responsibility for her. I was determined to be more responsible with my dogs this time around.

"Pook, how ya gonna do without your big backyard? Think you can make it inside this little place without resorting to your destructive habits of youth?" She had not chewed anything up in years. Pookie dropped the ball in my lap, and I rolled it across the living room. She acted like this was the best place in the world to play fetch, almost slamming into the dining room wall in her frenetic efforts to retrieve the ball as it rolled under the table. She seemed so easy to please. I wished I could be.

We established a walking routine around the apartment complex before I left for work and immediately on my return. My neighbors, few of whom had dogs, warmly welcomed us and seemed quite fond of Pookie and Dancer. Every evening I took the dogs to a nearby levee for a long walk, a soothing experience for us all. Pookie could exhaust herself retrieving balls on land and water while the quiet beauty and birdlife calmed Dancer and me.

After learning that my apartment complex was occupied by sex workers and pimps—kind though they were—John's former partner, Sidney, found the perfect garage apartment for the dogs and me in the neighborhood where he lived in Houston Heights. We prepared for move number four.

In this apartment, Pook was tall enough to see out windows in all directions. She kept an eye on the birds, squirrels, and life on the street. We could safely walk to a high school track nearby and to a vast park that ran alongside a bayou, and we could walk to friends' homes. Two of the most important lessons I had learned about being a responsible dog owner were to provide plenty of exercise and socialization opportunities with other humans who loved dogs.

Often on a Friday, I would head home, load up the dogs, and take off for Galveston in time to walk beside the ocean for

Dog Love Stories

sunset. The sounds of waves breaking and rushing were like music. Pookie would pursue seagulls who taunted her until she broke into a full chase. Crabs munched on my apple peels, their high-story eyes on me the whole time, until scampering away and disappearing in a flash. The dogs would romp and play and, of course, roll in decomposing fish. Thank goodness I had a truck with a topper where I could sequester them until a good spray-down at home. Once, Pookie drank some salt water, and the resulting puke found its way into the crevices of my truck bed, requiring a massive cleaning later. Still, it was worth it, for them and me, to air out on the beach at the end of long, tiring weeks.

Summer held plans to go clean out Sidney's grandmother's farmhouse in Goliad, then later to Rancho Viejo in far West Texas. The travelin' trio we were, me and my dawgs. Lazin' on the farmhouse's front porch with coffee in the morns and iced tea in the afternoons, a dog on each side as I rocked in the porch swing, put me in the center of dog heaven. Sometimes Pookie would take off through the yard's gate and slip under the barbed-wire fence to sniff around in the pasture. I liked that my apartment dog had this freedom. However, she kept a close eye on me, and if I went inside for any reason, boom, she was back on the porch! She liked to roam and wander as long as we could keep eye contact. She appeared to like the experiences of connection, safety, and security with me as much as I wished to offer those to her. She wanted her freedom, but not too much of it.

Later, at Rancho Viejo—when we were indeed in the wild, wild west—Pookie demonstrated this same concern, only it took her longer to seek the cool of shade, unlike her new desert dog-friend there, Hank. Back in Houston, between Goliad and West Texas, Pookie was back on her leash on our walks and resumed her good behaviors without a hitch. Once off-leash in the far west, she stayed close by, as though aware this was no place to

Pookie

stretch her freedom. Again, I thought of how my earlier dogs had experienced freedom: Dabb never had a leash and roamed free in my childhood neighborhood; Bandi-Lune once hopped the fence at our fourplex and made her way to the beach on her own while I was at the university all day; I leashed Dancer when she first became our dog, then later wore it around my waist, and subsequently forgot it altogether on our walks; and Bebe yodeled like the part beagle she was while careening through the fields on a bunny chase, reliably returning to Dancer and me as we moseyed on.

In Mississippi, I discovered Pookie could run through the state park and would come when called. On one visit there, I found Pook about to pick up a sleepy water moccasin. "No! Come!" I screamed, careful to be succinct and stern. Pook pivoted from the snake and came right to me. "Geez, Pookie, am I glad you listened!" I felt such relief that her military school training with Dan still held. Thank God she had heeded my command.

I liked giving Pook occasions to be unleashed, as long as I could pay close attention and keep her and other dogs and creatures safe. Allowing my dogs opportunities for freedom felt essential, but I realized the risks and only took them when my dogs demonstrated learned behaviors.

Pookie, Dancer, and I returned to Houston at summer's end and embarked on another school year together. They were back in the garage apartment for long days as I commuted to the high school where I taught and worked. I fretted about them being inside for so long. Still, I remained committed to taking them out in the mornings and immediately on my return, then giving them significant exercise in the evenings—walks and a lot of ball throwing. At four years old, Pookie was more mature and had retained her training despite my lapses.

Dog Love Stories

As recounted in Dancer's story, one day after arriving home from work late, I found Dancer standing in a corner, unresponsive, behavior the vet believed was a possible brain tumor and/or stroke. From the moment of finding her and during the ensuing week of her care and the decision to put her to sleep, Pookie's behavior changed drastically: she observed everything; she was not clamoring to get out on her walks; she pulled like old times to get home, anxious to get back since Dancer could no longer go with us. Once we arrived home, Pookie immediately went to her sister and lay beside her with little interest in eating.

On Dancer's last night at home, Dancer crawled onto Pookie's back while they were on the couch. Pookie stayed there all night without moving with her sister on top of her.

"I want to be like you, Pookie, for the people I love. Patient. Steady. Committed to their end-of-life journeys." I babbled through the night to both dogs and myself, dozing repeatedly, shifting my position while Pookie remained still. By morning, her face was devoid of joy. She grasped that our lives were changing.

I brought Dancer's dead body home from the vet so Pook and I could sit with her, remembering how Dancer and I had spent time with her sister Bebe after her death. Pookie sniffed Dancer all over, then lay down next to her, the same sad look on her face I had seen that morning. On our way to bury Dancer, Pookie moved slow, with a noticeable lack of energy. I kept trying to make eye contact with her as I usually did with our communications, but she looked away. She came when I called, jumped in the truck when encouraged, but was unwilling to connect with me.

Plain and simple, dogs grieve. People that debate this have not lived through the death of a dog and then watched how that dog's companion reacted. I had seen it now with three of my dogs who had lost a companion who they were *always* or often with. Pookie's love for Dancer moved me and kept me aware that

Pookie

it was not I who had been the center of Pook's universe. Pookie had been Dancer's dog more than she had been my dog, 24/7. It gave me pause to even try to calculate all the hours they had spent together in Pook's four and a half years, and I had never once observed a fight, simply their immense affection for one another. If only I could claim the same in the closest relationships I had had within my species.

In the subsequent months, Pookie and I had to find a new way to be together as we had rarely been with only each other. I walked her as usual, but she would often lie down at the track while I ran, right where she and Dancer used to tumble. She chased a few balls but walked rather than running them back to me. At home, she was not comforted by my sitting with her or when I put my face in her fur. She abided it but sighed loudly and looked away. I did not get so much as a nuzzle. It bugged me that I wanted her to comfort me, while I was unsure how to comfort her. I began sitting with a little distance between us, most often on the kitchen couch, and talking to her softly about Dancer.

"Dancer sure loved you, Pook, and you loved her too. Remember our days walking on Double Horn Road when she had to keep pushing you to quit rolling onto your back? Then in Mississippi, she stayed in the backyard all day with you when I had to tie you up to keep you from crawling over fences. She never complained, did she?" I gave Pookie's ears some gentle rubs. "And the three of us had such good times on our trips last summer to Goliad and West Texas. You two were perfect for each other. We were lucky to have Dancer, weren't we?"

I gave Pookie time and space and quit trying to force her to do what she didn't want. I put food out to eat when she was ready. I tried to keep everything else consistent: feeding times, longer walks, time on the couch together, frequent visits with friends Sidney and Michael and Kelly. Kelly stopped in during my long workdays to see Pookie and even started keeping Pook at her and

Dog Love Stories

Michael's home several times a week. Over the next three to four months, Pookie slowly emerged from her grief, and I rediscovered the strength of relationship that can occur between one dog and one human, like what I had experienced with my dogs Dabb and Bandi-Lune many years ago.

Pookie and I took off for an Austin visit when school was out. Shawn was now living there, and that's where Dancer was buried with a lovely tree planted on top of her. I wondered if it had some buds.

One morning Shawn, Pook, and I went hiking on a trail that ran alongside Barton Creek. The day held blue skies, a comforting breeze, and running water nearby. Shawn was telling me about his world when we stumbled upon a guy standing near the water, his fishing tackle all set up, swiping a fillet knife on his trouser leg. He had a faraway look in his eyes and in a strange monotone voice uttered, "There's a lot of fish in there."

He did not make eye contact. After Shawn responded, "Well, that's great!" we moved right along, giggling nervously, and when out of earshot, commented that the guy seemed stoned.

Then Pookie yelped.

"Pookie!" I screamed, as Shawn and I turned in the direction of her panicked cry. Pookie came running toward us, one side of her face flapping, blood flying in all directions in the sunlight. I was on my knees when she ran right into me. I saw that the skin on the right side of her face looked like it had been filleted. Shawn took off his T-shirt, and we pressed it against her wound. She was shivering. I hoisted her into my arms, and we began walking back, passing where the guy had been fishing. There was no trace of him.

Shawn and I took turns carrying Pook. She weighed sixty pounds, half my body weight, but I needed to hold her. I wanted

Pookie

her to feel my arms around her. I remembered feeling like I could lift a car years earlier when I carried Bebe from the street where she had been hit to my car. Pook was still and quiet. I reassured her softly that everything was going to be okay. "I love you, Pookaburra. I love you, girl," I repeated. Luckily, we had just started on our walk and were not far from my truck. In she went, partially in Shawn's lap so he could keep the pressure on her wound while I drove to an emergency vet I remembered from my Austin days.

The vet said it looked like a sharp knife had slit her face, that maybe she had turned her face right before impact, which helped keep the cut shallow. He could not see any eye or nerve damage. He flushed out the area, placed a tube in her face, then temporarily patched up that side. "Once you're in Houston, see what your vet says about irrigating the wound twice a day for ten days and then pulling the tube out. I'm giving you some antibiotics for her as well. She's a lucky dog."

Oh, Lord. Dancer had only been dead for about five months, and I could have lost my other dog? My vulnerability was hovering over me like a menacing cloud. I realized I had been so involved in my conversation with Shawn that I had not paid sufficient attention to my dog off-leash. I knew better; when dogs are off-leash, you must keep your eyes on them.

Once back in Houston, Pookie and I got into a rhythm of the nursing routine, always on the kitchen couch. "Let's see, Pookaburra, I'm going to flush this wound out and clean you up again," I informed her as I arranged the towel, medicine, and bowls of warm soapy water and clear water. She was not crazy about this, but she complied, and it gave us hours of one-on-one time together. "I'll pay more attention on our walks, girl, because you are too precious to me to have you injured again or to lose you." Stroking her velvety soft ears became her favorite way of receiving affection, something I did after nursing her, and I would lay my head on her back. Like she had done with Dancer, she would hold still. "I'll do my best to be a better dog mom, Pook."

Pookie began reciprocating my affections. The smile returned to her now-scarred face. With permission, I took her to my high school a few times, demonstrating her discipline for my students.

"Sit," I'd tell her, then do an easy toss of the ball in my classroom. She would sit there quivering until I said, "Okay!" then race to the ball and bring it back to my outstretched hand. "See," I told my students, "if my dog can refrain from going after something she desperately wants, so can you." Teachers were always trying to influence our students to walk away from fights when provoked and, of course, the temptation of drugs.

Pookie would spend the rest of the class on the old couch I had brought into my temporary classroom building, along with various standing lamps, so we did not have to use the buzzing overhead fluorescents. Their absence helped us all relax more, but not as much as having Pook in the classroom. The kids took turns sitting beside her on the couch and on the floor, and she relished all the attention, generous with her nuzzling, licks, and satisfied groans. The use of "emotional support dogs" was not yet widespread, but clearly, Pookie was a pioneer in demonstrating the idea.

Daily exercise was an integral part of our life, vital for both of us. One of our favorite places to walk was along a bayou in our neighborhood where I threw balls for Pookie to retrieve. Periodically, the water in the bayou would be full and moving along fast—depending on Gulf Coast storms—partially covering the walkway that stretched beside it at the bottom of the steep concrete slope. One day, a ball I had thrown rolled by accident down a slight grassy knoll right into the bayou's slope, plopping into the fast-moving water. Ever the diligent Labrador retriever, Pookie dove in after it.

Pookie

"Pookie! Come!" But she could not hear me over the rush of water. I ran along the canal, delirious with panic, watching as the water swept her along. "Help me! Help!" I screamed at the top of my lungs as I ran at the top of the bayou, keeping my eyes on my girl. I couldn't get ahead of her; if I had gone down the slope, she would have been way ahead of me in a flash. Pookie would flail at the side of the bayou in efforts to get out, but the power of the water was too strong for her. I began contemplating jumping in myself. It wouldn't be my first time trying to save a dog in the water.

Suddenly, way ahead of us, a runner was creeping down the steep slope sideways, keeping one hand on the ground. He reached the water ahead of Pookie with his arm outstretched. In a matter of seconds, she was within his grasp, and he gripped her collar and began dragging her out of the water and up the slope. Her feet barely touched the ground, but the runner pulled, even when she collapsed on her belly, gagging. I was waiting for them at the top, Pookie now breathing heavily on her side in the grass. I pressed my face in her neck amidst my litany of, "Thank you. Thank you. Oh my God, you saved my dog! Thank you so much." I looked up to take in the face of this incredible person—only no one was there. Puzzled, I twisted around and checked all directions. No runner, only a few people walking, no one in running gear, ANYWHERE. Only a few minutes had passed from the time of his dragging Pookie up the canal's slope. Pookie's hero in the blue-and-yellow running shoes had evaporated, yet his wet tracks were still on the concrete of the bayou's banks. Someone had been there!

Pookie was still flat on her side. She did not appear injured, only exhausted. Her belly was red where it had scraped the concrete while the runner was dragging her. My girl lifted her head and nudged me. "Oh, Pook, I never thought your ball would roll down into the canal! Girl, I was about to dive in and come after you. We both would have ended up in the Gulf of Mexico!" Pookie got to her feet and shook. I laughed nervously as a spray of water glowed myriad colors in the sunlight. "Who was that guy, Pook, and where the heck did he go?" I looked around again, then up, half expecting to see a guy dressed in running shorts, shoes, and angel wings hovering over us in the sky.

I mumbled prayers of gratitude all the way home, wondering what in the world just happened. Maybe Pookie had her own guardian angel! Perhaps this was Dancer's doing, or John's. Those thoughts helped me relax and breathe deeply after this close call. From the horrible man with the knife at Barton Creek to this miracle person beside the bayou, my dog was still alive, thank God. Once again, I vowed to be more vigilant.

Pookie and I soon experienced an unexpected pause in our lives: I had an emergency total hysterectomy when a tumor that turned out to be benign was discovered on my uterus.

Kelly and Michael cared for Pookie as usual. I heeded the "don't drive for six weeks" and rested at home, missing the first two weeks of teaching in the new school year. Friends stayed over the first week and continued to help in the weeks after, but Pookie and I were on our own for the most part. It was heaven. We relaxed. I could toss balls and was able to lengthen my walks gradually. I felt my entire physical-mental-emotional-spiritual system recalibrate.

I prepared lessons for the substitute teacher and kept up with my graduate courses, but I was not commuting daily or navigating 180 students a day. I did not have to hear bells, buzzers, school fights, alarms, horns, sirens, and the screech of tires. Leisurely naps became the norm, sitting quietly on the kitchen couch with Pook's head in my lap became a daily habit, and my headaches eased. I experienced what it would be like to live with less stress, less rush, and deeper breaths. Throughout the subsequent school

Pookie

year, I fantasized about what I could do to help life feel more spacious.

The tenant in the house in front of me moved out, and my landlord encouraged me to move up front. "You'll have a backyard for Pookie!" he pointed out. Being able to open the door and let Pook out, giving her a place to lie in the grass and bask in the sun—maybe this was the more spacious life I had envisioned. Pookie and I spread out in the house, loving every inch of it, even if it was way more room than we needed for the two of us.

The house was full of windows, partially covered with white cloth shower curtains I'd found at a Target store. I worked at the computer on my thesis until my back hurt, then crawled into the deep claw-foot tub with a ceiling fan over it, one hand hanging over the edge on Pook's head as I relaxed in humid Houston's spring afternoons. We were in our own house, just the two of us, and it felt like we were all the other needed.

By now, I was seeing a therapist regularly—sometimes taking Pook with me—getting guidance for navigating stubborn abuse memories, discussing my migraines and why I might be having them, and working toward having more of the life I wanted.

Even with my master's thesis complete and a slight bump in pay with the additional degree, rent was eating up too much of my paycheck. I wanted to save money and figure out how to have that more easeful life I had fantasized about after my hysterectomy. Move number seven for Pookie. She did not stress when I schlepped the boxes out of the attic, but I did. It seemed like an ongoing adventure for her, but I wished I hadn't moved from the last garage apartment.

My new upstairs garage apartment was only blocks away and across the street from a park. Its best feature, however, was that the house next door had a pond with running water under my bedroom window. Listening to the water was almost as calming as knocking four hundred dollars a month off my rent. Also, with some of the extra money, I hired a dog walker to come by on the days I had to be at work for over ten hours because of meetings, a class for teachers I was leading, or parent-teacher conferences. It relieved my stress substantially to know that the dog walker was coming by to take Pookie out and give her some company on those days. Pookie and I were both calmer with this arrangement.

No longer being in grad school allowed me to tap into the dating scene. Despite being open to dating people of any color and gender persuasion, I still wasn't having much success. I was just about to give up when a dog-loving physical therapist invited both me *and* Pookie to dinner. That seemed promising until her groomed, fluffy, perfumed dog decked out with bows greeted us. Her dog sniffed Pook's earthy smell that lingered from a mud puddle she had plopped in earlier, a few clots still hanging on her belly. My date winced, and we didn't make it to dessert before my early exit. I decided that dating was overrated.

I was now coming up on eighteen years of having migraines. Every time I thought I could blame something—two marriages, two divorces, sexual abuse, Mississippi, the stress of teaching, graduate school, my reproductive system, my lousy dating experiences—once that situation was changed or improved, the headaches would still be there. My therapist suggested I think about a major life change that could allow me to have an extended pause.

After a great deal of thought, I talked to my principal, who was aware of my migraines, and told her I was thinking of taking a year off from teaching. This idea had been bouncing around in my head since the weeks after my hysterectomy. She offered to hire a yearlong sub and guaranteed I would have a job upon my return. I began calling it my sabbatical, even though I would receive no pay for the year.

Pookie had become my bodhisattva. She loved me however I was: happy or sad, headache or not, secure or insecure, confused

Pookie

or clear thinking, accepting or hard on myself. Her constant, unconditional love taught me to forgive myself more often, not set such high standards, and acknowledge that I had mental health challenges and could navigate them, even when I did not always make the best choices. I vowed to take care of myself in part so I could take care of Pookie. After all, I had been in therapy, finished grad school, held down jobs, and arranged for this sabbatical.

I sent out a letter mentioning that I was looking for a place to stay with little or no rent for a year, preferably in the country. By then, I had saved enough for another move, to pay for utilities and food during a year off, and then to move back to Houston or somewhere else at the end of that year. A few ideas and offers floated in, but one from my sister Pamela felt like the best idea. Move number eight for Pookie took us to Gainesville, Texas, where both my sisters lived, to move sight unseen into an old mobile home in the country they had cleaned up for me. Almost everything worked in the trailer after a plumbing fix here and there. I unpacked and settled in for the year. My rocker went on the front porch where I could gaze across several fields at the longhorns grazing. With one of Pook's beds beside me, my hand stroked her velvety ears, and I breathed deeply. We were a team playing "slow down and live." In the evenings, we soon realized we were in the middle of a firefly hatch, leading me to name our new home ground Firefly Fields.

Growing up outside of Abilene, Texas—hiking through fields, exploring a creek bed and the dump nearby, riding my bike for hours on dirt roads—I used to roam and wander outside of my assigned boundaries. Now I was doing the same, but with no limitations imposed by my mom. Pookie even ventured out on her own. She would mosey across the road, slip under the barbed wire, and sniff around in the field where the longhorns were fenced. Mama longhorns shifted their heavy heads to peer at her, then resumed munching grass, despite their young calves milling around next to them. Pookie was going on nine at this point and moving more slowly, and those big animals seemed to grasp that she was of no danger and didn't pay her any heed. She seemed welcome, but I never took my eyes off her and breathed deep sighs of relief once she was back on our rickety old front porch.

She was not welcome, however, on my bike rides. I loved my one-speed clunker and pedaled in the evenings to the sister that lived closest to me, only about two miles away. It was much too far for Pookie, plus I huffed it for the exercise. But we spent the rest of our empty days together, roaming the fields and the creek near where the trailer perched, and lounging on the front porch.

During this time, I decided to have a portrait made of Pookie and me. Her face had taken on a look of sunny disposition, and I suspected mine had as well. We were in sync. Spending most of our days together had made us a happy duo. It was not difficult for the photographer to catch this delight on both our faces in several photos, pictures that I have cherished in subsequent decades.

One dusk, skidding in from my bike ride, a gigantic copperhead greeted me curled up on my back porch. Holy moly! Normally I used that door and knew Pookie was probably right on the other side waiting for my return. The snake had no plans to move. I walked around the trailer to the front door, thinking that I had better not leave my screen door ajar, and called my neighbor.

"Must be an ole feller," Frankie evaluated. "Probably been under this trailer for a lotta years, but if you don't want it to slide right back under there, I'm gonna have to take care of it here," and he popped off a shot.

I felt bad thinking the snake had reigned under this vacant trailer for so long, and then Pook and I came along declaring

Pookie

it our territory. Even so, I couldn't stand the thought of tripping on that humongous critter when taking Pookie out for a pee before bed. What if she tried to nuzzle it like the water moccasin in Mississippi? But Frankie was probably right. Several nights later, a bunch of growling and screeching woke me up. Then the odor began wafting through the trailer. I had seen possums slip under the trailer, and apparently, skunks were competing for the space. That snake had probably held court down there for years, holding the skirmishes in check and the skunks at bay, but my awareness of that snake's role in some sort of ecological balance was zip at that point. I was trying to be responsible for my dog's and my safety most of all.

My regrets surfaced again when a skunk angrily sprayed Pook one afternoon. Considering she had savored wallowing in disgusting dead fish at the coast, oddly she was uncomfortable with this stench. I almost puked while bathing her in tomato juice in the tub, a remedy that did not achieve the desired results. Pookie stood there with her eyes closed as I soaped, scrubbed, rinsed, and poured tomato juice on her over and over. She still smelled like skunk, and now, so did my bathroom.

One morning I walked out on the front porch to head out to the archery range I had set up, and there was a dog on Pook's pillow! The little heeler popped up and ran to us, wagging his nub of a tail. His auburn eyes looked at us through a black mask.

"Well, who are you, pardner?" I inquired. His body went into a wag. I looked around but didn't see anybody out wrangling cattle. Pookie gave him a sniff and a nudge, then settled onto her pillow and looked at him with curiosity. I decided to go ahead with my archery and see if he took off or if an owner showed up.

Zorro, as I took to calling him, stayed close when we were outside. He sat with us on the porch and waited for us to come back out after we went inside. Pookie had never had a male dog

Dog Love Stories

companion, and she clearly liked Zorro, tussling, playing, then allowing him to curl up next to her on her pillow. I knew I could not let the two of them venture into the field of longhorns. I had seen how the cattle gave Zorro the stink eye. While he could easily escape, Pook was not as agile. I would not take a chance that she might get caught in a stampede. The days of field sniffing for Pookie were over, either temporarily or for the rest of our stay, depending on whether Zorro stuck around or not.

About this time, I hung a map and marked areas to consider for teaching positions for the next year. Although it was comforting to know my principal was holding my Houston teaching position for me, I wasn't sure I wanted to return to Houston. I marked places where I had close friends—Taos, Durango, Denver—and decided I would explore those areas. After moving to Mississippi where I did not know a soul, I vowed never to do that again. However, taking a different job meant I had to commit to searching and ultimately interviewing.

My migraines had improved until the stress of looking for a job hung over me. I was in my late forties and realized if I was going to make a change, I needed to do it now or never. Résumés went out, and come spring, interviews were scheduled. Pookie stayed at my sister's, Zorro went on the lam as he occasionally did, and I hit the road. After interviewing in Durango and Taos—neither school appealing to me—I was off to Denver for two more interviews. I landed a job at a charter school. The next step was searching for a place to rent that would allow for a dog. A four-hundred-dollar pet deposit nixed the idea of bringing Zorro, regardless of how fond Pookie and I were of him. I rented a duplex with a small yard for Pookie that was close enough to my new job to allow me to ride my bike. Driving back to North Texas, I felt my spirits lift. I would be in the same city as Carolyn, one of my closest friends. I could relax for a month before packing and making the big move.

Pookie

Pookie didn't seem to like the idea of this ninth move here in her tenth year. Her face started drooping, and she spent more time on the front porch with Zorro, noticeably uncomfortable when navigating packed boxes accumulating in the trailer. Although I appreciated having spent a year without working, I was ready to be back in the classroom and in a work community again.

The Denver duplex was an old home turned into an upper and lower residence. We were downstairs, much better for Pook, who was now having trouble with her hips, sometimes limping along. One day I threw a ball for her to fetch, and she sat down and stared at me. I could almost hear her saying, *Done. I'm not chasing balls anymore.* I tried a few more times, but she didn't budge. Dogs, I realized, have a sense of their limits and can accept their aging with more grace than humans sometimes do.

In our new abode, when the back door was open in warm weather, Pookie could push on the screen door and head outside to do her business or lie in the sun. She was lonesome without Zorro and would stand by the fence and wag her tail when other dogs walked by. I was familiar with her capacity for grief and how she could draw into herself. But Denver was more expensive than Houston, and getting another dog was not in our near future. However, when Pook was blue, I felt blue. She was my ballast at home and in my life. Her perpetual optimism during my sabbatical year had nourished us both, and I focused on what could lift her spirits. We walked mornings and afternoons, and I spent part of every evening relaxing and talking with her on the floor and couch. "How you doin', Pook?" The sound of her tail flop-flop-flopping as I chatted with her became a measure of how content she was.

"I'll do everything I can for you, Pookaburra, to help you through lonesome times, just like you've done for me." She looked at me with trusting eyes, counting on me to do what was best for her. Dogs don't gradually grow less dependent on us as children do; our dogs always need us.

We were close to one of Denver's beautiful city parks, and Pook enjoyed her daily walks, which we kept up come snow or shine. During my first spring in Denver, my principal stopped by my classroom after school one day and asked if I had a snow shovel. "Might wanna get one," she encouraged. "Forecast shows a spring snowstorm. What a way to start spring break, eh?"

Ace Hardware was on my way home, and snow shovels were on special for only five dollars. From there, I went to stock up on groceries in case there was heavy snow and I couldn't drive, especially since I had little experience driving in snow. Plus, I knew Pook was almost out of dog food, which was a gamble I would not take. From there, Blockbuster. I grabbed about six movies to watch. After unloading at home, Pook climbed into the car, and we headed to the park. Months ago, I had traded my Nissan pickup for an all-wheel drive Subaru, an easier climb for Pookie and certainly a better choice for Colorado weather such as the forecasted snowstorm.

The wind came up with a biting chill. I had never been in a snowstorm and wondered what it would be like, especially living alone. During that first year in Denver, I had dated someone who turned out to be a poor choice. The most egregious flag was when we traveled to Texas for a visit at Christmas. The guy arranged for a neighbor to come to feed his dog and Pookie—both staying inside his large home during those winter days. Pookie had never shown an affinity for his dog but tolerated him. When we returned a week later, Pookie was frantic when she greeted me at the door. His neighbor had not let the dogs out regularly, and the dogs had peed and pooped throughout the house. They had been given water but not fed as instructed. This was on top of a week

Pookie

without any exercise. Although Pook was not able to count the days, she knew I had been away too long.

Why hadn't I talked with this person to gauge her level of responsibility and commitment instead of relying on someone else to arrange my dog's care? Why had I not called this woman to check on things while we were away? Because of my negligence, my dog suffered. A memory of leaving Dancer at the goat farm surfaced, and I recalled how her anxiety led to hives upon my return.

Pookie and I immediately headed home. I felt shaken by my irresponsible care of the most precious being in my life. Pookie was vulnerable to my life and decisions, just as Bandi-Lune had been with the poor choices I had made with her. I had made my promises to Pook, but whether I would keep them was not up to her but me. When I got her home, we curled up on the bed, and I buried my face in her neck.

"I'm so sorry, Pook. I made such a big mistake. I'm soooo glad you are okay."

She licked me frenetically like she was trying to reassure herself of my presence. I was so glad to be with her, so relieved to feel her in my arms, though deeply disappointed in myself. *Buck up*, I told myself. *Let these times of brokenness and vulnerabilities help steer me to make healthier choices, like not dating that guy any longer.*

As Pook and I walked around the lake that evening before the snowstorm, I mulled over the memories of that dating fiasco and felt at peace with being a single woman with her beloved dog, come what may in the way of snow.

Three to six feet of snow paralyzed Denver and the surrounding areas for three days. It was one of the worst blizzards in over a century. Lucky for Pook and me, we did not lose power like thousands of others. I shoveled a trail lined with four-foot walls of snow outside our back door so she could go out to pee and poop. A snowplow broke down in front of our house. Cars, including mine, were buried in snowdrifts. People were skiing down the streets, sometimes over cars. We sat in front of our living room window and watched the show—warm, cupboards and dog food bin full, a queue of movies to watch, and thank goodness, a snow shovel to keep clearing Pook's path.

During this extensive time indoors, I began considering whether I could buy a home. I had never owned a house alone, and this felt like an important step as a single woman. Interest rates were reasonable, and I learned I could buy something with a low down payment and pay less on a mortgage than I was paying for rent. I began looking and soon settled on a fifty-year-old townhome. Although it was three levels including a full basement, the ground level looked appealing for Pook. We both missed her ability to climb stairs, but the ground floor had large front and dining room windows for her to peer out and a dog door in the kitchen that opened into a small backyard where she could lie in the sun. Move number ten for Pookie.

Pookie was slowing down significantly as she approached thirteen. She limped, slept more, and stared into space. She did not always hear me come into the house, but once she realized I was there, a grin crossed her face, and that tail started flopping. She could sure hear me well enough to know when I was about to get off the phone; something about my tone of voice or words I predictably used made her pop up and be ready for a walk or some one-on-one attention. She came to own that ground level, and we spent time together reading, grading papers, watching TV, napping, visiting with friends, and having meals. We had become each other's hearth.

Bill, my ex-husband, from whom I had divorced in 1994 and with whom I had not spent more than a few hours in over ten years, had been installing printing presses in France. Knowing my love of French, on an impulse, he offered me a trip to France. I was

Pookie

hesitant and wondered what it would be like for us to spend time together again, but with my quarterly break beginning the next day, I decided to take the chance. I made careful arrangements for Pook to stay with a dog-loving and dog-respecting friend, booked a flight two days hence, and landed in Paris three days later.

During the days, I roamed the quaint streets and shops of Lannion, the small town in northwest France where Bill was working. In the evenings, we went to his favorite café, tucked away on a side street with no sign, and ate whatever meal the proprietors had prepared for that day. Our conversations opened with balance, depth of flavor, and smoothness, just like the delicious four-dollar Bordeaux we consumed. Over the years, we had both reflected on our lives, our mistakes, and our dreams. We shared what we had learned during our time apart over these long, intimate dinners while being waited on by doting French restaurateurs who had grown fond of Bill during his months there.

Pookie had been receiving good care while I was gone, but on my return, I started worrying about my girl, who was getting thinner.

My Denver neighbors on each side of me, cat people, were stellar. They liked Pookie and greeted her affectionately on our comings and goings. But soon I began receiving phone messages saying that right after I left for work in the mornings, Pookie would go out back and start barking at nothing, just standing there, *Arf, arf, arf, arf, arf!* When either of my neighbors went out to talk to her, she would quit, but once the neighbor went inside, the barking resumed. Her consistent, monosyllabic barking was what my good neighbors heard until they finally left for work themselves.

She didn't do this at all when I was home. What was she saying? *Come back, come back!* Or maybe, *I'm lonesome!*

There was a no-kill shelter across the street from my high school, and I wandered over with a few students one afternoon.

Dog Love Stories

A brown male dog about the size of Dancer and Dabb was in a kennel with a sign that said BITES. *Would the similarity to Dancer feel good to Pook?* I wondered. *Surely such a little dog could not have that much bite in him.*

I returned to the shelter the next day with Pookie. The shelter workers were timid around the little biter, whom they called Rusty. They were also incredulous that I was even interested in him. I took the leash and led Rusty out to my car. When I opened the hatch and helped Pook out, she sniffed him, then strode on ahead. We made it around a couple of blocks while Pookie put up with him. Rusty strutted proudly at her side and looked at her every time he hiked a leg. *Maybe he'll grow on her*, I thought.

The adoption process for the kiddo I later named "Gavroche" was arduous, and that's part of his story. With Pookie distracting him, I managed to get him home. He ambled in and acted like it was his penthouse, and Pookie and me his bitches. She harrumphed and lay down, giving him a stern eye and me the stink eye. Despite having explained my intentions to Pook for days, I continued with my diatribe about how another creature would give her company all day. In that respect, Gavy's presence indeed curtailed Pookie's irritating barking, although if Gav was in the backyard at the same time as my neighbors, he acted like he was out for the kill.

Christmas holidays were coming up and I invited Bill, who had completed his work in France, for a visit to Denver. With Gavroche not fond of men and Pookie weary of life, I wondered how this would go. On a recent slow walk with just Pook and me, she had crawled under someone's front hedge and would not come out despite my coaxing. Finally, on my hands and knees, I gently tugged her out. "What's this about, girl?" Puzzled, I tried my best to read what she was communicating with this strange behavior.

Bill's arrival perked her up. She waited patiently for Gavroche's histrionics to dissolve, then she ambled over to Bill and

Pookie

placed her head affectionately in his hands. She remembered him. Bill teared up, and I marveled at my dog's memories despite their years apart. She had only seen Bill two or three times in the ten years since we had separated and divorced, and then not for very long. Seeing my dog-soulmate connect with a former human-soulmate touched me deeply. Over the next few days, Bill's presence put a sparkle back in Pook's eyes, though not a spring in her step.

Soon after Bill left, Pookie's noticeable decline sent us to the vet. "Her weight loss and lack of energy are most likely signs of organ failure and/or possibly cancer, not just old age," our vet counseled.

I looked at my beloved dog and saw her hip bones and ribs protruding through her thinning coat and body. Even her head looked bony now. She still ate and drank, though in small amounts. She no longer wanted to go for walks and needed me to lift her onto the couch and sometimes even to take her out back to do her business. I was surprised at how light she was.

"Any measures we could take at this point probably won't give her that much more time. I can run tests and do surgery in efforts to extend her life, or you can keep her comfortable for as long as possible without taking these steps," the vet encouraged. I wondered how comfortable I could keep her with Gavroche around, but he had come to stay, even though Pookie seemed ready to go.

One cold and snowy January evening, I heard the dog door flap while I was upstairs. Surprised, I ran down and found Pookie lying in the snow in our backyard. The temperature was ten degrees. "C'mon, Pook, you can't stay out here!" She laid her head down and would not budge. "Okay, I think I understand, girl. Let's go in and talk." I hefted up my beloved and carried her inside with tenderness.

I thought of how Pookie trusted me with her care and was

now asking that I let her go. Her soulful eyes reflected my pain with her decision and reminded me how she could feel what I was feeling. "To love what lives a shorter span than you necessitates loss," author Mark Doty wisely wrote.[1] That is one of the biggest lessons of being a dog owner, recognizing that you will most likely outlive your dog, even if they have many strong, healthy years.

This experience was not the first time I recognized that my dogs carried for me my will to live. Dabb, my first dog, had done that, then Bandi-Lune, and later Dancer. The depth of love I experience with each dog gives them this power to infuse meaning and vitality into my life. In the past week, my Houston therapist had written Pookie a letter where he explained, "Just between you and me, even though she's reading this note, I know that you are hearing these words. You live within her because you have loved each other." My dogs become a part of my DNA, our lives entangled so deeply that it feels like one huge love snowball, and right then, I was trying to push that gigantic snowball uphill.

"I promise I'll call the vet in the morning, Pookaburra." We were inside now, where I had covered her with a warm blanket. She laid her head in my lap, and I buried my face in the folds of fur on her neck. "You've given me so much, Pook. God, I hope I've been as good for you as you've been for me. I can't imagine the past decade without you." Pook had stood by me through ten moves, five towns, five jobs, and a divorce in the past thirteen years. I thought of the almost nine years Pookie and I had spent together since Dancer died. I curled up beside my girl and stayed there with her all night. She shivered and twitched, wrapped in her favorite worn wool blanket.

Letting go. My animals have given me much practice at this, but still, at fifty-one, I did not feel any better at it. Each time grief hits, it is as though I have never let a dog go before. Each time I find myself saying goodbye, it is not just to the dog but

Pookie

also to the years and what those years have held while we were together. At that moment, a new beginning was being forced upon me, whether I was ready for it or not.

Lying there with my girl, I began to recount Pook's life story to her—which was my life story too—the words later becoming her obituary. Occasionally, she would open one or both eyes and give me a single lick, as though that was all she could manage. In the morning, I called the vet, who said he would come to our home later that afternoon. I asked Carolyn and another friend to come help: Carolyn to stay with Pook and me during the vet's visit and the other to take Gavroche on a walk during Pookie's dying experience.

Pookie had not eaten or had a drink in over twenty-four hours. She had not moved except for those precious licks on my face. It occurred to me that letting Pookie go was the hardest thing I had ever done. I stroked her velvety ears and slobbered all over her face, kissing her nose and the scar on one side of her face.

As we waited on my friends and the vet to arrive, Gavroche kept his distance, occasionally coming to give Pook a sniff and a gentle nudge. "Thank you, Pookie, for your patience in these last weeks with Gavroche." Pook opened her eyes and looked sternly at Gavroche, and I imagined her telling him he better be there for me after her death, or else.

"Pookie, will you please be my guardian angel? Soon you're going to see John and Dancer. You'll meet Bebe, Bandi-Lune, and Dabb. I loved them all, Pook, but with you, our time covered so much ground, so much heartache, so much joy, so much growth. Now it's time for you to go, my precious girl. Find the comfort you deserve. And once you feel up to it, chase a gazillion tennis balls. Jump in all the puddles, lakes, and bayous you want. Drink salty ocean water. Roll in dead fish. Wander amongst the longhorns. Eat pizza off the counter. Win every tug-of-war. Hump all the teddy bears and pillows you see. But check in on

Dog Love Stories

me every so often, Pook, and let me remember the comfort of those warm furry folds on your neck. And if it's possible, please help me learn to feel life as soft as your velvety ears," the very ears I later stroked as the vet injected the medication. Pookie let go willingly and with ease, her body becoming lifeless in my arms.

I had heard about a dog leaving a paw print on your heart, but I had no idea how deep the indentation could be.

Pookie
Soulmate
1990–2004

SIX

Zorro

(met him in 2001 while I had Pookie
and before getting Gavroche)

"Well, who are you, pardner?" The screen door slammed behind me, just after Pookie slipped out to check who this stranger was on our porch. The boxy blue heeler wagged his body and what was left of his docked tail as if he had been waiting on us to get up and out.

"You got a cowboy close by?" I stepped off the porch of the trailer where I was spending my sabbatical year and surveyed the fields on three sides. Nary a cowpoke nor a pickup truck in sight anywhere. I glanced down at this handsome masked visitor. Pookie had lain down off to the side of her bed, kindly leaving room for our guest, who came and lay next to her.

Pookie was already nuzzling the little cowdog whose coat was an array of luscious blacks, coppers, and tans. He looked strong and healthy, and most likely not from eating field mice. It really did look like he had a black mask on his handsome face that surrounded his striking auburn eyes. No wonder Pookie was smitten.

"So, Zorro, where the heck did you come from?" Surely, he didn't just plop on our front porch out of nowhere, but at the moment, he was settled in with Pookie, acting like he had arrived at his predetermined destination. I called the owners of the land where I was staying to see what they might know.

"Plenty of heelers around these parts, but not one who lives close by. We'd know if there was." I detected a hint of concern since these landowners had a herd of steer, and heelers can take to a job of herding without provocation. "Coulda been pitched off a flatbed when the driver took a turn too fast."

Maybe a walk would show me a cowboy or repairman close by. When I started down the steps, both dogs hopped up. Pookie took the direction I was heading as a sign to venture into the longhorns' field, one of her favorite places. From the moment of our arrival, they never paid my old slow-movin' Lab much mind. She was only out for a sniff, not to try to round up any cattle. But this morning she had a perky compadre, and the big mommas looked antsy, moving near their calves and hanging their heavy racks low, giving Zorro menacing stares. He looked ready for a chase, muscles twitching in that athletic frame of his.

"Oh, no, buckaroo! We won't be having any of that around here."

I called to Pookie, who had already ducked under the barbed wire, and she looked back with a look that said, *What? I haven't even started sniffing!*

"Not today, girl. You and Zorro are going to stay right beside me." We moseyed down to the mailbox, and I looked up and down the dirt road that held no evidence of a truck Zorro might belong to.

Zorro

Back at the trailer, I gave in to Zorro hanging out with us. At least for the day. He strutted and teased, an admirable flirt, and Pookie was clearly enamored, practically batting her eyes at him. It was like watching *Lady and the Tramp*, only Pook was three times Zorro's size and probably more than twice his age. Pookie was ten, I was forty-nine, and Zorro's age was a mystery. Didn't seem to matter to either of them. He was even nosing me along with his herding moves, his eyes twinkling in that dark mask. This dude was on cloud nine.

I put out bowls of breakfast. Zorro waited for Pookie to eat, then stepped over to his bowl and politely chowed. Every kibble disappeared. I moved to my rocker with a hot cup of coffee, glasses, and my book. Zorro and Pook settled back on the bed like they had been together for years. We looked the picture of domestic tranquility, together for barely an hour.

Soon enough, days clicked by. I started refilling water bowls several times a day and buying more dog food. Zorro clearly preferred staying outdoors. The few times he came inside he lost his bravado, jumping every time the refrigerator made noise, and refusing to lie down. Outdoors, he came to attention, hind legs slant and taut, head alert, ready to bravely zip off somewhere.

Pookie stayed inside when I took my evening bike rides, too old to run the four miles I rode. Zorro started coming along with me, anticipating the directions I would take and getting ahead, often glancing back with an expression that said, *You comin'? What's the holdup?* If a car or pickup came by, he took off like a bullet, disappearing in clouds of road dust. Back home he responded to his name, but on the roads when I hollered, "Zoroooo!" as loud as I could, he didn't slow a speck. This would not do. I had budgeted carefully to be able to take a year off from working, and I did not have the money to pay for a dog getting hurt from chasing vehicles. Zorro was going to have to buck up

Dog Love Stories

to the frightening fridge and stay inside the trailer when I took my evening rides.

Occasionally, Zorro disappeared for several days; then he would be back on the porch a few mornings later with a look that said, *What? Y'all are my place in the world!* Pookie would be visibly relieved. I suspected he had a second home somewhere, or another source of food, or maybe he had a part-time job on another spread. After some vittles, he would settle down for a snooze with a look that said, *Just back from the cattle drive, ladies, and plenty tired.*

Our world began to revolve around Zorro, like we were his property. In his book *The Dog Who Came to Stay*, Hal Borland wrote, "There are dogs that a man owns and there are dogs that own a man."[2] The way Zorro had shown up on our porch like he knew just what he was doing, and the way he so confidently became part of our little family, it felt like he owned us. I started wondering how to handle the months ahead. I had trips scheduled where Pookie would be staying at my sister's. In May, I would be moving back to Houston or to another place where I might snag a teaching position. Wherever it was, it would be in a city and, without a doubt, this little zipper was a country boy.

When I would be gone for a week or two, despite having a neighbor put food and water out for him, Zorro would disappear until I returned, never looking skinnier for his absence. Although Pook and I had come to love our masked man, it was not likely that he would be a permanent member of our family. Our reunions, however, were always celebrated, the three of us delighted to huddle together once again on the porch. Pookie would take on a prissy walk, Zorro a strut, and even I would feel a bounce in my step.

After traveling to Denver in April for interviews, I accepted a position, found an affordable place to rent, then returned home to prepare for the move. The duplex I leased stipulated one dog with a hefty four-hundred-dollar deposit. It had not been easy to find a place that fit my budget, and I was relieved to discover something close to where I would be teaching. I drove back to Texas to pack up.

As boxes accumulated on the porch, Pookie and Zorro moved to the grass, quietly watching the commotion and sensing my stress that surfaced with every move. My heart had been aching for days while watching the two lovebirds whose destiny was doomed. Any move is destabilizing for a dog, but separating two dogs can be disastrous. I was not sure how to ease the impact of such a big change for Pookie and Zorro.

I took plenty of breaks to sit with them. With a hand on each dog, I blabbered on about what was going to happen. "We got some big changes comin' up, Pook. Of course, you're gonna come with me to Denver, and Zorro, you're gonna go live with my sis. I can't take you, boy, though I sure wish I could." As I choked up, Zorro's eyes sparkled, and Pookie comforted me with licks, both aware that I was worried about something and trying their best to cheer me up.

My stomach twisted into gnarly knots. My oldest sister, who lived about four miles away, had agreed to give Zorro a home, but he would be staying with us for our last night. I wanted him to be present through the entire moving process, hoping that it might help him understand our absence later. After all, dogs do have memories.

On our final night, I got up and slipped out onto the porch. There he was curled on Pook's outdoor bed. I lay down with him. "Zorro, living in Denver wouldn't work for you. You'd have to be indoors all day, and you don't even like being in a house. You'd have to wear a collar and walk on a leash, and I doubt you've ever done either." He nosed my face and sighed in what felt like an affectionate but hopeless gesture. "You wouldn't like it, Zo, and I wouldn't like how unhappy that would make you. The country is the best place for you, pardner." Zorro sighed again and laid his head in my lap.

The next morning, my sister came to take him home. My truck was loaded, and I was ready to leave. Pookie followed me over to say goodbye to our masked man. He stood up when she approached and gave her a herding nudge, almost like, *G'on, honey, I know you got someplace to go. I ain't gonna forgetcha!* I walked Pook to my truck, patted the seat for her to hop up into the cab, closed the door, and walked back to Zorro. He was watching like this was the most important event in his life. Maybe it was.

"Damn, this is hard, Zorro. You are one of the finest men I have ever known. You helped make this past year one of the best of Pook's and my life. God, I hope we see you again." I bent down and put my face to his and heard a soft whine, then stood up and turned toward the truck, forcing myself to walk away before I changed my mind. I was convinced having Zorro watch us leave was better than if we ghosted him. Dogs are so much smarter than humans give them credit for.

My sister sat on the porch with our stalky cowboy, who looked more serious than I had ever seen him. I pulled out of the drive. Pookie stared straight ahead as I kept glancing in my rear-view mirror. There sat our stoic boxy heeler who had befriended Pookie and me for eight months, warming our hearts and souls with his free and loving spirit.

Suddenly, an eye-opening gut punch hit me. *Zorro knows what's happening! He's been left before! During those unexplained absences, he was returning to check on a previous home! Another family had also packed up to move to a city, leaving the country and their loyal country dog behind!* Sure, I was guessing, but my intuitive hunch felt spot-on. I could hardly bear these thoughts, but I knew Zorro was resourceful and resilient.

His eyes remained locked on the truck until we turned onto

Zorro

the county road, then I lost sight of him. I reached over and stroked Pookie, trying to comfort us both. "He's gonna be fine, Pook. He's goin' to a new home. He'll miss us, and we'll miss him, but he's a country gentleman, not a city slicker."

Once we were settled in Denver, I often found Pookie standing at our side gate, wistfully watching dogs pass by on the front walk, probably hoping Zorro would soon be showing up.

Several months later, my Texas sister came home from work to find Zorro's lifeless body outside her door. There was no evidence of a snakebite or impact from a car. The vet said Zo could have died from dust inhalation resulting from the little buckaroo's bad habit of chasing vehicles on my sister's busy, dusty road. Soon after we moved, however, my sister had told me that Zorro's previously perky behavior had gone mopey, and she assumed he missed Pookie and me and, with time, would get better.

Maybe something else had been wrong. Or maybe Zorro died of a broken heart.

Zorro
Free Spirit
? to 2001

SEVEN

Gavroche Napoléon

(met him in 2003 while I had Pookie)

"We'll come with you to look," announced two of my students who insisted I begin my dog search right away. Paul and Kristin had noticed my sagging posture, red eyes, and long sighs between an incessant chewing of the insides of my cheeks. They had heard an earful about my dog Pookie's decline at thirteen years old. She was no longer interested in chasing balls and had taken to crawling under bushes and lying down on our walks until I coaxed her out. I felt the urge to get another dog to prepare me for the loneliness that occurs when a beloved dog dies. Coincidentally, the Denver Dog Shelter was just across the street from the high school where I taught.

We walked over to the shelter after school. One kennel had

a sign on it: BITES. Inside sat a small, snarling, brown rat-terrier mix—the shelter's best guess about this captured street dog.

"Ha!" Paul announced. "This guy's like me, brown and tough! Check him out!"

We sat in front of the kennel and whispered softly. At first Rusty, as he had been labeled by the shelter, lunged and barked viciously, then finally sat down and glared at us. We kept up an easy chatter. Paul put the back of his hand to the cage. "We both brown boys, dude," he sweet-talked Rusty. "I ain't gonna hurt ya." Rusty gave him a sniff and a faint wag. "Yeah," Paul concluded, "he the one. Just like some of your students!" Blonde, demure Kristin concurred. I had my doubts.

As I watched Paul schmoozing with street dog Rusty, I was reminded of how kind Paul was to his fellow students, gangsta persona and all. Author Mark Doty writes, "It seems that compassion for animals is an excellent predictor of one's ability to care for one's fellow human beings."[3] Sadly, little did we know then that Paul would be shot dead on a Denver street a few years later, tragically mistaken by a gang for someone else.

I returned over the weekend with Pookie, thinking she might like this little guy since he looked a lot like her sister who had died years ago, Dancer. Rusty was leashed and handed over by a volunteer. I kept my hands away from his mouth, spoke in a low murmur, and moved extra slowly. We walked out to the car, and I let sixty-pound Pook out. She no longer needed a leash, and she limped beside us. She gave a cursory sniff to seventeen-pound Rusty, who wagged his tail and hopped up to give her face a lick. He politely kept Pookie's slow pace as we took a short walk and even let me pet him several times. *Maybe he isn't so bad after all*, I thought. He kept looking back at Pookie. *Perhaps Pook would come to like Rusty. Such a small dog can't be that bad, can he?*

With Pook back in the car, I returned to the shelter with Rusty and announced that I would like to adopt him. The

Gavroche Napoléon

tired-looking woman behind the desk looked alarmed. "You do? We're waiting on the shelter's vet to get here to give that dog a rabies shot. He bit an employee this morning! Are you sure you want *that* dog?" She spoke with such emphasis her bun popped a hairpin. "He's been living on the streets for over a year, dodging the dogcatcher, too aggressive to catch. This little guy is pretty bad! Are you sure?"

I thought of students I'd had over the decades who were often described as "bad." Rarely did they turn out to be as tough as predicted. Patience, taking time to listen, and recognizing that I knew little about their worlds helped me to gradually come to understand them better. Was that what Paul meant when he commented that Rusty was like some of my students? Just another misunderstood dude with a 'tude?

"I'm going to try," I responded hesitantly.

"Well, you know," she answered, "they say the problem is usually bad homes, not bad dogs. If you can give him a good home, he might come around. I sure hope so." Her doubts were reflected in her voice as she handed me paperwork to complete, then slipped the wayward pin back in her bun.

After being assured that I could bring Rusty back, although without a refund of the adoption fee, the transaction was complete, except for the rabies shot. Before the ink was dry, the vet charged in, pumped up a needle, and swooped down for my little guy. *Snap!* Rusty bit him like a snake on its prey.

"Shit!" the vet yelped, jumping back. A staff member handed him a pair of thick rubber gloves, and the vet aggressively poked Rusty, then rushed off, grumbling as he checked out his hand. The hurried vet had even made me jumpy. He had not so much as addressed Rusty. No wonder the little biter fought back.

Once at home, Rusty ambled in like he owned the place, hopping up on furniture, sniffing a few toys, and finishing the kibbles in

Dog Love Stories

Pook's bowl. Pookie sighed. I kept my hands off him unless he came to me. Later, when I crawled into bed upstairs—a place Pookie could no longer come due to her instability on the stairs—Rusty didn't even look at the bed I had made him on the floor but looked up at mine instead. "Okay, c'mon," I relented, impressed that he had asked. He hopped up and crawled under the covers next to me like he was burrowing for safety. A couple of times during the night, I bumped him with my leg, and a snarl would wake me. *Oh yeah*, I remembered. *I'm sleeping with a fighter.*

At one point during that touch-and-go night, it occurred to me that Rusty's name should be Gavroche. I had taught the novel *Les Misérables* in upper-level French classes for years. My students were always drawn to Victor Hugo's character of the young, sassy street orphan who steals bullets from the king's soldiers for the revolutionaries. In France, Gavroche symbolizes la liberté and is a full-fledged hero with his own postage stamp.

Gavroche responded quickly to his new name. He was riveted by Pookie, lunging at her then nuzzling her as she returned his attentions with threatening growls. Pook looked at me perplexed as if asking, *Why is he here?*

"You may be too much for Pook this late in her life, Gavroche, but I promise I'll do what I can to help you two become friends."

Gavroche never gave up on his dreams of Pookie relenting and loving him despite their age and size difference. He pranced around her and hiked his leg so high outside that he sometimes fell over. Pookie would give me the side-eye as if repeating, *Remind me why he's here?*

"Okay, Pook. You were barking every morning when I left for work and the neighbors were pulling their hair out! I thought a companion might distract you, and it's worked. You aren't barking anymore!"

Harrumph! She let out a long, loud sigh.

Gavroche Napoléon

One afternoon while I was checking my mail, Gav quickly slipped out the front door and took off toward busy Fourteenth Avenue. I rushed out and grabbed him seconds before he would have run in front of a car. *Snap!* His jaws clamped down on my wrist.

"Ow!" I screamed. "Dammit, Gavroche!" I felt mad and hurt but refused to let go of my saving grip on him as cars sped by. I continued to holler at him as we returned to my house until the fear and anger in my voice shushed me. He cowered while watching me rinse my wound. Angry bite marks bled onto the back of my hand. An ugly bruise was already surfacing.

I plopped down in a chair, my chin trembling as Gav approached, sniffed my hand, and licked my fingers. "All right, all right, I'll take that as an apology." How could I blame the little fella? He had been surprised by my attack from behind and did precisely what had protected him on the streets. He was an under-socialized and fearful street dog who had defended himself for over a year and survived. Being kicked and swatted had made him reactive. Gavroche could switch to that place in a nanosecond. *How am I going to make our time together one of connection and not reaction? Can I come to love and accept him with his past just as I hope someone will someday do with me?* I considered how touchy I could be at times, my past rearing its ugly head out of nowhere when triggered. Maybe what I was wanting for Gav is what I wanted for myself. Maybe we would shape each other into someone better.

I could only guess what his previous experiences had been and how he was now experiencing me. I wanted to learn what he was communicating with his snarls and snaps and take time to consider his perspective and not just try to overpower him with my commands, control, and dominance. I wouldn't want anyone yelling at me as I had at him. I yearned to communicate *with* him, not just *to* him. Although I wanted to respect his threats,

I took my responsibility seriously for keeping him safe and me bite-free.

My writing group was scheduled to meet at my house that week. I wondered how Gavy would be with strangers. As people arrived, I instructed them to *not* pet my new dog, and everyone obliged. But when the only male member of the group walked in, Gav started barking hysterically and would not stop. Uh-oh. Men, apparently, he did not like. As I coaxed him upstairs with a treat, I could hear the collective sigh of everyone there.

Once the last person had left, I went upstairs and discovered Gavy had unleashed his anger by pulling off my bedspread, tossing shoes around, and yanking things off the nightstand. Nothing was ruined; the boy had just made a holy mess. He darted downstairs and gave the place a full perimeter sniff, then plopped down and looked at me as if saying, *I tried my best to get down here to protect you.* Pookie groaned and laid her head down. Gav strutted over and gave her an affectionate nuzzle as if to say, *I'll protect you too, honey.* He wagged his tail and pranced around, clearly pleased with himself.

"So, you're a biter and protective and you have a temper, do you? Looks like we need to keep working on trust." Gav's good behavior had never been rewarded, but he had learned to shape the reactions of others with those snarls and snaps, and either get away or get his way. I had my work cut out for me.

I had recently reconnected with my ex, Bill, after an invitation to visit him in France where he was temporarily installing printing presses. He was coming to visit me in Denver soon. Hmmm, how would Gav be with a man *staying* in the house? I called the shelter and mentioned my concern. "We'll take him back if he gets aggressive, but we can't give you a refund." The last thing I wanted to do was give up on him, just like another person adopting him would probably do.

Gavroche Napoléon

The day Bill arrived, I handed him some dog treats as soon as he entered the house. Gavroche started barking like a madman. "Don't look at him," I instructed Bill. "Move slowly and place a treat on the floor." Bill listened carefully, ignored the little yapper, and moved at a snail's pace. "Talk to me and slowly place another treat on the floor." By the time Bill and I reached the kitchen, Gavy was quiet. We kept talking, and Gav sat down by Bill's feet, staring at him. Then Bill dangled his hand at his side and soon got a nudge for another treat. The next few days, Gavroche followed Bill, who kept a few treats in his pocket, around the house, accepting Bill's easy and kind touches and reciprocating with occasional licks.

What a reminder that dogs don't fake whether they like you or not. Taking the time to understand them can make a difference. Gav was inspiring me to look at how to connect and communicate with dogs in new ways. Perhaps our dog–human relationship would improve in due time, despite his lack of experience with humans and mine with aggressive dogs.

Thank goodness Gav liked Bill and Bill liked Gav.

Two months later, with Gavroche fully ensconced in our home, Pookie began fading rapidly, and I made an appointment for a vet to come to our home to administer euthanasia. I kneaded my chest with the heel of my hand as my heart squeezed, then made plans for a friend to come and walk Gav while the vet was there. The rest of that day and night I spent curled up next to Pook, Gavy joining the puppy pile, exactly as Pookie and I had once done with our dog Dancer, miserable from a stroke, the night before she was euthanized. Pookie barely moved, occasionally giving me a nudge or a lick. Gav sat and stared at us, not bothering Pook, then lay directly behind her, providing warmth to her backside.

After the vet left the next day, taking Pookie's warm body with him, Gav gave the house the once-over after returning from his walk. *Where is she? She was just here. I still smell her.* He gave every room a thorough sniffing, checked all Pook's beds, went outside several times to look around, then plopped down beside me. I wished I could have let him sniff Pookie after she had died. But the vet had other appointments, and we didn't have that opportunity.

Finally, I persuaded Gavroche to curl up next to me as I lay on the couch. "You wonder where your gal is, don't you? She's gone now and won't be back. But I'll look for another sweetheart for you soon; don't you worry," I said, my voice struggling between sobs. Gavy watched as though he'd never seen a human weep. Maybe he hadn't. He placed a tiny paw on my leg, and I stroked him with gratitude and reassurance of what I hoped would be years of companionship. How had he learned to love like that without any practice? "Oh, Gav-roni," I whispered in the tenderness of the moment, this nickname coming out of nowhere.

Then, as if I had reminded him about Pookie, he leaped off the couch to go outside and look one more time.

About three months later, I could tell nine-hour days alone in my townhome were too much for Gav. He moped. His zeal for life was diminishing. He was used to roaming a neighborhood and being the tough guy on the block. True to my promise, at least I could give him a companion to keep him company during my long absences.

I returned to the Denver Dog Shelter. I was told about a Lab and taken to her kennel. Leashed up, we took off on a get-to-know-one-another walk. Her one-year-old seventy-plus pounds just about pulled my shoulder out of the socket. Geez. I thought of how hard it had become for me to lift Pookie's sixty pounds in and out of my car after she couldn't jump up any longer. Returning the Lab to her kennel, I noticed a smaller mid-sized dog hunkered down in the adjoining kennel. SERENA, the sign

Gavroche Napoléon

read—a red heeler mix. She came when I spoke to her. Since I had a leash in hand, I decided to take her out without going back up front to tell anyone at the shelter.

She was a delight, beautiful, and easy on a leash. We walked to my car, where Gav was waiting in case I wanted him to get to know a possible new companion. Off the three of us went, sashaying down the sidewalk like we had been walking together for years.

"Whaddaya think, Gav? You two seem compatible to me." Gavy looked back at me, an undeniable grin on his face.

After I put Gav back in the car, I happily waited in a long line at the very busy shelter to tell the flustered woman at the front desk I wanted to adopt Serena, who was sitting patiently at my side. I noticed a familiar unraveling bun before the woman even began to speak. "Who let you walk that dog? We have five adoption applications for her that we're in the middle of checking!"

"Oh, I should have asked. But she was in a kennel next to another dog I had been given a leash to walk. I took her out without permission." The woman sighed, clearly exasperated. I babbled on. "I walked her with my other dog, and they got along so well. I got that dog here several months ago."

"You got another dog from us? Who was that?" she asked nonchalantly as she shuffled papers without looking up. By now I recognized this was the woman who had discouraged me from adopting Gavroche.

"You called him Rusty, but now his name is—"

Her head snapped up, a pin flew out of her bun, and she interrupted me. "Rusty? You're the teacher from across the street who adopted him? And you kept him! He's the worst dog we've had here in a long, long time!"

"Yeah, he's been a handful for sure! But he made the cut and is a permanent part of my family. My other dog died several months ago, and he's pretty lonesome."

Dog Love Stories

"Well, sorry about your other dog," she offered with an authentic look of kindness. "Let me check on something. Could you have a seat over there?" She gestured toward the waiting area.

Serena and I sat down. She was so easy, slightly timid, nothing like Gav had been. I gently ran my hand down her back, and she cast a soft look my way. Suddenly, the woman from the front desk was moving a chair beside me. She leaned in and whispered. "We try so hard to get all our dogs into good homes, but we just never know. So, when someone comes back for another dog after successfully homing one of our dogs, especially a tough one like Rusty, we are so relieved." She reached over to run her hands over Serena. "Rusty is lucky he got you, and we want Serena to be a part of your home too." Leaning in, her eyes lit up, and I realized her job of placing dogs was important to her.

Apparently, Gavroche's bad-guy reputation was working in our favor.

After completing the paperwork and paying, I danced out to the car with Serena. Gav was ecstatic, licking Serena's face like she was his long-lost love, his sadness about losing Pookie long gone. Next to his mix of browns and tans, her coat was a light red, almost amber. "What if we call you Amber and drop your shelter name?"

Gavroche resumed his strutting and nuzzling, but if someone moved a little too quickly on the periphery of his vision, those lips curled back in a nanosecond and *snap*! It was a reflex Amber and I were both learning not to provoke. With my constant demonstration of security and love, and now with another canine companion, he began to slowly transform; we were both changing as we got used to each other. I was as responsible for him becoming tamer as he was responsible for me becoming more open to having a totally different kind of dog—one unlike Dabb, Bandi-Lune, Dancer, Bebe, Pookie, or Zorro. Plus, as I worked with him, I often thought of my own abuse and how learning trust and gentleness with myself had helped me heal from those early experiences.

One morning at home, I sipped coffee while we were all sitting together. Gav appeared unusually lethargic. I had noticed his breath smelled sour the night before. With his eyes on me, I slowly reached over and touched his muzzle. He whimpered. I gently lifted his lip and saw inflamed gums.

"What's this, kiddo? Looks like a problem to me." I glanced at the clock. It was 7:00 a.m. Luckily, someone answered at the vet. After letting my school know I'd be late, I drove Gav over.

"I'll need to anesthetize him to get a better look, but he clearly has some dental issues." I was glad Gavy felt too bad to bite the vet during this brief examination. We needed her on our side at this point. But Gav was acting subdued like he was already medicated. He turned anxious but trusting eyes toward me as I stroked his now-glossy brown coat.

"It's all going to work out, Gav-roni. You'll see. And you'll be back at home this evening." I turned and left him on the table with a vet tech, hearing a faint whine as I walked out the exam room door. Maybe he was getting a shot, or maybe he wanted me to stay. I whipped around and caught his eyes just as the medication closed them. My heart lurched as memories flashed of being with Dancer and Pookie as medication eased them out of life. Then I remembered Bebe as she faded next to me on the way to the vet after being hit by a car. "Damn," I mumbled under my breath, walking to my car, "sure doesn't take long for even the orneriest of dogs to find his way into my heart."

About an hour later, I got a message at school to call my vet.

"Do you know if this dog has been kicked in the mouth? His baby teeth are embedded in his gums and compromising his adult teeth. The baby teeth and a few adult teeth need to come out ASAP. His mouth is severely infected."

Dog Love Stories

I confirmed her guess about him being kicked—per the stories I'd heard from the shelter—and, without hesitation, approved the dental surgery. "Can you give me an approximate cost?" I inquired nervously.

"At least five hundred." It hit me that I was about to deplete my shallow savings account between Pookie's vet bills, adopting Gav and Amber, and getting all their shots and heartworm meds. But these creatures were my family, and with full awareness, I had taken on the responsibility of their care. Along with the label of teacher, stepmother, sister, daughter, and friend, I was also a committed dog parent.

Gavy was groggy but waggin' that tail when I rushed to the vet that afternoon. He winced when I bumped his muzzle, with no attempt to snap. But his painful mouth wasn't keeping a smile off his face. My little guy was happy to see me and to be going home. Amber gave him the sniff-over once we walked in the door and eyed his soft food with envy later that evening. Like me, she was visibly relieved to have her man back.

Bill and I had begun a long-distance relationship while he installed printing presses around the States. During this time, I found some land in the San Luis Valley, four hours south of Denver, that I wanted to buy. After visiting the area with friends who had land there, the lure of this West Texas–like area that offered spacious views hit me. The property I found overlooked a varied landscape of plateaus and round mountains south to New Mexico, the towering Spanish Peaks to the east, the San Juan Mountains and twinkling lights of Alamosa to the west, and four fourteen-thousand-foot peaks standing guard to the north.

I had not yet been able to build my savings back up after dog care, so Bill offered to go in with me on the purchase. After six months of seeing each other again, I wondered what that would mean for us, but I wanted the land and felt happy to be spending

Gavroche Napoléon

time with Bill, so I accepted. Several months later, I found an old twenty-five-foot trailer in perfect shape and moved it up to the six acres. The first time Bill saw the spot, he tagged the area Graceland.

Almost a year after bringing Amber home and not long after purchasing Graceland, Bill moved in with us. We were becoming a four-creature family. When Bill and I started talking about living together as a couple once again, I emphasized two things that I could not change: I came with dogs and many LGBTQ friends. Although Bill and I were committing to a monogamous relationship with each other, he knew I had been in relationships with women in the past. By then, neither of these conditions surprised Bill, and he was welcoming and comfortable with my preferred company, canine and human alike.

Many a weekend we slipped out of Denver to head four hours south, dogs in tow. We found our spirits revived by the Milky Way, coyote calls, and the remote solitude of Graceland. The dogs loved being outdoors and having mountain trails and campfire times the city life could not provide. But on one visit when I had gone without Bill, Gavroche wandered off while I was packing up to leave. I was impatient to get to Denver before dark and have time to prepare lesson plans for the following day.

"Gavroche!" I hollered down the road and mountainside for three hours. "Dammit, Gav." Although I was pissed at him, my heart throbbed. I was also angry at myself for not paying closer attention to him. His seventeen pounds were perfect coyote or eagle bait. I started unloading the car to stay the night. No way I'd leave without him, especially knowing there was a chance he might show up later.

Suddenly, Amber dashed off up our rocky drive. I looked up, and there he was, strutting down the road while nosing his gal, who was delighted to see him. He swaggered up to me, cocky and happy with himself for having been bravely off on his own.

Dog Love Stories

"Damn, Gavroche! Where the hell have you been?" I was mad but couldn't scold him for coming back. Whose fault had it been, after all? "Buddy, I thought we had lost you." I started crying in relief and sat down on the front step of the trailer to give my little dude a rubdown. "Just don't expect to get a second chance at one of those freedom forays. From now on, when we're at Graceland, you're on a leash!"

A month later, a car hit me while I was cycling to work. For six weeks I had to wear a clunky brace on my fractured left ankle, making the only bathroom on the second floor inconvenient. Besides, the old townhome's tiny backyard was proving to be inadequate for two dogs. I began to search for a one-level home with a bigger backyard and soon found an old place that fit us just right. Bill and I had decided to remarry, having discovered that the deep roots of our affection felt like home for our hearts. We liked the idea of starting fresh in a home new to us both. Our new home had a garage, a large back porch with more space outdoors for the dogs, a front porch with a view of west Denver, a warm and spacious kitchen, and best of all, it was one story. We settled in in no time.

We had to buy a fridge for this home and immediately regretted our purchase. For some reason, whenever the icemaker cranked on, Gav went into full attack mode, lunging at the fridge like an army of ice cubes were about to stampede. No amount of reassurance calmed him. We finally gave up and did our best to laugh these histrionics off. It could be worse, we figured.

Once ensconced in our new place, Gav's true colors emerged. He began insisting he be fed plenty of food and right on time. After all, he had been a successful street scavenger when the dog shelter finally snared him. Since I limited his rations after he began looking like a football, he spent an inordinate amount of time hypervigilant in our big kitchen, waiting for anything to

Gavroche Napoléon

fall onto the floor as I sliced veggies and prepped meat. He ate everything, even lettuce and broccoli. We learned to never reach for anything that had fallen. It would have been like sticking our hands into a shark pool.

After dinner, Gav humped, like clockwork. He traveled from kitchen to porch to living room to bedroom, wherever he had a dog bed and could drag his blanket. We used to say he had a bitch in every port. He would pull his blankie around (a gift from my sister embroidered with JESUS LOVES ME), roll onto his back, and hump himself breathless. Gavroche tested many a guest's reserve with this blatant demonstration of sexual urges, clutching his Jesus blanket while working those little hips and exposing a neutered pink, swollen penis that seemed much too big for his little body. "Avert your eyes," I often warned, as it was a difficult sight to behold. At last, after a significant amount of this exertion, Gav would pass out, snoring contentedly. "Mr. Man," I tagged him.

But Gav was grateful and never let a day go by without expressing his love with stinky licks, loving eyes, and wide, sweet grins. One quickly forgot his demonstrations of sexual prowess when he grabbed his adored monkey, whose nose he would suck on as he self-soothed, his small paws wrapped tenderly around Monkey's neck. The guttural noise he made right as he fell asleep, the monkey falling to the side, always made me smile. Monkey Man became another nickname.

Dog doors made all our lives easier. Bill and I worked full days; the dogs had the run of the house and could slip outside as needed. When I arrived home, the dogs and I piled into the car and took off for Rocky Mountain Lake and Park where we could circle the lake for a two-mile walk. I once heard how walking two dogs was like flying two kites, and sometimes that was the case, but I did get Gavroche and Amber used to sticking on their own sides,

Dog Love Stories

although we frequently had to pause so Gavroche could hike a back leg to pee.

"Enough, already!" and I'd give him an impatient tug after ample markings. This was not behavior I was used to with girl dogs.

You don't understand, he seemed to say. *I must leave my message*, or his pee-mail, as I had heard someone label it.

Bill wasn't born into the world of dogs. He didn't grow up with a dog. He never had a dog of his own. His first experience with a dog had been Dancer. Now, he fed Gav and Amber when I was away, occasionally taking them on walks, but not to the vet unless I was not there, and it was an emergency. He never got down on the floor with our dogs, kissed their noses, or babbled on about how much he loved them. He called them good dogs and petted them on the head when they begged for his attention, but he gently pushed them away after their second or third request.

Bill landed in between what I call a dog tolerator and a dog lover. He liked Gavroche and Amber and could handle being in charge, knowing that the dog lover (me) would soon be home. Of course, I had warned him numerous times that if he ever became the full-time dog caretaker—like if I died—he better take on the role wholeheartedly or I would never let him get a restful night of sleep. The curious thing was that our dogs loved him regardless of how much attention he gave them.

Soon, however, the refreshing remarriage Bill and I had entered in 2006 began feeling rocky. Bill had bought an industrial sharpening business in Denver that worked primarily with printers. I had left public teaching to work with an educational consulting company as an evaluator of teachers seeking alternative licensure. When the 2008 economic recession hit, we catapulted into financial crisis. Bill's once-thriving business was flailing, and I was laid off. As I began a full-time job search, Bill

Gavroche Napoléon

was forced to apply for bankruptcy. Our stress levels skyrocketed. When tension in our home raised the decibels in our voices, we began to hear the flap-flap of the dog door as Gavroche and Amber made quick exits, regardless of winter temperatures.

The sound of that flap became like a red flashing warning sign for us to calm down.

After closing his business in 2010, Bill began experiencing chest pains while out walking the dogs one evening. At the time, I was in Texas visiting my parents. The next day, he drove himself to see his doctor who immediately put him into the hospital. This averted death by a life-threatening heart attack, Bill's second since he'd had one while we were divorced. I got the last seat on a late flight and made it home in time to catch Bill right after surgery. We were only fifty-seven at this wake-up call.

The dogs were hungry and anxious when I arrived home alone that night. "Ohhhh, you two, it is so good to see you," I cooed and cried. "I'm so sorry your humans have been this stressed. We'll find a way to calm things down. Life has too much to offer for either Bill or me to kick the bucket this soon." Gav and Amber pawed and licked me in relief.

I also felt they were assuring me that they would have my back, but I knew they could not help pay the bills. I wasn't able to snag a job, even at schools where I had previously evaluated the teachers. Was it my age, fifty-seven? Bill started a small mobile sharpening service, but his heart—literally—wasn't in it. Then my middle sister mentioned moving my parents to a house in Whitesboro, Texas, that would have space for a caregiver. It occurred to me that Bill and I could sell our home, move, and provide this necessary care while we got back on our feet. Maybe, I also thought, being around my parents would be fertile ground to write a memoir that had been waiting inside me about surviving the sexual abuse from my dad.

Bill had his doubts. "I don't know, darlin'. Living with your parents could be really stressful for you."

"True, but the house Pamela is looking at would give us our own sitting area and bathroom, and a door to the backyard. Our financial stress would decrease. You could do mobile sharpening, and I'd look for a job. I think I've had enough therapy around the abuse to handle Dad and Mom." It would be a stretch, but staying in Denver was also a stretch.

Soon we were settling into our new home in rural North Texas with my parents and their dog, Hank the Cowdog, a gangly outdoor seventy-plus-pound bluetick hound. Hank had roamed up to their remote twenty-five acres southwest of Fort Worth before they had moved to Whitesboro.

An enormous backyard spread out behind our new place. Amber and Gavroche were now on flea and tick medication since, unlike in cool, dry Colorado, we were now living in hot, humid temperatures conducive to those critters. Nevertheless, our dogs were not allowed inside. Since Hank was an outdoor dog, my parents chose to save the bucks and not put him on flea and tick meds, which would have also deprived my mom of the pleasure of picking ticks off him.

Our new shared home had a built-in laundry room attached to the house and garage. We put in another door with a dog door in it that opened onto the backyard so the dogs could come and go, and their room could stay warm in the winter. North Texas didn't get as bitter cold as Colorado, but its humidity sometimes made it seem just as frosty.

This was a whole new setup for humans and dogs. While Bill and I navigated my parents' habits and moods and they did the same with us, our dogs were no longer able to live alongside us. Instead, they were relegated to the "dog office," as we started calling their space. But the dogs and I missed each other's comfort. To help, I put rockers, side tables, and footrests on the back

Gavroche Napoléon

porch, making it a place where humans and dogs could all hang out in warm weather.

Hank and Amber, the big dogs, romped around more often together. Gav still strutted his stuff, but the move and the separation from Bill and me had him frequently sucking on his toy monkey for comfort. No longer were we seeing the fierce little street dog in him. Instead, he was either craving our company or self-soothing with Monkey. Occasionally, Monkey got in the middle of a tug-of-war game between Gav and Amber, resulting in numerous "surgeries" of holes and tears in Monk's body. Gavy would sit watching me stitch up Monkey, patiently waiting for surgery to be completed.

Then, poof, Monkey vanished! Nary a nose or a leg in sight. "Hank, Amber, did y'all take Gav's monkey?" I searched where Amber and Hank had been digging but found nothing. Did one of the owls *hoot-hooting* in the big trees most nights sweep down and grab his toy monkey? Better Monkey than Gav, whom I had worried about being outside but knew he hunkered down in the dog office at night. "You two look guilty as hell," I accused. "This is serious. Gav has had that monkey for five years! He *needs* Monkey!" Hank and Amber were a little too nonchalant about the missing toy, so I started slipping Gav into the house and our bedroom more often to help soothe his loss.

Pretty soon, another creature surfaced. Only this one was alive. A big fat bullfrog emerged from under the house's foundation. He would hop to the doorway of the dog office, holding the dogs captive inside. They would all freeze and watch the big guy—and I mean big! Maybe about one and a half pounds. Staring at them with intense, beady eyes, he made it clear he was a no-nonsense creature.

"Whoa, look who's paying a visit today!" I announced on coming out to feed the dogs. "Mornin', Frogman! You come to terrorize the canines? Did *you* steal Gav's monkey, or are you here to punish Hank and Amber for doin' so?" I even hesitated when stepping over the fella, wondering what calamity might befall a human for ignoring a stately bullfrog. One morning he hopped forward into the dog office, and Gav decided to challenge the dude, delivering a light bite to Frogman. Seconds later, Gav jumped back, slinging his head around, salivating, and gagging, but okay within five minutes. I soon learned that when a bullfrog feels threatened, it can secrete a toxin on the surface of its slimy skin. Frogman let the dogs know he was indeed the prince of their domain. He never wanted to move in, just give them the once-over and then be on his merry way. Gavroche learned his lesson, keeping his distance from then on.

In the cool of the mornings, the dogs and I would pile into the car and find our way to a nearby cemetery to take our daily walks. Rarely was another live person there, which allowed me the entire space to sing or cry loudly, according to my mood. Moving in with my parents had already proven to be way more challenging than we could have ever imagined. My dad, who had suffered from a lifetime of mental health challenges, was taken by EMTs one night after a mental breakdown to a psychiatric facility and from there moved into a veterans home. My mom's health was deteriorating with Lewy body dementia. My sisters and I were challenged with providing the best care for them and navigating one another, not having lived close to each other for over a decade. I still had not been able to find work despite ongoing efforts, and Bill lacked the enthusiasm to start a small business in a new area. We both grieved the loss of work and the community we had loved in Denver.

Among the four of us—Bill, me, Gavroche, and Amber—the dogs had figured out how to adjust best to our new and different life.

Graceland was no longer an easy jaunt south like it had been from Denver. From Whitesboro, it was a steady thirteen-hour

Gavroche Napoléon

drive northwest and a whopping 8,200-feet-plus increase in altitude. Rarely was I able to break away and make a beeline for Colorado, and when I did, it was with Amber but not Gav. The little bugger had to stay with Hank. Either Bill or I had to stay with my mom and Gav while the other got a break and a dose of healing Colorado beauty.

A year and a half after this move to Texas, Bill and I abruptly decided to move back to Colorado. On an unusual visit together to Graceland, we wandered into Alamosa and haphazardly looked at homes for sale. We were still broke, but we needed to dream. Only a month before, I had bought a laminated wall calendar for the next year, 2012, and hung it in the privacy of our walk-in closet. "Let's use this to mark what we want to dream about and do in the coming year, things that might help us feel some promise for the future." Bill was all in.

Before the end of 2011, I made an incredibly low offer that was accepted on a century-year-old home for sale that we had walked through in Alamosa. Bill moved in January to begin the required electrical upgrade, and I followed in May after my sisters and I found a suitable assisted living home for my mom. Dad was settled nearby at the veterans home. Both needed more care than any of us could provide while living with them. As usual, the dogs were enthusiastic about change if we were moving as a family. Luckily, the woman to whom we rented the Whitesboro house wanted Hank, even allowing him indoors. Quite a step up for that old country hound. Gavroche was happy to lose the competition for Amber's attentions.

Once we all arrived in Alamosa and got settled, the enormity of what we had lived through in the past three years hit Bill and me: losing our work in Denver, his heart attack, moving from a home and city we loved into a house with my parents in a small town we didn't love, the extreme challenges we faced while figuring out how to live with my parents, dealing with immense financial stress, and moving to an old home that needed massive repairs. We crashed. Then, my Houston therapist, with whom I had worked for fifteen years in person and by phone, closed his practice due to illness. I was bereft. Bill and I clashed, and the frequent slap of the dog door resumed as the dogs quickly exited on hearing our raised voices, reminding us again that we needed to calm down and recalibrate. I often followed the dogs out in my efforts to do just that and to take some deep breaths.

"Hey, you two. We're at it again, eh? I'm so sorry we're stressing you out."

Both dogs would nose me, anxious to know I was okay, and I would assure them I was. When I sobbed and slobbered in my fears, confusion, and depression, the dogs would come to comfort me, concerned about one of their humans. Gav was always the most worried and would jump up, making little whines as I kneeled between them. He absolutely hated it when Bill and I argued. For a tough dude, he sure had turned out to be a sensitive creature. "It's okay, Gav-roni. We're all going to get through this intact. Don't you worry." At least he didn't chew a worry spot like Dancer had done or like the cheek-chewing I had resumed.

I don't like making promises, like telling my dogs I'll get better, without doing what I can to make those promises happen. I asked new friends for therapist recommendations and soon found one. I explained to her that I had started writing my memoir but I was not strong enough to finish it. And now, coupled with cumulative stress, my life and marriage felt like they were barreling toward doom. By the second appointment, my therapist encouraged me to meet with both her and her psychiatrist partner and consider medication. I recognized that after decades of my flailing mental and emotional health, I needed help in any form. Over the following three years, I would crawl out of depression with sufficient strength to experience the deaths of

Gavroche Napoléon

my parents, a lifelong friend, and my beloved former therapist. I would adjust to a new community while living in a drafty old home in minus-forty-degree winter temperatures, the coldest I had ever experienced. Bill and I learned to lean in toward each other rather than pull apart during tough times, and our relationship grew more resilient. In addition, I was able to resume focus on writing my memoir. Gavroche's and Amber's eyes regained a glow as they again began sighing in relief and making playful bow-like stretches. They appeared to be more warmed by my uplifted spirits than the ample blankets I placed on their beds.

What is it about companionship with dogs that frequently helps humans feel better? The unconditional acceptance of dogs—how they love us regardless of how messed up we can feel—is daunting. And their patience with us is impressive, despite the lack of patience that humans often display toward their dog companions. Play and laughter also helped me—letting go of my worries, seriousness, and sadness, by grabbing a ball, a tug-of-war rope, or a squeaky toy, and playing! As I began focusing on the love and affection I felt for my dogs, I was reminded of that which I held for myself.

After attaching a greenhouse to the south side of our home—allowing me to continue gardening in this very different climate—we also replaced the old wire fence with a six-foot wooden fence in the backyard. Hearing what went on outside the fence or peering through an eighth of an inch space between slats simply was not enough for our dogs. Our fence contractor, who was aptly named Friend, suggested we put in doggy windows on two sides, giving the dogs views instead of blocking out so much of their world. Now my kiddos could keep an eye on the deer that congregated on the other side of the fence or speak their minds to whoever was walking down the alley. Along with these views, they also had a dog door in the kitchen that opened into an attached workshop, and another on the workshop's back door that opened into the backyard. The ability to come and go at will gave our dogs autonomy, thus making all our lives easier.

This helped significantly with dog sitters. When we were gone for one to five days, I would hire someone to come feed and sit with Gavroche and Amber twice a day and take them on walks without the person having to stay at the house, although that was always preferred. With Pookie, I had been spoiled by having close friends who usually kept her when I traveled. Now Bill and I were living in a different place where we knew few people; however, I soon discovered that my next-door neighbor had started a dog-walking business. She didn't have dogs herself but presented herself as a dog expert, so I hired her to cross the alley from her apartment several times a day to feed the dogs and to walk them once a day while Bill and I were away on a trip.

"I decided to leash your dogs and take them on bike rides instead of walking them," she let me know on the day we returned.

"At the same time?" I asked in disbelief. "Thirty-five-pound mid-size Amber running the same pace as sixteen-pound squatty-body Gavroche? He's fourteen years old, for God's sake!" Gav was still suffering from overexertion when we returned home. I could have strangled this "dog expert," but realized I had not done my due diligence about her claims. *Never again*, I thought. I began interviewing young AmeriCorps and Mennonite community volunteers and had much better luck, plus I felt better having someone stay *in* the house with my dogs.

Sometimes I boarded Amber and Gavroche, but I struggled knowing that they stayed in a kennel from the time the facility closed until the time they opened—7:00 p.m. to 7:00 a.m.—and only got recess an hour, maybe two, in the morning and again in the afternoon. My dogs were used to going outdoors at will when they needed to do their business, moving from bed to bed in the house, and not being around the noise of the boarding facility. Granted, they had both come from a shelter where chaos reigned,

Gavroche Napoléon

but for over a decade they had become used to a tranquil environment. When necessary, I boarded them, but I preferred having them stay safe and comfortable at home.

Thinking about who might take Gavroche and Amber if something happened to Bill and me was another conundrum, possibly more critical than choosing dog sitters. I had been going through home funeral guide trainings that included talking about having one's end-of-life wishes and affairs written down and organized. What about one's dogs? That would be one of the most important concerns for a dog lover like me. Who would take my dogs? Would they stay together or move apart? What would I want to be considered for each dog's home if Bill and I both died? Would anyone I knew take one or both? Gavroche's early reputation as a biter lingered despite his becoming a little lover; I wasn't sure anyone would want him. I started pointing out to friends what a cuddler he had turned into. Amber was a hiker and very sensitive. She would need an outdoors person and a quiet home space. Both dogs were used to having their attentive humans around often and being free to come and go outside at will.

"Gavy tells me you're his pick for a godmother," I hinted to friend Carolyn.

"Not a chance, Pat! That little biter?" Then she would give Gav some loving rubs. She laughed off my insinuations and never accepted, but I could tell she had a soft spot for Gavroche, and I let myself believe she would take him. Amber I didn't worry about. She was beautiful, quiet, and mystical in ways I believed would have several people vying for her. Expecting my dogs to stay together was beyond my expectations, although it would be my preference. All I could do was make note in my end-of-life documents about how important it was to me that my dogs each find loving homes conducive to their dispositions and then pray that would happen, whether they ended up together or apart.

Dog Love Stories

By now, walking my dogs regularly was as much a part of our routines as feeding them twice a day. We walked down a block, across the street, to the park, and onto the levee that runs alongside the Rio Grande River. Gav walked on my right and Amber on the left. Still, we had times of tangled leashes, usually when squirrels in the park tempted them or a passing dog was aggressive.

As idyllic as this place was to walk my dogs, there were problems. One morning the three of us were walking along when I noticed a young woman ahead on her phone with her rottweiler running free. He lifted his head and began running directly toward us.

"Stop him, please!" I screamed while high-stepping amidst his snaps and lunges toward my dogs and ankles. I had pulled Gav's and Amber's leashes in tightly while still giving them enough lead to avoid this dog.

"Come here, Sam! Stop it!" the woman screamed as she pocketed her phone and ran to us, reaching into the melee to snap a leash on her dog.

"I'm sorry," she offered nonchalantly once Sam was leashed and they were at a safe distance. "I didn't see you coming."

I ran my fingers over Gavroche and Amber, checking for bites. I could barely speak, my heart was pounding so loudly. Once I determined they were fine, I looked up and saw she had walked on and was back on her phone. At least her dog was leashed. Maybe she'd pay closer attention from now on.

Another time when we arrived at the park, I noticed a couple with their pit bull. I waited at a considerable distance to give them time to make it to their car and load their dog before proceeding. Behind my back, I heard screaming. Their dog had slipped out the back door before they closed it, and he was barreling in our direction.

"Snowball! No!" Both the man and woman were running

Gavroche Napoléon

toward us, but Snowball was rolling faster than an avalanche. By the time the owners leashed him, Gavy's ear was bleeding, and Amber was in shock. The man led the pit bull to the car.

"I am so sorry," the woman gushed, bending down to check the puncture wound on Gav's ear. "He slipped out of our car so quickly! What can we do to help?" she offered.

"I've got to sit down." I found a bench, sat, and caressed my dogs, trying to calm us all.

"I just need to sit here quietly with my dogs." She nodded kindly and walked back to her car. It took me a while to quit shaking. I petted Gavroche and Amber, checking if I had missed any wounds. "That was so scary, wasn't it? Thank goodness you aren't hurt."

The next dog confrontation was the worst. Farther out on the levee with cows grazing on the Alamosa Ranch Land on one side, Blanca Vista Lake on the other, and in between cottonwoods rustling in a morning breeze, we spied a woman with two German shepherds ahead. "C'mon, kiddos, let's pull off to the side." I moved down on the barbed wire–fenced ranchland side of the levee and waited.

Her dogs weren't leashed and soon came hurtling toward us. The woman had her earbuds in and walked right by us while her dogs lunged at us, backing us into the barbed wire. My jacket got caught, and I heard it rip as my fists tightened on my dogs' leashes.

"Please leash your dogs!" I screamed in a shaky voice, hoping she could hear me. She turned, ripped out her earbuds, and let them dangle around her neck.

"Just walk away and they'll stop!" she snarled. I could barely hear her over the raucous barking. Gavroche and Amber stayed quiet, their eyes wide and tails tucked.

"I can't get up the levee with them there. Please, just leash them!" I pleaded, gasping.

"Oh, go fuck yourself." She finally reached out, yanked her dogs to her by their collars, and leashed them. I was startled.

"What if you were an older woman walking your dogs and a younger woman came along with two unleashed big and aggressive dogs?" I struggled to find the right words, trying to communicate how horrible the situation felt.

She popped her earbuds back in and shot me a finger as she walked away.

My knees were shaking, but most of all my heart hurt from this latest encounter. What was going on in that young woman's life to leave her so calloused? Were those her dogs? I realized she had never called their names or said one word to them. Did she know what it felt like to be up against two vicious-behaving dogs who weighed more than Gav, Amber, and me altogether?

After seven years of walking in Alamosa, I became a hyper-vigilant walker, always looking for other dogs. I also started carrying a dog pepper spray and hoped that in an attack, I would be able to get the spray out of my pocket and release it while holding onto my two dogs. What I knew for certain was I would do everything I could to protect my dogs and myself.

Proximity to Graceland was one of the main reasons we moved to Alamosa. I could go up the mountain for the night or just for the day, and it was a dog paradise, although Gav remained restricted to the leash. He didn't care. He loved hiking with Amber and me and sitting by the fire as the temperatures cooled, all of us gazing out on the valley. Afterward, when I was inside writing while propped up on the bed, he lay beside me, twitching as he dreamed.

One afternoon a roar filled the air. I looked out the window behind me and saw nothing, then out the window beside me, and nothing again. "What in the world is that, Gav-roni?"

No sooner had the words slipped out of my mouth than the

trailer was slapped with the force of a dust devil that rocked us with a whirling dervish energy that left my hair standing on end. Papers were flying and dust filled the air. Gav's eyes bugged out, and Amber tucked herself farther into her bunk space hidey-hole.

"Whoa! What happened here?" I laughed as the trailer stilled and the dogs' eyes returned to a calm, questioning gaze. The inside of the trailer was covered in a layer of dust, with papers and clothes strewn about. I watched the dust devil dance down the mountain, moving higher in the air as it slowly dissipated. Out the back window, I saw how wood normally stashed beneath the trailer had been tossed out on a pushy whirl of air and was now resting ten feet from the trailer.

Later, still nervously giggling from the experience, I stepped out to release water from the trailer's tank before heading home. Leaning down to pull the lever out, I heard a noise and saw a slight movement in the periphery of my vision. "Oooh, a rattler!" I stepped back slowly and remembered I had on flip-flops. Never a good idea in the mountains, but I had just hopped up after the commotion and slipped them on to do a quick chore. "You musta been roused up by that dust devil. I bet you were hiding under that wood the wind whisked out."

I went back in and put on pants, boots, and work gloves, then returned to take a gander. It was a small critter, still coiled about five feet away. I reached slowly and pulled the lever, standing and observing its flicking tongue and intricate brown-and-tan patterns. Once the water was drained, I slowly pushed the lever back in and went inside.

"Let's take that as a reminder to always look under the trailer and not wear flip-flops. We are in the wild up here. And it's a good thing we keep you on a leash, Gav."

Gavroche was older than Amber, but Amber's health had begun failing quickly. The decision to put another dog to sleep was staring me in the face, and I could not bring myself to act on what would be best for Amber. Finally, after waiting too long, I put her to sleep. As with Pookie, I struggled to let her go, as did Gavroche. I hadn't taken him with us to the vet that day; I wanted to focus on Amber. Maybe I should have. When Bill and I returned home after burying his sister, Gav refused to relax. He walked to the door and back, checked her beds, and looked at me questioningly. *Where is she? Is she still outside, in the car?* I remembered how confused he had been after Pookie died and also how distraught Pook was after Dancer's death.

Why hadn't I taken him with us, believing how important it can be for a dog to sniff its dead companion?

"Come here, Roni-bony head." Where this nickname came from was a mystery to me—perhaps in my affectionate effort to calm him. "Your gal won't be coming home again," I slobbered as tears spilled. "It was her time to go, just like she's been asking. She hated leaving you, though, sweet guy. She sure loved you."

Gav sat there with his head cocked, listening but puzzled. He nosed me, then took off for another search. *Maybe she came inside. She must be somewhere!*

Oh, the heartache of losing a dog companion. Gav didn't keep me at a distance like four-year-old Pookie had after Dancer died, but he was more mature at almost seventeen. He had been with Amber for fifteen years, while Pookie had been with Dancer for only four! His grief showed in how he would sit and stare into space, but that could have also been his age. His eyesight and hearing had dimmed, and he sometimes ran into things. He had little doggie stairs to get on and off the couch. He glommed onto me a little more, and I made a point of giving him extra attention. When we went to the land, I lifted him in and out of the car, then in and out of the trailer, then back into and out of the car when we arrived home. My back ached. He waited patiently while I went hiking and showered me with affection

Gavroche Napoléon

on my return from those lonely, dogless hikes. But my little man still loved going to Graceland, and I loved having his company on the mountain.

When lumps started popping up on Gav's body, I decided to check in with our vet, a brusque but highly respected ninety-year-old Japanese man beloved in our small town.

"What do you think, Doc? Should I worry about these things?"

The doc ran his hands over Gav's body, then turned and addressed me. "He's ode! He's ode!" the vet hollered, waving his hands at me to leave. Since he was a one-person operation that day, I asked what I owed him. His hand-waving became more pronounced, gesturing for us to leave.

I think we better go, Mom.

"No kidding. Guess we got our answer to those concerns!" and I lifted Gavy into the car.

Amber died in January, and by May it occurred to me that I should get another dog to lift Gav's spirits and give him a chance to do a little training. Of course, as with Pookie, I knew I might have waited too long, but by then Gav was so good-natured and such a lover I could not imagine he would resist a new dog in our family.

I started looking online at who was in nearby shelters. After some research and conversations, Bill, Gav, and I drove the ninety miles west to Pagosa Springs one weekday to check on a dog that seemed like a match. She turned out to not be the dog for us—too big with too strong of a pull for me on the leash—but on the way back to Alamosa we checked a shelter thirty miles away in Monte Vista, and one pup caught my eye. Gav strutted his stuff and nosed her politely. I couldn't make up my mind, so we headed home.

"What do you think, Gav-man? Is she your new gal? You seemed to like her."

Dog Love Stories

Yeah, she's not Amber, but she has potential. I can see her with you, though, and that's what's important. You know, I'm an old man now, and I want to make sure you have another dog before I go.

Gav had a point, but only being five months out from Amber's death, I could hardly bear the thought of him leaving. Why had I gotten two dogs so close in age? I had gotten Gavy only months before Pookie died and later lucked into finding Amber after having Gav for only a short time. Now I was looking at getting another dog about the time Gav was ready to exit. He had fallen a few times lately and was also becoming incontinent. Other days, he'd perk up and want a walk, but I knew his days were numbered.

The next day, I returned to the shelter and got the black dog with a fluffy tail we had met there. She was smaller than Amber but almost twice Gav's size, her markings suggesting she was part cattle dog. Gavy nudged her gently and gave her welcome wags. Mercy became her name, and I hoped she would show mercy to her older brother, who was slowing down by the day yet never letting that precious grin leave his face. Gav was quite grandfatherly toward Mercy. She was curious about him and tried to get him to play, but he mostly wanted to doze or sit and watch her.

The decision to let Gav go was more challenging than all the work it took to tame him and help him learn to trust me. I'd given him my all through our fifteen years together after he had come into my life as a fierce little street dog. I refused to wait too long like I had with Pookie and Amber. Since their deaths, I was committed to honoring my dogs by respecting them with as dignified an end as possible. As he looked at me with so much love, the realization that his tough little spirit would soon need to move on was devastating, but his trust in me was complete. He had finally pivoted from being a biter to a lover boy.

It was the end of August, and winter would be dropping our temps within a few months. Gavroche was having trouble

Gavroche Napoléon

controlling his bladder and bowels long enough to get outside, which made for plenty of messy days and nights. Keeping him in our workshop, where it could get down to twenty degrees, and expecting him to go out the dog door to do his business in zero degrees or below felt unrealistic. Images of bony Pookie and demented Amber kept flitting through my brain, and I knew I wanted to usher Gav on before he was too ill. It's so damn hard to take that responsibility to let a dog go and know the best time to do so.

Are dogs aware of this quandary? Pookie had communicated by slipping under a bush and refusing to come out, then another time insisting on staying outside in ten-degree temps. Gav hadn't shown either of those behaviors. I had promised him he could trust me, and now I waffled on what that implied. Finally, I decided that it meant he would trust me to make the wisest, most caring decision, even when I felt helpless and insecure doing so.

Bill and I considered our options. He dug a hole at Graceland under our favorite piñon, then we discussed some more. Meanwhile, Mercy settled into our home, into our lives, and into Gavroche's life. He nosed her along but ignored her pleas to play. I imagined slipping in on more than one conversation between the two of them.

She's finally finished that book she's been writing but will need to travel to talk about it. You better buck up, darlin', and give her a ton of support.

Travel?! I love going places! Will I be able to run there? Mercy enthused.

You can run when you take her on walks and hikes, but you better always keep an eye on her. Don't get too far away. I mean it too. I've been loving her for sixteen years, so she has a lot to give to you. Fill her up and she'll fill you up.

I promise I'll keep my eyes on her and stay close, Mercy replied in all seriousness.

Dog Love Stories

As soon as I made myself known, Gav yawned like he'd been sleeping. "You can't fool me, you two sweeties. I heard you talking."

Soon, Gavy started barking loudly in his sleep. I wondered if the pack of dogs from my life was urging him to c'mon home, and he was telling them he was on his way. His life had passed in a flash right before my eyes. Fifteen years together felt like a blur.

I made an appointment for euthanasia.

As Bill drove us to the vet, Gav turned his little white-and-gray face to me as I sat in the back seat and gave me that unmistakable Gav-grin. He was just happy we were together going somewhere, and that I was sitting in back with him.

The vet came out to our car to give us privacy. I held Gav tight as the vet injected the first shot to help him relax. I considered how we were clearly Gavy's pack, and without a doubt, he had loved us all. He had packed a punch in everything with admirable bravado, but at his core, he was a scared street dog who wanted to feel safe and loved and be part of a family. He was a lucky, lucky dog, and our lives had been enriched with his feisty spirit.

"You are such a fine man, Gavroche. An incredible dog. I'll never, ever, ever forget you."

Bill was sobbing in the front seat. I sang to Gav and kept talking to him, wanting my voice to be the last sound he heard as his fierce and resilient spirit floated away with the second shot. The afternoon sun warmed me in the back of our Blazer as his body stilled in the grip of my arms. I continued to remember the quality of all he had been as I rocked and sang him love songs while Bill drove us home. I had never known a dog like Gavroche and doubted I would ever know another like him. When I've had a dog for so long, I feel the immensity of the years we've lived together and the love we have shared. The impact of the loss slams me.

Before heading to Graceland, we picked up Mercy, who hopped up hesitantly in the back of the car where I was still

Gavroche Napoléon

caressing Gav. She sniffed him and sat down off to the side. I felt it was important for her to be present for as much as possible with what was happening, like Dancer had been when Bebe died, then Pookie with Dancer. I still had regrets that Gav hadn't been able to sniff Amber's body before we buried her.

At Graceland, Gavy's open grave was waiting under the welcoming, sweeping piñon. I wrapped him in his worn-out *Jesus Loves Me* blanket that he had loved to hump. Bill and I were crying so hard as we bent over his grave that we could barely see where we were lowering him. His body was stiff and cool now, his grin long gone. Mercy watched quietly from the open window of the Blazer.

We shoveled dirt onto Gav's precious body, then covered his grave with larger stones to keep the coyotes from later digging him up. Bill and I helped each other carry over a larger rock to use as the gravestone. Earlier I had used a Sharpie to write Gavroche's name and dates on it.

I got down on my knees, propped up the rock, then tenderly looped Gav's collar over the top of the stone where it fit perfectly. The sun was setting, casting dramatic shades of yellows and pinks across the sky. The air was still, the valley calm below us. Mercy shifted in the car where she was watching us and whined softly.

Bill and I stood together in silence, holding hands, this experience of life and loss full within us. I focused again on the dense, gray gravestone looking so stately there on our mountainside, announcing one beloved creature's precious time on Earth.

"Damn, Gav, I'm sure gonna miss you."

Gavroche Napoléon
Dude with a 'tude
2001–2018

EIGHT
Amber Grace

(met her in 2004 while I had Gavroche)

Amber tiptoed into our world like a graceful princess with dainty white stocking feet. That she even came to be part of our family was an unexpected blessing that resulted from my adopting and keeping the snarling, snapping Gavroche. When I first saw her cowering in the far back of the shelter's kennel, she looked at me with such tender yearning. Her expressive eyes, outlined with dark hairs that contrasted with her amber-colored coat, looked as though someone had applied eyeliner around them.

Gav got him a fine gal with Amber Grace—that middle name spontaneously occurring because of her manner and how she became my steadfast companion at Graceland, our mountain retreat. Dogs don't appear to recognize their size differences. Gav sure didn't. His sixteen pounds compared to Amber's thirty-five didn't faze them. She calmly watched him prance and strut, full of the bravado of a fifty-pound dog. As told in Gavroche's story, sometimes he hiked his hind leg so high he fell over, perhaps in attempts to stake his claim to Pookie then Amber by marking at the same level of any big dog that might wander along to sniff and know that he, Gav, was their man.

Despite Amber's demure demeanor, she liked to bark in the tiny backyard behind my Denver townhome. I resisted discouraging her since she had run off several cars that had taken advantage of the inviting, dark alley on the other side of my fence. Drivers brought whomever they had picked up from Colfax—the street two blocks over that sported a selection of sex workers. My regular Sunday morning chores included getting out the dog pooper-scooper to pick up the used condoms tossed out around my car. Eventually, I hung a sign on my fence: PLEASE DON'T THROW OUT USED CONDOMS! Amber, however, was my best deterrent, although my neighbors preferred sleeping through the night in silence over the barking of my vigilant dog.

Amber's guard-dog duty contributed to my looking for another house, hopefully without the alley activity. Amber was happy to have a more spacious backyard at our new place. She would lie nearby and watch me garden for hours on summer weekends, popping out the dog door onto the covered back porch or into the fenced-in dog run we built at the side of our home. As with previous dogs in whatever space they used, I kept a pail and a scooper handy to clean up after them every other day. I did this to keep poop from being tracked inside and because I believe dogs prefer ample, clean spaces to do their business.

During teaching months, Amber and Gavroche waited until I arrived home to promptly make our way to Rocky Mountain Park for a walk around the lake. One afternoon, binoculars around my neck and holding a dog leash in each hand, we were stopped by two older men out for a stroll.

Amber Grace

"She is Russian! That dog is like Russian dogs!" exclaimed the men, with strong Russian accents, nodding in agreement as they stood and admired Amber. Gav sat down and watched, looking from them to Amber as they continued.

"Dog like that lived with czar and family!" one of the men announced.

"What kind of dogs were they? Do you know?" I queried, curious about their adoration and whether I might get confirmation on Amber's breed.

"No, no, don't know. Very beautiful, though. Same dog, we are sure," the other guy added, looking at his companion, their heads bobbing.

Amber inched closer to them and allowed each to give her some respectful strokes. They spoke to her in Russian, and she listened demurely as if she understood. Maybe she did for all I knew. The guys were behaving like they were in the presence of royalty. I was impressed. Even Gavroche appeared awestruck. *My girl? I knew she was special!*

The two men continued their animated conversation with each other in Russian, watching us amble away. The shelter had labeled her a red heeler, which I could see, but she had more stature than the heelers I had known and was far more gorgeous, though seemingly humble about her beauty. She had a few white spots on her nose and a couple of amber spots on her white stockings, but the rest of her was a luscious amber coat except for the white tippy-tip on her swirling tail—a characteristic of basenjis that a few owners of that breed had pointed out. Then, of course, there were those striking black-outlined eyes.

Weeks later we were stopped on our walk by a six- or seven-year-old boy who emphatically cried out, "A dingo! Look, Mom and Dad! A dingo!" As he ran up to her, I put my hand on Amber's head to assure her all was fine.

"Move slowly so you don't scare her, okay? Let's see how she feels about you," I instructed. Amber sat down and watched. Gav also plopped down, perhaps feeling ignored but watching this familiar scene of Amber's adulation. "Put your hand out like this and let her sniff it." As the little boy did, Amber gave his hand a slight nuzzle. Then I encouraged him to pet her softly on the top of her head. She pressed herself into his tiny hand, and his eyes widened and glowed. A giggle erupted.

"Oh, indeed it is, Robbie!" I could hear the dad's Australian accent. He turned to me. "Have a dingo, do you?"

"Well, not that I'm aware of, but apparently, she looks like one!"

"Oh, she definitely does," the mom added. "We're visiting from Australia, and we've seen plenty! Our little fella has been homesick, and it looks like this will help."

The little boy continued to pet Amber as he oohed and aahed, talking to her in a bubbly voice. Gav watched with no observable reaction. "Good boy," I reassured him. I could imagine him calculating all the attention his gal was receiving.

Geez, again? Yeah, she's pretty, that's for sure. Go ahead, pet her all you want. But she goes home with me, hear?

Russian royalty or a dingo from the outback, I sure didn't know and didn't really care, but I enjoyed the speculation. I never thought about having my dogs' DNA checked back then. It didn't matter to me; plus, it would have been expensive. Instead, I saved more for vet visits and vaccinations. Hearing the assumptions about Amber's origins was entertaining. What pleased me most was observing the pleasure of people who assumed she was from their country, who saw something from their background in her.

As we walked away, I checked in with my girl. "Whaddaya think, Bertie Grace?"—using her nickname. "Would you rather be Russian, Australian, or American?"

Amber looked up at me and I imagined her saying, *I just want*

Amber Grace

to be yours. Despite the adoration, Amber maintained her humble and reflective demeanor, which only added to her mystique. "Oh, you are, girl. You are all mine and, of course, Gavy's!"

Amber adapted with ease after her adoption. At her first visit, the vet mentioned how Amber's timid behavior seemed like a dog who had been kept isolated, like dogs she had treated who had been rescued from basements. "She's got a chip, you know. I had to call the shelter to check on that, and they said they had made several calls and left messages, but no one called back. Either her previous owners dumped her, or she escaped, and they didn't care."

I could not have found a better-behaved or more stunning dog than Amber. No wonder there were five applications for her when I spied her at the shelter and lucked into becoming her owner, that tale told in Gavroche's story. In no time, Amber became a part of our family. We were like two couples living together: Bill and me, and Amber and Gavroche. Gavroche used his monkey to self-soothe, I sat on a pillow and followed my breath, Bill watched football, and Amber watched us all. She didn't push for dinner like Gav and, despite loving her walks, didn't claw at the door. She wagged her tail when either Bill or I came home but didn't jump on us. Instead, she waited patiently until we settled down, and would come sit beside us, looking up at us lovingly.

I had learned from adopting Bandi, Dancer, and now Amber that dogs are often abandoned despite their penchant for loyalty, love, and good behavior. While Amber slipped seamlessly into our home and lives, I had relied in the past on the current dog to train a new dog. Dabb, my childhood dog, had no other canine example to follow but lived most of his life outdoors. My second dog, Bandi-Lune, meek and submissive from being isolated like Amber, adjusted as an only dog with ample attention and companionship. The dog after Bandi, Dancer, pranced into my life as an already well-behaved shelter dog who must have been trained by a previous owner. Although Dancer provided an example of good behavior for Bebe and Pookie, Pook definitely needed more training, and I never regretted getting her trained. Zorro was an outdoor dog, period. Then came Gavroche and, well, you've heard his feisty story. Although Pookie showed him how to use the dog door, he had to learn to refrain from his impulse to bite. Rarely had I read about training dogs, but I did watch and ask other people how they worked with their dogs, and I'd occasionally seek a vet's opinion.

Sometimes I learned that a dog couldn't have certain freedoms—like Gav not being allowed off-leash after wandering for three hours during a visit to Graceland. By the time Pook was eight, she had learned to stay right next to me off-leash or wait in the car, even with the hatch up, without jumping out. Bandi had preferred to remain in my car when we traveled and would jump out the window to do her business and hop back in on her own. I liked giving dogs choices if these choices didn't endanger their lives or mine. Amber proved to be an honor student, grasping on her second try with the dog door that she was free to go outside whenever she wished.

When we took family weekend forays to Graceland or when I went alone, Amber—or Bertie Grace, as I had taken to calling her—was my constant companion. She could remain off-leash since she stayed close. When we hiked, I kept her leash handy in the back pocket of my hiking vest, allowing her to trot along beside or behind me. Often, I would stop, wondering where she was and sometimes calling her, only to turn around, look down, and discover her directly behind me. Maybe she was a heeler.

One morning as we clamored down Oak Road east of our land, Mounts Little Bear and Blanca looming directly behind us, I noticed Amber's ears perk up right before she froze. "What's up,

Amber Grace

girl-dog?" I followed her gaze, and about one hundred feet ahead of us was a small round dark body rolling around in the road. The road we wanted to turn onto to get back to Graceland was between us and the little critter. "Whoa," I uttered, reaching around to grab the leash out of my hiking vest, clasping it onto Amber's collar, adhering to the better safe than sorry adage. "Let's back up, Bertie. Where there's a baby bear, there's a momma close by."

I tried to walk back uphill as quietly as Amber, but rocks tumbled from my clumsy efforts. Pulling Amber over to the side, we turned to look, and the little bear scrambled across the road—a ball of black fur, just like a stuffed animal. Had his mom already crossed over? After about fifteen minutes with no further bear sightings, we cautiously approached Graceland's road and turned west to head back to our trailer. Amber rushed ahead of me, frisky with our encounter and eager to be home. I could hear her: *Gav, I smelled a bear and saved Mom! It was right in front of us, and I stopped her from going any farther!*

You don't say. I could have taken down any bears, darlin'. Too bad I wasn't there. But truth be told, Gavroche spent most of his time now on the bed in the trailer.

After our hikes, Amber would tuck herself into the bottom bunk area where I had placed Pookie's big ole blue bed. If a thunderstorm rolled through our corner of the valley and lightning cracked, she hunkered down far in the back of the bunk area, squeezing between the bed and the wall. "It's okay, girl," I would reassure her, lying down to stretch and reach as far back as I could to touch her. "Ain't nothin' gonna hurt you while I'm around."

Why some dogs are afraid of thunder, lightning, and fireworks and others aren't is a mystery to me. Gav reacted to lightning with a slight jolt, but Amber would tremble and hide with any booming sounds. My other dogs hadn't cared about booms, so I didn't pay close attention to storms when I got Amber. The first time a thunderstorm rolled in while we were out on a hike, she took off toward the trailer. I called, but to no avail. Luckily, she was at the trailer door when I arrived and jumped inside and into her bunk hidey-hole, pronto. After that, when I saw thunderheads, I leashed her quickly, just in case. What if we were too far out, and she took off, burying herself in a rock cave, and I never found her?

As recounted in Gav's story, the 2007 to 2009 recession kicked Bill and me in the butt. I had been looking for a job for months when Bill closed his Denver business and then had a heart attack. We needed to make some big changes fast. My parents needed caregivers, so we packed up and headed to their small town of Whitesboro, Texas, two hours north of Dallas near the Texas and Oklahoma border. The farther we got from Denver, the more I worried. We loved our life there in a home that fit us just right. We had tried so hard to get back on our feet and were now unsure of what lay ahead.

"Okay, kiddos, we're off for a different kind of adventure. I need y'all to be really good sports in our new home, in a new yard, living with my parents." Like most of their lives, what was happening to Amber and Gav was out of their control. Neither dog had met my parents. Amber and Gavroche sat up and looked out the windows as Bill and I each drove our own car to North Texas. They listened to me ramble on, talking to myself as much as to them. I knew it would be essential to help them adjust and thrive and not suffer from upcoming changes. I hoped I could do the same.

The idea of moving into a house with my parents so we could provide their care seemed good from afar, but the tension escalated once we were all living within the same four walls. The dogs, however, were relegated to the outdoors and that small laundry room we soon labeled "the dog office" off the garage. This was a problem. My dogs are therapy for me, especially when

Amber Grace

I'm in stressful situations: playing with them, talking with them, making up our conversations, petting them throughout the day, and experiencing how I love them, and they love me. Plus, their social time with humans is just as crucial for them. Depending on the season, I could sit with them on the back porch, but come late morning, afternoon, and early evening it was *hot*. This was Texas, and the metal roof over the back porch blazed. Amber and Gav were confused at suddenly being ostracized to the outdoors.

The problem was my parents' lanky ole country dog, Hank, who had never been allowed in the house; hence, *no* dogs were tolerated inside our shared home. Spending so much time together outside, Hank and Amber got eyes for each other, and little Gav-man was left out. Didn't matter one iota to Hank that Amber was taken; he moved right in on her. They romped in the huge backyard and chased squirrels up trees while Gav sucked on his toy monkey. But once I loaded up my two to go for a walk, just the three of us, Amber batted her eyes again at Gav. Hank had never been walked on a leash, and I wasn't willing to start training his seventy-plus pounds. Holding three leashes, like flying three kites, was not in my skill set.

Within months I was doubting our decision to move to Texas and live with my parents. The shifting North Texas ground kept our bedroom suite door from clicking shut, and we felt the loss of privacy. Bill and I still needed work, so he tried to get some small-time knife and scissor sharpening going. I expanded my job experience to tutoring high school students. Most often I huddled over my writing desk or piled the dogs in the car for a walk at the cemetery.

I could let loose and scream or cry loudly at the cemetery on the edge of town. I wailed, and both dogs watched and worried. I would sit on a headstone and assure them I was all right, but doubt filled their furry faces. Gav's grin was now infrequent, probably resulting from Amber's lack of attention and the dogs having to stay in the backyard and dog office. Amber's beautiful, expressive eyes twitched with concern. As my feet pounded the cement, gravel, and dirt roads at the sprawling cemetery, I prayed like my life depended on it—and boy did it. Interspersing my prayers with songs helped the dogs relax, and I imagined their conversation.

Okay, okay, sounds like she's gonna make it. Whaddaya think, Amber?

Yes, I agree. She gets better out here where it's just the three of us and all these dead people. Well, and those big oak trees and the birds she talks to. By the time we leave, she's happy again.

What's wrong with anthropomorphizing our dogs' thoughts? Who says dogs don't have feelings? Pookie clearly demonstrated deep grief and depression after Dancer's death. Over time, Gavroche's snarl had been replaced with that unmistakable grin full of delight. Amber displayed gentle support and love whether we were roaming mountains or I was experiencing relief at the cemetery. Perhaps my recognition of these traits of comfort, joy, satisfaction, and acceptance in my dogs came from a yearning to be experiencing those traits myself. In all our times together, surely our behaviors came to mold who the other became.

Sometimes I had to get the hell out of town and back to Colorado to achieve some sanity. Bill would assume parent and Gavroche duty, and Amber and I would load up the Outback and take off. My intentions would be to stop somewhere between Whitesboro and Blanca, Colorado, and find a cheap no-tell motel, the kind where you want to fall straight to sleep so you don't notice the grimy surroundings. But once I was on the road, my pedal foot would get heavy for the thirteen-hour drive in my anticipation to be back on the mountain. By the time we arrived at Graceland, I would just about pass out from the 8,200-foot gain in altitude.

Amber Grace

Amber would land lightly on Colorado soil, stick her nose in the air, and take a big sniff. *Ahh, junipers, piñons, desert dust, scrub jays.* Long, groaning sigh. *We're home, Mom,* I could just hear her saying.

I would moan as I straightened my body and held onto the car as my world spun. After unloading, turning on the propane and fridge, feeding Amber, and putting together a dinner, I would build a fire. A walk could wait till morning, a safer time than dusk to be out with my dog in the wild. Sitting by a crackling fire with Amber by my side, food in my belly, and a glass of red wine in my hand, we would silently let our eyes stretch across the miles in front of us. Before long, nighthawks whooshed, and the western sky filled with a palate of colors that slowly faded until stars began popping out. By the time the fire was nothing but hot coals, the Milky Way would be blasting over our heads with a gazillion sparkling stars in a majestic arc. Amber and I would crawl into the trailer, and if I were lucky, she'd hop up in bed, circle, and curl up beside me, something she would sometimes do on the first night we arrived rather than head to her bunk space.

"Oh, girl, I'm so happy to be here with you. This is the most beautiful place on Earth for me, even more so when you're with me." Little did I realize how this relief of being in Colorado would eventually draw us back to the state. I pressed my head into her soft fur and felt immensely grateful, even though the last eight months had been some of the toughest in my life thus far. Amber groaned contentedly before falling asleep. I wasn't far behind.

It had probably never been a good idea to move to Texas, but by then, I had learned that nursing regrets rarely brings about something better. After eighteen months in Whitesboro, once my parents were settled into care facilities, Bill and I moved to Alamosa, a college town barely forty minutes from Graceland on the western side of the San Luis Valley. We continued to feel pummeled with what to do with our lives. The outdated home we had bought in Alamosa, however, held onto all four of us "for better or worse," words Bill and I hadn't included in our wedding vows but words we were learning to embody. The vacant century-year-old house required an electrical upgrade but was livable, with its buckling panel walls and fifty-year-old gold carpet showing well-worn paths. Drop-tiled ceilings covered up cracks that revealed an attic insulated with old quilts. With buckets of paint and willing friends, we painted walls made of horsehair and mud.

The good part of "better or worse" was having Graceland nearby. Getting up there regularly to hike with Amber, doing some meditative archery target practice, and staring at a fire and the Milky Way helped recalibrate my flailing mental health. The bad part of "better or worse" was the hefty weight of depression that couldn't be assuaged by Bill, the dogs, or the promises of what our home could become. In addition to starting a business of writing and officiating memorial and wedding ceremonies as a celebrant—something I completed the training for while in North Texas—I was still applying for other work in my field of education. At the same time, Bill struggled to establish his sharpening business in Alamosa as we tried anything to ease our financial woes. Somewhere amidst all this, I thought it best to not give up on my goal of writing my memoir about surviving sexual abuse, so I started plugging away on that as if this endeavor would somehow lift my spirits. Soon, I hit a rock-bottom low.

Phone conversations with my Houston therapist from the nineties stopped when he retired due to illness. I was not getting therapy, and after the experiences of the past few years, my vulnerable mental health needed serious help. As ungrounded as he felt, Bill talked me up from some low lows that scared us both. After quick exits through the flapping dog doors, Amber and

Amber Grace

Gavroche would reappear and slip their soft heads onto my lap, licking my arms and hands and looking up at me with their desperate yet hopeful faces. *We're worth it*, they seemed to be saying. *We know you can get better.* These were times that brought author Anna Quindlen's words about her beloved dog to mind: "In a world that seems so uncertain, in lives that seem to ricochet from challenge to upheaval and back again, a dog can be counted on in a way that is true of little else."[4] However, despite my canine support, I needed something more to land me on my feet.

After committing to therapy and a cocktail of meds tweaked to the lowest level that could still be lifesaving and supportive, I was soon able to grow my celebrant business while writing my memoir and renovating our old home. Bill and I grew stronger together, and the dogs became calmer. I moved Amber's bed—Pookie's old blue bed—under a repurposed dining room table I used as a desk. As I worked on my book, I kept my feet on or under her, stroking her back or warming my toes. When I reached an emotional impasse in my writing, I'd reach down and rub her ears, then hold her beautiful face in my hands and thank her for being my muse. She'd reciprocate with a lick and lay her lovely head onto my foot. Gavroche would watch from the side of my desk where he lay on Dancer's well-worn green bed, flopping his tail and grinning.

Life was finally on the better side of "for better or worse."

My sixtieth birthday occurred the first summer we were in the San Luis Valley. The passage to sixty and the journey to Alamosa had been challenging with some hard lessons along the way. I had heard of ceremonies called "cronings" that serve to mark one's transition into eldering, and I was drawn to the experience. Because friend Nancy was also in her sixtieth year, we decided to plan an event together. We invited twenty women we felt close to and dedicated several days to reflection and celebration at Graceland, led by a fellow celebrant.

It was a moving experience, particularly one evening when Nancy and I acknowledged and thanked each person who had come and shared how they had contributed to our lives. As we sat in a circle around a fire under the blazing Milky Way, I watched as my normally timid dog worked the circle, moving from person to person, allowing time for each to pet her. Her amber coat reflected the fire's light and her eyes shone. Were her actions for her own pleasure, out of her love for me, or some kind of indirect expression from me of my gratitude to others? What she was doing felt intentional; normally she liked to get in her hidey-hole come dark. When she had gone round the circle, she came and sat beside me. Resting my hand on her warm side, I could feel her energy vibrating. "You're my Spirit Dog, Bertie Grace," I whispered in her ear, and I thanked her for walking me to cronehood.

Alamosa was a unique community, unlike any I had lived in before, and I had lived in plenty of others. So many people had stayed here for decades or been here their entire lives. Most in the community were active in a variety of service organizations—the community garden, Habitat for Humanity, a homeless shelter, the Rio Grande Farm Park, a dog shelter, an immigrant resource center, their churches, and more. In my efforts to meet others and feel grounded, I joined a book group that had been meeting for forty years. I began attending the Unitarian Universalist church—located a half block away—having grown fond of one during my time in North Texas. After one of my celebrant teachers told me about Threshold Choirs—choirs that sing to comfort at the bedsides of those dying or suffering—I investigated this national organization and began the steps to start one in Alamosa's active and generous volunteer community. I had sung to my mom when visiting her nursing facilities, as well as to a student

Amber Grace

and to a friend when their life support was discontinued. I knew the value of soft, comforting songs in these situations.

Amber and Gavroche benefited from my song practice: I sang at home, on our walks, sitting by the campfire, driving to and from the land, and as they closed their eyes at night. They knew the sweet tones and melodious sounds that contrasted with the angry voice that sometimes accompanied my times of depression.

Mom, I sure love that you are singing more than you're crying now, I imagined Amber expressing as she nudged my hand onto her head.

Yeah, Gav added. *This is the good life!* That Gav-grin was planted on his face. Although healthy food, regular walks, updated shots, and vet exams are all very important to the health of one's dogs, it was easy to see how peaceful, comforting, loving attention can be the most vital.

Our lives spread out in the San Luis Valley. We were renovating approximately one room a year in our old home, slowly seeing the house reengage with what was surely a glow from its past. The previous owner, an elderly woman who had grown up in the house, stopped by soon after we moved in and hesitantly asked if she could see what we were doing to the house. She walked through rooms in a daze, both dogs following her with curiosity, brushing a hand along the walls as she repeated, "This was such a good home." I took comfort in knowing these old walls had held her family with such love. I felt the metaphorical arms of my home's walls supporting me, Bill, and our pups. We were home, finally. Like Gav had said, this was the good life!

Mild-mannered Amber must have felt protective of our new home, judging by her daily reaction to the mailperson dropping the mail in our mail slot on the wall. As soon as she heard the creak of the flap lift, she'd tear into the living room and attack the front door with a fury we never saw before or anywhere else again. I thought of Gav barking hysterically at our fridge's icemaker in Denver. I pondered what precipitated these random reactions with dogs.

What popped up for me was how my dogs were able to read my behavioral cues better than I did theirs. I tried to understand and curb these weird habits and convince them that no one's life was in danger when the icemaker came on or the mailperson dropped the mail in the slot. Eventually, we quit spraying water and dispensing a loud "NO!" and simply got used to the situations.

Several years later, after Amber had died and Bill and I were finally renovating our funky fifties living and dining rooms, friend Carolyn suggested I preserve a section of the large area on the front door where Amber had regularly tried to claw her way to the mail aggressor on the other side. I thought about my otherwise meek, gentle red heeler as I carefully painted turquoise around a heart that displayed Amber's signature scratches on the door's natural wood.

But Amber's more gentle side dominated, whether trailing behind me on our mountain hikes or when we were snowshoeing. On those snowy days, she learned not to follow too close behind, or she'd get an unintentional kick from my flapping snowshoes. Dressed in her cobalt-blue wool cape with side pockets for who knows what and its Velcro attachment under her belly, she'd prance at a safe distance and occasionally stray to check out a smell. But my little blue riding hood was always easy to keep an eye on. We loved to wander along winter paths in the utter silence only snow can create, pierced by the crunch of my snowshoes or the raspy *kee-eeee* call of a soaring hawk. Amber tread noiselessly in the snow, like she did in our lives; except, of course, for the attacks on the front door.

I recognized the differences between my dogs just as parents can appreciate those between their children. Amber Grace was

Amber Grace

unusual in how demure she remained, usually meek and quiet and not begging for attention, conceding to Gavroche and other dogs. Although I had tacked Grace onto her first name because of her graceful manner and because she came into our lives when we bought Graceland, I also started to feel the name fit for other reasons. It held spiritual meaning, like saying grace before a meal. This connected grace with expressing gratitude, which I certainly felt about Amber. Her muse-like presence under my writing desk was a gift all on its own. She was simply there, as though offering herself to support the challenging journey of writing a memoir about a life like mine. Just saying her name became a prayer of thanks; the power of emotion in expressing her name opened my heart in bigger and better ways. "Oh, Amber Grace," I prayed.

Within six years of landing in Alamosa, that prayer changed to, "Whatcha doin', Bertie? You okay?" As Bill and I sat at our kitchen table for dinner, Amber would poke her head out the dog door, then return for a sip of water, back to the dog door, sip water, dog door, water. We laughed about it in the first few weeks, wondering what she was hearing—since her hearing had diminished—plus puzzling over what was making her so thirsty. Ha ha. After months of this behavior, I counted the repetitions one evening: twenty times. We quit laughing. When she started searching for her dog bowl—always in the same place—this was no longer funny either, but heart-wrenching.

Her vet explained we were watching the fast progression of doggie dementia playing out in front of our eyes. Suddenly, at sixteen years old, she was displaying puppylike behaviors I had not seen before: biting my hand softly when I returned home and playfully rolling onto her back for tummy rubs. The trouble was, she couldn't manage to get back onto her stomach without help. She would curl her lips back into an innocent grin that made me break out in nervous giggles. "Oh, Bertie Grace. You're still happy, aren'tcha?" But I was beginning to feel that dread of soon losing an aging dog.

Late that summer, I took Amber camping to an area in the Rio Grande National Forest with my friend Cathy. I pitched my well-used blue tent in a grassy meadow where I could hear the water rushing, then made warm, comfy beds for Amber and me. We loved our times together in my tent's sapphire world.

The next day, Cathy, her corgi Pats, Amber, and I took off with poles and lures. Despite Cathy's patient instruction and my earnest efforts, I never mastered the fly-fishing throw. I decided to take a hike while she continued to fish.

Amber was slow, but I still loved being outdoors with her. I was slower, too, with a knee that ached from old athletic injuries. The trail along the river was smooth, and the song of the water carried us along. I had the ashes of both my parents that I had stashed in a plastic bag on a bookshelf after their deaths. The bag contained a small mixture from the two that I had kept out of the containers my sisters and I had buried beside their gravestone in the Whitesboro cemetery where I used to walk. I didn't have a plan for what I'd do with the ashes but hoped an idea would come to me at some point. My dad loved the outdoors; my mom did not, but she knew that I did. Maybe that would be enough to justify dispersing the mixture outside. What else was I going to do, surreptitiously sprinkle her ashes under a bright new carpet or between a gaudy floral bedspread and some ironed polyester blend sheets, things my mom took delight in? I decided the flowers and green grass of a riverbank would be suitable substitutions. I tossed the mix over the water and the lush bank. Amber and I watched as their ashes floated away like the wisp of a cloud on a gentle breeze. With my hand on my girl's head, I felt the relief of a deep breath in that soft afternoon air with the refreshing smell of running water. *Relief is a part of healing*, I reminded myself.

Amber Grace

My parents took their first and last ambitious camping trip when I was two. We drove to Colorado with gear tied to the top of Dad's black 1954 Chevy. I have pictures of Dad setting up the big heavy canvas tent while Mom, always in a skirt, stirred something in a pot over a camp stove on a picnic table. My ten-year-old sis must have had the Brownie camera. In one picture, I'm on my dad's shoulders as he stands in a mountain stream, much like where I was right then. I became lost in the memory. I like to imagine us laughing and him sweeping me off and playfully dipping my feet into the waters. Mom would be watching us, happy to have the family outdoors somewhere new and beautiful. But more likely, I would have been afraid of Dad being mad at me again for crying after forcing me to get into the stream. Mom would be slamming things around at the campsite, angry and uncomfortable about being outdoors, having been forced by Dad to go camping. "Forced" is the operative word.

By my mid-forties, my parents and I had established a tactic of "no asking about and no talking about" my abuse allegations. So I quit asking questions, but I refused to recant, and they didn't admit. We made nice, with periodic daggers flying. This tactic made it possible for us to be around each other. By dispersing their ashes that afternoon, I was making nice, no daggers, even if Mom would have rather been in a floral bedspread.

Later that night, tucked into our blue world, some part of me knew this was my last campout with Amber. Having her beside me that afternoon had helped me feel stronger and safer. Now I pulled back my sleeping bag, like opening a door and welcoming her in. She curled up right next to me. I wrapped my arms around her and took comfort from her breathing. Her coat smelled like meadow grass and river mud and water, a fragrance that lulled me to sleep.

I soon began noticing that Amber was having trouble getting onto her bed, and since it was under my desk, I moved it out to the side. She'd almost make it fully onto the bed, with only her hips hanging off, then lie and stare at me with eyes full of puppy dog affection. Her fur had lost its sheen and thinned. Her hips suddenly seemed bony and her face white, and the carpet was often damp from her seeping bladder. I remembered how thin Pookie got in her last months and my reluctance to let her go.

How do we mark the beginnings and endings that unfold in our lifetimes? How can we describe our different selves across the years? Amber was my eighth dog, meaning I had been through six deaths, since Gav was still with me at the time. She was sixteen, not young for a mid-size dog. How did I keep missing my dogs aging? They would seem okay, until one day they weren't. Did my denial persuade me to not notice the signs: the cloudy eyes, dulling coats, observable skeletons?

My grief started bubbling up as I reflected on who I'd been with each dog I had lost: A little girl terrified of being bereft without the comfort of her dog Dabb. A confused young woman who couldn't manage the responsibility of her dog Bandi and so gave her up but never forgot about her. Hearing a car thud into Bebe one quiet Saturday morning and holding her head while rushing to the vet, hoping to make it in time, but didn't. A newly divorced teacher discovering her dog Dancer stricken by a stroke upon returning from a long workday and making that first difficult decision to euthanize a beloved dog. Nine years later, wanting to ignore Pookie's nudges to let her go, paralyzed with the thought of no longer having this soul companion who had offered so much strength and love. Now Amber, my muse, always there with her loving, gorgeous eyes, who had shadowed me for fifteen years from Denver to Whitesboro to Alamosa to miles on mountain paths, watching me find my ground physically and metaphorically.

It was already December, and the ground had begun freezing. Fly-fishing Cathy offered a place on her land at the edge of Monte

Amber Grace

Vista Wildlife Refuge to bury Amber when the time came. That meant digging the hole right away. Once dug, I visited it one evening under the faint light of a new moon. I circled the space, wondering if the time was near. Oddly, I had stuck some dirty socks in my pocket before leaving the house, ones that had been on Amber's bed all week—favorite socks I had worn with her on walks, hikes, camping, and snowshoeing. Maybe by tucking them into her grave she could sniff her way to a familiar-smelling, but new, home. It was a crazy idea, but I was desperate to do anything for comfort around her impending death. I often left socks previously worn on my dogs' beds when Bill and I left on trips, something that might remind them of my presence and impending return.

Despite recognizing that this was harder for me than for Amber and that in no way was I doing her wrong by deciding to let her go, I struggled with making the call. Guiding our dogs' health decisions, and hopefully letting them go before they are in too much pain and too uncomfortable, is exactly what I have directed that someone do for me. After watching Amber deteriorate for another month, I finally scheduled the dreaded appointment for euthanasia.

On that January day, I wanted to give her a last walk. We moved slowly to accommodate her careful gait and to navigate ice patches. Gav on my right, Amber on my left, as usual. Suddenly, I lurched forward as if lassoed from behind, my feet unable to separate. I crashed ahead, still holding a leash in each hand, one elbow hitting the sidewalk and the other some grass. Pain seared in my left elbow to the point that I had to hold onto my bowels and stomach contents.

"What the hell?" I couldn't separate my feet. I saw the loop of a shoelace on one foot's shoe caught on the too-large open hook on the other shoe. I had to pop it out of the hook to be able to part my feet. Not a well-thought-out design on these brand-new hiking boots. As the pain subsided, I pulled my phone out of my back pocket and called Bill. I was only two blocks away from home, right in front of our neighborhood mortuary.

Bill came to pick us up. After an X-ray and close look in the emergency room, I learned I had a fracture, best healed if kept in a sling for six weeks to keep me from using my left arm. Left: Amber's side on walks. This morning's stroll would have been her last.

When I returned home, I had an hour before we needed to leave for our appointment at the vet. Amber was sprawled out near her bed, only her head and front legs on it now. I lay down next to her, placing my injured elbow held in a sling on her bony body. Gav sat off to the side, and I remembered how he had also watched my last hour with Pookie before she was euthanized. As I petted Amber, I noticed her hair falling out in clumps. Every day it was something new. Her cloudy eyes, so beautifully outlined in black on that now-white face, were still so loving. She licked my left hand, which was now swollen and bruised.

"Thank you, my love, for all your care and support in our fifteen years together. You helped me finish my memoir, Bertie Grace. Finally, it's out there to do whatever good it will do, and I'll never forget how having my feet on you as I wrote it helped me get it done. Your ears were within reach for a rub or the side of your face for a kiss at the most needed moments." Amber nudged my painful hand onto her head, and I caressed her ears. I tried to imagine what she might be saying if she had words, but I heard nothing except my sobs. Still, her eyes held such love.

"I'm gonna bury a manuscript copy with you, Bertie." I picked up the one I had printed out for her. "I'm turning it to the section that describes one of our visits to Graceland so you can show it to all the other dogs I have loved and who are also in my story. You remind 'em how you've all played a part in keeping me alive." Gavroche's tail thumped, and I told him, "You, too, Gav-man."

Amber Grace

Amber looked at me with her dark, willing eyes and licked my nose. I thought of how she and Gavroche had walked me to the sharpest edge of my life thus far, one I had come close to jumping off, and how Amber's tender companionship was now leaving me a much stronger person.

Bill pulled the Blazer up close to the house so I could load Amber. I had encouraged Gavroche to say goodbye inside, but neither dog knew these were their last moments together, did they? Gavy could tell we were going somewhere, and he wanted to come, but I wanted to be alone with Amber and Bill, no Gav distraction. Kneeling beside the two, I made up what I wanted their conversation to be:

Maybe you'll remember me better wherever you are going, darlin'. I won't ever forget you.

I'll never forget you either, even if I can't remember what I'm looking for outside the dog door or if I already had a drink of water!

Well, you've been my best gal. Nobody gonna replace you. Just know that.

Although I was crying amidst this little fantasy, Amber nudged Gavroche to seemingly comfort him. Just a little touch of her nose on the side of his face right before I opened the front door. Gav sat down and watched us go—no grin, no wag. "I'll be back, Gav-man," and I closed the door with a soft click.

I walked in to tell our rural vet that we were parked out front, as he had requested. I crawled in back with Amber before he stepped out to explain what he would be doing: give us ten minutes alone, next come out to provide her with a shot to subdue her, then return to inject the medication that would euthanize her. He was a big, burly guy with a gentleness about him. When he left, I began singing, one song after the other—cheery made-up songs and sleepy Threshold Choir songs. In between, I nuzzled Amber's neck and cried while Bill let loose in the driver's seat, blowing his nose into one Kleenex after another. He had become more of a dog lover than he liked to admit.

The vet returned to give the first shot. Amber loosened in my arm. I managed to keep the left, slinged arm free to stroke her lovely head and continue singing and telling her thank you for who she had been in my life, in Gav's life, in Bill's life, and for all she had given us. I didn't think she could become limper, but when the vet came out with the final injection, her head rolled off my arm, and her weight doubled.

Oh, to hold a dog in your arms and let them go like this is unlike anything else I've ever experienced, and experience this I had with Bebe, Dancer, and Pookie. Now I had to say goodbye to my precious Bertie Grace, who had tiptoed into our lives with the elegance of a Russian princess.

While my left arm throbbed, my right arm ached from Amber's weight, but I refused to let her go as we drove to Cathy's. My face was wet and my nose draining, and I couldn't move the hand of my arm in the sling up to my face to wipe it. As I brushed my face across Amber's neck, I could feel her body's heat dissipating. Even her coat seemed to be stiffening. *Is that possible?*

When we pulled up to Cathy's home, Bill backed up to the gravesite. I looked out to see a bench beside the hole and a vase of flowers in front of an attractive wooden marker engraved with: AMBER GRACE EAGLE. Cathy had thoughtfully prepared it all.

Cathy helped me grab my side of the sheet Amber was on, and then the three of us carefully unloaded her from the back of the car, carrying the uncharacteristic heaviness that she was to her grave. Once there, we repositioned ourselves to lower her with ease, letting go of the sheet's sides once she was at rest on the ground. I was glad her face was partially uncovered for a last glance. Still, when I stepped down into the grave to place my

Amber Grace

manuscript on top of her, I closed her black-rimmed eyes, then pulled the sheet gently over that snow-white muzzle.

"Oh, Amber Grace," was all I could say, over and over, like a prayer carrying her to someplace where I believed a whole pack of wagging tails was waiting to welcome her.

Amber Grace
My Muse
2002–2018

NINE

Mercy Mercy Me

(met her in 2018 while I had Gavroche)

Run! Leap! Soar! Twist! Pounce! Mercy flies, front legs reaching forward and back legs stretching behind her, her attention rapt on some sound only she has heard in the field. Suddenly, she pivots in midair and dives, her nose disappearing in a clump of grasses, likely searching for a field mouse. After adopting Mercy, I gradually learned what she had an affinity toward, and it wasn't chasing balls.

Morning walks are her time of utmost pleasure. Of course, she's not trying to impress me, though I chuckle watching her air-bound antics. But what impresses me is how she keeps an eye on me in case I call, "Come!" on seeing another dog or a family of geese dawdling in the reeds. A treat awaits her compliance.

Dog Love Stories

Then, after an intermittent time on the leash, she takes off again running in a wide circle at full speed, even managing to scoop up snow in her open mouth without breaking her jaw while in a full run.

Mercy and I share this penchant for the outdoors. Here in this bowl of the San Luis Valley with the Sangre de Cristo Mountains towering to the east, Blanca Vista Lake and the San Juan Mountains to the west, the Collegiate Peaks farther north, and New Mexico plateaus to the south, this is where we both feel most alive. I watch Mercy's activity and remember how it felt to run full speed on a soccer field or across the finish line of a 10K race or marathon. But now, I relate more to her propensity to be alert—listening intently, smelling, and scanning for movement. Every cell is at attention with her, and I watch and imitate.

What we focus on, what grabs our attention, says something about our lives. After a lifetime of taking notice and attempting to understand dogs, this dog is now helping me be attentive to what I experience as the holy outdoors. While she watches what skitters on the ground, I watch the northern harrier hawk flying low, perhaps looking for what she has flushed out of the grasses. I listen to the cacophony of red-winged and yellow-headed blackbirds, search for the powder-blue patch that identifies the blue-winged teal, and call out a morning greeting to the resident red-tailed "hawky-hawky," as Bill affectionately calls every species of hawk. I notice the flash of a yellow warbler, luxuriate in the friendly swirl of swallows on a summer morning, or catch the eerie sound of the Wilson's snipe hiding in the grassy field. One winter morning a great horned owl soared silently beside me as I walked on the levee, its brilliant golden eyes illuminated by the rising sun. Then, suddenly, a loud scraping sound split the morning air, even stopping Mercy in her tracks, as the lake's ice cracked and curled like a frozen wave breaking.

For me, this is how I experience walking my prayers, with my

Mercy Mercy Me

ears and eyes wide open. I have deepened my relationship with the earth I walk upon, this land I call home, the creatures with whom I share it, and the air I breathe. Mercy and I are collaborators, accepting these mystical invitations from nature to be as present as possible.

Adhering to my pattern of getting a new dog while an older dog—this time Gavroche—was still around, Bill and I planned a trip to the Pagosa Springs shelter, two hours west of Alamosa. I had found a mid-sized, mixed-breed dog online who had been discovered living in the woods. The nice-looking female was described as shy and sweet. I began the application and approval process, getting everything squared away before we left in case we were to leave Pagosa with a new dog.

Excited but anxious, I discovered a dog who pulled so hard on my shoulder that I realized a forty-five-pound mid-sized dog was too big for my aging body. Gavroche was with us for the meet and greet, and he looked at me with alarmed eyes that stressed, *Not this one!* After thanking the shelter, Bill, Gavy, and I loaded up and took off. As we drove home, my spirits got edgier.

"Let's stop at the Monte Vista shelter and see what they have," Bill suggested, doing his best to curb my sour mood.

The barking was deafening as soon as I stepped out of the car. I dragged myself to the office and asked if they had any female dogs who weren't pit bulls. This was clearly a pit drop-off and a shelter where you don't have to be preapproved for an adoption, especially if you're willing to take a pit bull.

"Got one female who isn't pit. Wanna see her?" the male staff mumbled. He looked like he had spent the night in a kennel.

As he opened the gate, I walked toward a small black dog who rushed at me, pushing her head between my legs as if she couldn't bear the noise, while tucking a fine-looking fluffy tail. I rubbed behind her ears and tried to see her face. Maybe if I took her on a little walk and got someplace quieter, we could get to know each other a bit. He leashed her up, and "Mercedes" and I took off.

She was excited to get out. Bill lifted Gavroche out of the car, and we all took off on a stroll. Even pulling on her leash, Mercedes's twenty-seven pounds didn't strain my shoulder. Gav tried to edge closer to her, focusing on this lively gal who exhibited an enthusiastic demeanor with her chance of escape from the raucous shelter.

It was already closing time, so I returned her to the staff guy, asked when they opened the next morning, and said I'd think about it. I liked Mercedes, and her backstory didn't indicate abuse, something I had decided I would avoid after my experience with Gavroche. But I was still grumpy and needed to shake off the day before I could consider adopting a new dog.

That night I couldn't get Mercedes out of my mind: how she responded to my touch, was the perfect size, appeared happy, and how she and Gavroche got along. The following day, I was at the Monte Vista shelter before the gate was unlocked. I waited. Mercy bounced around upon seeing me. *You came back! You came back!* After taking care of payment and papers, my new pup and I headed to the car where I had a crate ready, and I lifted her in with ease. I talked to her all the way to Alamosa, telling her more about Gav, Bill, and her new home.

I showed Mercedes the house, the dog doors, her bedroom (the crate), the backyard, the water bowl, and most importantly, I sat on the floor with her and Gavy. Gav looked miserable as she lunged at him, trying to get him to play.

Calm down! he implied, backing away.

"Gav-man, this is exactly what you did to Pookie. This dog is younger than you and has more energy. Be patient and help her settle in. Okay?" But his memory most likely didn't hold a place for Pookie anymore, now fourteen years after her death.

Mercy Mercy Me

Mercedes morphed into Mercy that first day, a new name close enough to her old one. The first friend I told about Mercy exclaimed, "Mercy me!" *Oh*, I thought, *Mercy has a middle name.* Then the next friend responded with, "Mercy, mercy, me!" and I realized I wanted the entire phrase. Mercy Mercy Me jumped right into her name, ready to be whatever we wanted to call her, which was most often simply Mercy or Merce (rhymes with "purse"). Several nicknames were already springing up. With two distinct blond spots above her eyes, she became Miss Polka Dot Eyes. One floppy black ear led to Miss Floppy Ear. And with that impressive fluffy tail, Miss Fluffy Tail was tacked onto the list. Best of all was observing her propensity to delicately cross her front legs when lying down, such a prissy gesture for Little Miss Cross Her Legs.

I was glad to know Mercy's original name. From the shelter, I learned Mercedes had been picked up five times wandering around Monte Vista, often landing at Sonic, where she snagged fries and burger bites from customers. Mercedes's owner, a woman in her eighties, paid the fifty-dollar charge to get her dog out of the shelter four times, then on the fifth time, relinquished her. After googling the phone number on Mercy's collar and finding the address of Mercedes's old home, I drove by and discovered there was no backyard fence. I noticed an open field next to Mercy's former home, perfect for her hunting forays. Bill and I had noticed how Mercy slapped at our front door early in the evening, looking at us with a pushy expression that seemed to say, *Time for me to go hunting!* Or maybe she was saying, *I need to get to Sonic!*

Gavroche lasted almost three months after we adopted Mercy, a little longer than Pookie lasted after I had adopted Gav, but still not long enough. It's hard to divide attention between a dog in his last months of life and a new dog. Neither displayed jealousy toward the other. Gav was patient with Mercy at home and welcomed us when we returned from walks. After he died, Mercy conducted a few searches and sniffed his bowl until nothing was left to smell. Gav's absence didn't impact her despite my heart remaining tender for months. But Mercy was a distraction, and she was eager to explore her new life, quickly becoming an excellent walking companion, except for some leash aggression.

On morning walks, Mercy began looking back at me with a yearning to speed up. "This is as fast as I can go," I informed her as she pulled at the leash. I was now wearing a brace on my painful left knee, a nagging injury leftover from running and soccer days.

Can't we go faster? I'm hearing and smelling things and want to check them out! I began letting her have the run of the levee after allowing her off-leash a few times and observing how she kept her eyes on me and responded to "Come!" *I'll keep an eye on you, don't worry! Gavy made me promise to do that!* Without holding her leash, it was easier to use my binoculars, and Mercy could cover more ground and follow her nose and ears. We were both relieved to have this freedom.

Soon Mercy's behavior began to confuse me. Her amiability with nonaggressive dogs when off-leash, like at the dog park or a boarding facility playground, contrasted with her aggression when on a leash. I remembered how valuable Pookie's training had been in helping her to calm down. Had I gotten training for Gavroche, he might have given up his aggressive penchant much sooner. I hoped to take Mercy on my upcoming book tour, so I sought training.

The first trainer recommended an e-collar operated at low intensity with kindness. Still, I grimaced with even a slight zap in my palm when holding the collar and pushing the control button. A beeper also let her know a shock might follow, giving her a chance to change her behavior before a zap. Mercy learned to come to attention with just a beep and no shock. Regardless, I sought another trainer.

The second person used so many treats I thought Mercy would puke on our drive home. I began carrying them, however, and they effectively distracted her when we saw another leashed dog. Yet if the dogs were too close, she would bark and lunge. If I simply yanked at her leash when she did this, it felt like I was trying to impose my will on her rather than teach her something, plus it had her gagging even in a harness.

"Maybe Mercy is being protective of you," a few folks surmised about her aggressive behavior toward other dogs.

"I don't think so. Off-leash, she's calm and happy around other dogs." I simply wasn't hearing from Mercy: *How do I protect myself or you from these other dogs when I'm leashed up!*

The best solution was guiding her off the levee and closer to the lake where she would be more likely to remain calm and less likely to make a mistake. I also started using a harness with two places to attach a double leash, allowing me to both hold onto Mercy and redirect where she looked. I chose to follow author Suzanne Clothier's sensible instruction, "If you show a dog a more comfortable and productive way to experience life, he is usually quite glad to trade in his confusion, anxiety, anger, or fear for more pleasant feelings."[5]

Walking Mercy through the park one day, a guy working on a nearby fence yelled, "We have a dog who looks just like that one in the shelter!"

"Really? Do you work there?" I questioned after being knocked out of my reverie.

"Yeah. Somebody dropped off an identical dog to yours yesterday. Must be her brother!"

"Hmm. Maybe I ought to go look." It occurred to me that another dog might curb Mercy's propensity for leash aggression.

Dog Love Stories

Indeed, the little guy was almost identical to Merce in size, markings, and colors, with a slightly boxier face. I went home, talked to Bill about the fella, then brought Bill and Mercy to the shelter. The male dog walked well without tugging. I couldn't tell if Mercy recognized him like a sibling, but the two were amiable. We took him home and named him Ruffino, after one of our favorite Chianti wines. He immediately seemed like the perfect companion for us all: excellent leash behavior, house-trained, didn't chew or bark, and liked to play with Mercy.

Eight degrees in Alamosa is not that cold in the context of San Luis Valley winters. But eight degrees in the evening hours felt plenty chilly as I stood in our backyard, clad in my robe and furry house shoes, watching Ruffi watch me.

"C'mon, Ruffi. Do your business already." Orion was popping out in the night sky. Ruffino looked at me, then turned and, with a hop and one touch, soared over our six-foot wooden fence in two seconds.

After four days of chase and catch—not easy for Bill's and my sixty-six-year-old knees—with one of us zipping out of our yard the moment Ruffi's paws hit the fence, we gave up. I addressed Ruffi directly, "Geez, little guy, you couldn't find a better home than ours. Why do you want to bolt?" I was afraid Mercy would watch and learn, and my heart would become increasingly attached to Ruffi who would soon disappear or be hit by a car. I couldn't bear the thought of losing one or two dogs, especially Mercy, to whom I was already attached.

I returned Ruffi to the shelter as a flight hazard and later learned they found him a country home nearby. The difficulty of making that decision nagged me: the roots a dog can put down so quickly, the initial dream with every adoption of the years to come that a dog and I will share, along with the wonder of how our love will most assuredly stretch boundaries beyond fur and skin.

Mercy Mercy Me

Only four days with this dog, and I still cried on relinquishing him.

In early 2019, not a year after Mercy had come to live with us, I had a total knee replacement on my left knee. I wondered how Mercy would react to my being propped up in bed for hours, the required ice machine used at that time circulating cold water on my knee. Her concern was observable, and her vigilance admirable. She stayed on the bed with me except for her walks, delicately resting one of her front legs on my injured leg. *I'm right here, Mom, keeping an eye on you.*

Maybe her leash aggression did reflect some level of protectiveness.

Before the surgery, I was concerned that Mercy wouldn't get her regular exercise while I healed, so I hired an Alamosa AmeriCorps volunteer to walk her daily. When Amanda came in, Mercy would fly off my bed to greet 'Manda and get outside. Knowing Mercy was exercising helped me feel better; I imagined her running-leaping-pouncing in the melting snow and mud at this time of year. When she and Amanda returned and after 'Manda gave Miss Muddy Paws a good cleaning, Mercy rushed back to her post in the bedroom smelling of snow, chilled air, and damp earth—a balm to my spirit.

Amanda referred me to a dog DNA operation, with a coupon for a discount. Why not? People often asked what breed Mercy was, but I had no idea: small, black, some border collie–like markings, smart as a whip. I was nonplussed when the results came back: husky, I could see, even Australian cattle dog, but miniature poodle and Staffordshire terrier? Her absolute love of and comfort in snow convinced me of the husky designation. How she grabbed my heels around the house when she wanted to go on a walk persuaded me of the cattle dog category. Perhaps her size and intelligence could be from miniature poodle. But

Dog Love Stories

Staffordshire terrier, part of the all-encompassing label for the many "bully" breeds? I couldn't see it. "Almost all dogs in the valley have some pit in them," I heard from another local dog-lovin' friend. "No gettin' around it. Too many pits around here."

Four months after the 2019 knee surgery, my memoir was published. Although I finished it in 2017, the next year and a half was spent on final edits, formatting, cover, acquiring blurbs, scheduling readings and interviews, writing articles for publicity, and more. I had no idea how much was required to publish a book. Mercy romped along beside me on the last year of this journey, providing almost as much emotional support as Bill.

Amanda left after her year of volunteer work in our valley, so Bill walked with Mercy and me until I got stronger. Mercy kept her eyes on us as we trailed behind. She learned to loop around and run full speed back to us, over and over, to expend her energy. Soon Mercy and I were back on the levee alone, which allowed me quiet time for reflection, so necessary since *Being Mean: A Memoir of Sexual Abuse and Survival* was now in circulation. The delight I felt in watching Mercy's attentiveness and boundless energy outdoors filled my cup to the brim. Later, I discovered how this comfort and grounding I experienced on the levee supported me while speaking at events in Colorado, New Mexico, and Texas. At least one person approached me at each book reading to share their own abuse experience. Soaking up the beauty on the levee and Mercy's joy at being out there strengthened my courage to trust myself to speak my truth.

In the fall of 2019, I had readings and speaking engagements scheduled in Arizona and California, where I also planned on visiting friends. Mercy would accompany me as well as an emotional support dog for me and, hopefully, for others. She responded to commands and behaved well on a leash, although her leash behavior was still iffy when another leashed dog appeared. I was

Mercy Mercy Me

willing to take my chances, keep the double leash on her, and keep my pockets full of distracting treats.

Then wildfire season started. Hundreds of fires began burning across California, eventually leaving many thousands of acres of burned land. Air quality was horrendous. Vacation rentals were being sought by people evacuating from their homes. Bill and I carefully reconsidered our journey and our lodging reservations. It wasn't the time or place for travel, we concluded. I canceled my plans. Although we hadn't lost our home or animals to fire—only a book tour—I still felt walloped by disappointment.

Driving out of the Walmart parking lot one day soon after, the dog shelter across the highway caught my eye. "Think I'll stop in and see who they have, not that I'm looking for a new dog. I'm just curious. Maybe comforting a few dogs will make me feel better." I knew I'd get Mercy a companion someday soon, just not yet.

I petted some of the dogs outside and was impressed by a beautiful white German shepherd mix. "She's up for adoption," a staff person informed me. "Wanna walk her?"

She had to be at least seventy pounds. "No, no, I'll just rub her ears. Really, I'm only here to look around." Then I meandered inside and walked down a narrow corridor between kennels of barking dogs. I remembered how loud the shelter was where I adopted Mercy.

See me! Hear me! Touch me! Take me! I took a deep breath and put the back of my hand up to cages, allowing dogs to smell and lick me. So many lost, abandoned, or abused dogs, with their desperate eyes begging for attention to get out. I was reminded of when I was ten years old, and a friend and I sneaked up on the parked truck of the dogcatcher while he was out on a hunt and let the dogs out. With a handful of treats, we lured six or seven into her garage, then watched the dogcatcher angrily stomp around looking for the result of his day's work. Even now I wanted to take them all, tell Bill we were going to have a really big family. I winced and pulled my heavy feet along, attempting to communicate kindness with my eyes and a soft voice that was barely audible over the rowdy barking.

I stopped beside a cage with a little blonde huddled in a back corner, big brown sad eyes watching me. ON HOLD, the sign read. APPROXIMATELY THREE YEARS OLD. I stuck my fingers through the gate, and she came over and gave me one lick. "Who are you?" I asked. There was no name on the sign. She lifted her wide head and stared at me as if she were so tired of her journey. Maybe she was pug? Her tail didn't curl, but her nose had a slightly smashed look. I had never given a pug or any toy-like breed a second thought. At this point, the only thing she had in her favor was her size, about seventeen pounds. Still, something about her defeated disposition made my heart ache.

On my way out, I interrupted a lively chat among workers and asked about the pug-like dog. "Oh, yeah. We found her wandering the streets of Alamosa on a ten-degree night. Has a chip, so we called the number. Guy had no idea how the dog got to Colorado. He's in Texas. Said it was his girlfriend's dog, and he'd be here to pick up the dog by tomorrow. We told him if he's not here by then, dog's up for adoption."

I thanked the guy and left. Once home, I talked to Mercy about a possible sister, someone to play with like she had tried so hard to get Gavroche to do.

I'd really like that, Mom. My walks are special, but that's just not enough activity for me, and you won't play run-around-the-dining-room-table with me for very long.

Bill and I also discussed adding another dog. "Sounds like a nice dog, darlin', and Mercy sure has enough energy for some company."

I gave it a full day, then I returned to the shelter with Mercy. "Guy didn't show up or call back, so she's up for adoption. Hasn't left any messes in her kennel, so she's house-trained."

Mercy Mercy Me

"Let me introduce her to my other dog, take her for a walk. Would that be all right?"

Leashed up, I led the boxy gal out to the car. Mercy hopped out, and after a sufficient butt-sniff, the three of us sauntered on. Mercy set the pace with an extra prance in her step and more fluff to her tail. The pug mix followed and had a good pull on the leash, looking like a little muscled bulldog from behind. The two dogs seemed fine around each other. One small, one mid-size. One blonde, the other black. One scrunched-up pug nose, a long nose on the other. They both had a floppy ear. I decided to go for it. Why not? We were stranded at home and winter hadn't set in yet, so I had time for some outdoor training with a new dog. Adopted dog in tow, as soon as we arrived home, the little gal walked inside and promptly peed and pooped. Mercy looked at me with a face that said, *I didn't do it.*

"Goodness gracious!" I exclaimed, and the dog turned those enormous brown eyes on me, alarmed, then slipped into a fit of snorting backward sneezes. "Goodness!" I repeated, pausing as I sat beside this wide-eyed little stranger on the floor, and gently rubbed her body to help calm her. Were these nerves? I scooped up the poop as Bill sopped up the pee, and I led the girl out back, plopping her poop on the ground and letting her sniff it outdoors. I had heard this can help dogs understand where they should poop. She peed again, then began the backward sneezing once more. "Goodness!" I reiterated, shaking my head. She looked up and inched toward me, and I wondered how it would feel to call goodness to me daily. "Well, if that's your name, honey, you'll have to calm down and quit peeing and pooping in the house!"

Goodness didn't pee or poop again inside, and the dramatic display of backward sneezing stopped too. Over the next few days, Mercy threw a few toys at her and repeatedly stuck her tug-of-war toy in Goodness's face, but Goodness displayed little interest. Once or twice, she grabbed the rope and gave a threatening growl, but soon backed off. Mercy looked at me, bereft.

That dog only wants to sleep, eat, poop, pee, and sniff!

"I'm sorry, Merce. She doesn't seem to be much of a player like we hoped, but she is sweet!"

Sweet! Who cares about sweet? I want a dog to run with! That dog's a dud!

"Now, Mercy, she's just different than you. She clearly needed a home. I think she's older than they told us. We won't be taking her back. Maybe she'll play the more comfortable she gets. You'll get your walks, and I promise to play run-around-the-dining-room-table with you more often."

Mercy gave in and adjusted to having "that dog" around, even though Goodness never became a player. "Goodness Gracious," I announced as an exclamation while looking at my new dog. "We'll make it work out."

Soon, a song for each dog came out of nowhere for me to sing to Mercy and Goodness on our walks. The pleasure I feel speaking *for* my dogs is tantamount to that which I feel singing to them. Mercy's song is fast, one that suits her gait. It sounds like what she looks like, a fast tempo ending in a high, dissonant note like a dog caught in a high pounce:

> Mercy—Mercy, Mercy Me, oh my oh,
> Mercy—Mercy, Mercy Me, oh my oh,
> Mercy Me, Mercy Me, Mercy Meeeeeee!

She is usually off running when I get to the end of the song, and I sing loud enough for her to hear. If she isn't too far out, she glances back on hearing her singsong name. It becomes like the background score for her hunting frenzy.

Goodness's song fits her moseying pace perfectly: slow, and best sung in a goofy style with a bit of a gravelly voice on the last line:

Mercy Mercy Me

Puggy pug pugworts,
Puggy pug pugworts,
She my little puggy dog.

Who doesn't like being sung to or having a song created just for them, as if we are in our own Disneyesque musical? When the three of us are out there on the levee, surrounded by the dazzle of nature with swallows swooping, geese quacking, and the blue sky comforting, these silly songs add a playful skip and a bounce to our steps.

Mercy might be disappointed that Goodness doesn't like to play that much, but the two watch each other inside and outside and often sleep next to one another on the couch. Theirs is a peaceful, mutually acknowledging coexistence, one where they both have their own theme song.

A year after my first knee surgery and two months after adopting Goodness, another surgery became necessary in hopes of correcting the original, which hadn't gone well. Mercy donned her nurse cap and resumed her bedtime vigilance. This time, Sacramento friend Sharon came to help Bill with meals, keep me company, love on Goodness, and walk Mercy. I noted to Bill that although I didn't doubt that Mercy loved me, what she loved most of all was getting outside to run and explore. It was as though her job was hunting, and she couldn't miss a day of work, and I refused to let her.

In March 2020, six weeks after the second surgery, Bill, Mercy, Goodness, and I packed up to head to Boulder, a town just west of Denver, staying there with friends Annie, Patty, and their dogs. It is always a relief to visit dog-lovin' friends where our dogs are invited, and we don't have to leave them behind. But dogs have to be well-behaved enough to be welcomed, and our girls had made the cut.

Dog Love Stories

I had been invited to testify at the Colorado State Legislature for House Bill 1296 in hopes of eliminating the statute of limitations for sexual abuse allegations. The timing so soon after surgery wasn't optimal, but I wanted to participate in this decisive event in Denver. When my turn came, I asked the committee members not to put a time frame on when someone finally feels she can let her guard down and speak up about her abuse or assault. The problem, I clarified, isn't that survivors should speak out within a particular time frame. *It takes time to get to a safe enough place to disclose.* Limiting how long survivors have to speak up allows perpetrators to feel power and control. I also mentioned the financial burden placed on me because of the sexual abuse I had experienced: I had spent many thousands of dollars on mental health treatment. I didn't mention that the amount would have been so much more without the dogs in my life, despite that being true. Even having my dogs with me on that trip bolstered my courage.

How does having a dog/horse/cat/bird—fill in the animal—help soothe someone's experiences of trauma or a difficult life? There is science behind this claim, but I speak from personal experience only. As a human who has struggled for stronger emotional and mental health, having dogs has been crucial in helping me want to stay alive: caring for them, playing with them, loving them, feeling loved by them, and having my hands on them. Dabb buffered my traumatic childhood experiences as my first experience of love. With Bandi's companionship, I felt strong enough to be single and move to California. With a hand on Dancer, I learned to calm down and breathe through the loneliness and fear of becoming single again. Pookie also supported me through a divorce, as well as getting a master's, and ten moves, always my steadfast companion. Goodness prompts laughter with her funny little pug behaviors. And Mercy wants my hand on her as much as I want to put my hand on her. How

Mercy Mercy Me

do I know? She continuously bops my hand onto her body with her pushy nose so I will run my hand over her silky fur and gently rub her ears. Together, our eyes get droopy, and our breaths deepen. We calm.

I had rescheduled the 2019 canceled engagements in Arizona and fiery California for spring 2020. Bill and I would be leaving soon after our return from Boulder. But as with people worldwide, our plans once again came to a screeching halt with warnings about the highly contagious coronavirus. Breathing the same air as others indoors became dangerous. Stay home! Wear a mask everywhere! Don't touch your face, eyes, nose, or mouth! Wash your hands and use hand sanitizer! We even began wiping down our groceries and our mail. Some claimed there was a low risk of dogs transmitting the virus to humans. On the rare occasions when we were around others—indoors or outdoors—we stayed the recommended six feet apart. Thousands of people were dying every day across our country and the world. On my levee walks, I watched the helicopter for medical evacuations regularly *whop-whop-whop* into Alamosa. We were officially in a pandemic.

Months went by, and soon, a year. Bill, Mercy, Goodness, and I sought refuge at Graceland. This was no time for travel, but with our land close by, we could get out of the house and even meet friends Becky and Maggie from nearby Questa, New Mexico. They pitched a tent, then Maggie stretched out in the lounge chair with a book, and Becky brought out her guitar. Bill napped in the trailer, Goodness chewed on a deer bone, and Mercy worked at pulling the piñon sap out of her paws. Under the sweep of the piñon tree, I pondered Becky's lyrics with my feet propped on Gavroche's grave. A blue sky hovered over the valley, stretching to New Mexico's plateaus and round-topped Ute Mountain. The coronavirus pandemic felt far away, except for our diligent six-foot distancing.

Dog Love Stories

Sometimes Mercy and I left Bill and Goodness at home when we went to Graceland. Becky and Maggie showed up ready to work on one of those trips. "Show us again where you want to create a Medicine Wheel," Becky asked. I had told them on their last visit about this idea, one begun with my friend Nancy years earlier when we had carefully marked the east and west points on the fall equinox when the sun rises due east and sets due west everywhere on Earth. I had already cleared most of the cactus from this level area surrounded by piñon and juniper and shadowed by peaks overlooking the valley. The land was still studded by rocks of all sizes, this being the Rocky Mountains.

"Do you have a hoe? We brought shovels." Maggie hopped up, ready to work.

"Always have one on hand, but I don't want you to work! You need a rest from farming!" Maggie spent her days irrigating forty acres of grass and alfalfa fields on her farm in northern New Mexico. "Besides, I can't do much since my knee is still healing from surgery." This job would involve moving some damn big rocks.

"I'm getting my gloves," Becky insisted.

We began by using a rope to define the circumference of the circle. Becky held the rope in the center, and I took the other end and walked around, marking the points of the four directions. It was a June afternoon and at 8,200 feet altitude, already hot. Maggie and Becky couldn't be stopped; I worked until my knee warned me to quit. Lying in the trailer icing it, Mercy's paw predictably resting on my leg, I could hear the *clop, clop* of the hoe and loud sighs from both my friends hefting large rocks. Maggie finally took a break, but Becky was determined to move one last enormous rock that blocked a path. I walked out to encourage her to take a break.

"Almost got it. Where do you want this beauty?"

"Good God almighty! Don't lift that creature! Can you roll it to the circle's center?"

Mercy Mercy Me

She heaved it out of the mountainside and rolled it five feet to the middle, right next to a big rock Nancy and I had used to mark the center of the east–west line. I helped situate the stones side by side so two people could sit together, back-to-back, one looking north and the other south.

"There, you have a Prayer Circle," Becky announced softly in respect to the space she and Maggie had largely created on their own. Prayer Circle, she said. It did make more sense than a Medicine Wheel. I had walked a few Medicine Wheels in my days, but I was only barely familiar with the traditions of how Indigenous Americans used them. But prayers I walked daily, and I liked the idea of doing so in a circle while showing respect to the cardinal directions. As a gardener since my twenties and the granddaughter of two farming grandfathers, eyeing the directions of the sun's journey felt like part of my history.

There were still rocks to move to complete the inner path of the Prayer Circle and the four paths to the center. It would take several more visits to complete—a few yucca plants and prickly pears would need to come down in the paths—but the foundation was there. By evening, we were ready for a ritual to incorporate the circle into the side of the mountain. Becky—a songwriter and recording artist—got her guitar. Then she, Maggie, and I walked the circle in silence, stopping at each direction. Mercy joined us, walking the path exactly as we did, looking from one face to the next every time we paused. The sun dropped, the air stilled, and nighthawks swooshed. Becky walked to the center and sang a blessing song about "witnessing the work of our hearts and hands" in a prayer of gratitude for each other, the circle we had created, and the holy outdoors surrounding us.

On our visits to Graceland, Bill and I now walk our prayers in the circle. Mercy stays on my heels when I'm on the path, waiting for me to walk to the center and sit, as is my habit. Then she runs to me, anxious for an ear rub as I say prayers of gratitude

Dog Love Stories

for having her in my life, Bill in my life, and for having this sacred place to walk prayers.

Besides prayers for the pandemic to end, I also prayed for the protection of Graceland and lands on fire far and near. Fires were burning in the west, in New Mexico, and had desecrated a large section of La Veta Mountain Pass to our east, far enough away that we felt safe, but close enough that I could see red in the sky. Some days the smoke hung in the air, obliterating day views of the valley and the nightscape's clarity.

Coupled with fire concerns was the number of times vandals descended upon our trailer. Despite the glory that Graceland offered, the land, the trailer, the humans, and our dogs were vulnerable there. Perched on the side of a mountain with horrendous roads, the county sheriff and his deputies, not having four-wheel-drive vehicles, didn't rush up when called. For a dozen years we'd never worried about people stealing from us; suddenly, it became a regular occurrence. Neither did we lock the trailer, since we were told thieves would simply break a window to get in. We had done so much work keeping mice out, we sure didn't want to take that chance. Once, someone squatted in our trailer for weeks, leaving it a disgusting mess and taking whatever they wished upon leaving. Soon silverware, knives, clothes, the battery, propane tanks, and even three wheels disappeared. I started propping up a note inside explaining how sacred this land and trailer were to us and asking whoever came in to please shut the door. Subsequently, regardless of what was taken, the door was consistently closed. One prayer answered.

Going alone to Graceland no longer felt like a good idea. I couldn't run anymore with a perpetually healing knee, and Mercy wasn't big enough to be an effective guard dog. Despite her loud bark at home behind our fence at whoever walked down our alley, I rarely heard a peep out of her at the land. In the past fifteen

Mercy Mercy Me

years, we'd seen numerous coyotes, a bear, a mountain lion, several rattlesnakes, and elk up there. But it took human intruders to persuade Bill and me to buy a gun to take to Graceland. After I learned to use it, even sleeping with it nearby didn't assuage my fears of being alone in a remote place on the mountain where people had stolen from us at least a half dozen times.

On a solitary overnight trip to Graceland, I maintained hopes that firing the gun into empty space rather than at someone would be enough to scare any creature away. Then, one morning, I got to check that out. Resting in bed with my coffee and journal, Goodness at my side, and Mercy at my feet, Mercy suddenly bolted off the bed and out the screen door. A pack of four wolf dogs, owned by a neighbor southwest of us, was stealthily walking in front of our trailer. The animals occasionally broke out of their pens. Suddenly, there went thirty-pound Mercy after almost three hundred pounds of wolf dogs.

"Mercy!!" I screamed, cramming my feet into my Merrells, grabbing the gun, and running out the flapping door. My knee buckled in pain, but I kept moving, hollering for Mercy as she veered left through the trees while the wolf dogs ran straight ahead, disappearing in the distance. I pointed to their right and fired. *Boom! Boom!*

Mercy, who hates loud pops, quickly circled back to me. I wanted to wring her neck but knew that wasn't the thing to do since she had come when I called. "Damn, Mercy. You can't do that!" My heart raced, and my hands shook. I held onto my little husky and kissed her forehead. She slapped a paw onto my arm and looked at me proudly.

Couldn't let them think they had free rein up here, Mom.

Later that night, Mercy and I were sitting around the propane fire ring. She uncharacteristically crawled into my lap, a little too big but still snuggling while hanging off both sides of my thighs. Between the vandals and the wolf dogs, as I sat there staring at the fire, I felt my peaceful solitary sojourns at my sacred site slipping away. Periodically, Mercy let out a low snarl looking beyond the light, making me worry about what might be out there. Finally, after too many snarls at the dark, we were both ready to curl up in the safety of our beds in the trailer.

It was my last time to spend a night alone at Graceland.

Six months later, I was pacing the Prayer Circle mumbling prayers for Bill. After two heart attacks in a decade resulting in two stents, Bill's cardiologist detected a blocked aortic valve. A replacement valve surgery was scheduled. Because of the pandemic, restrictions were placed on how many visitors were allowed into the hospital and the residency area where patients' families could stay. Friends Annie and Patty drove over ninety miles from Boulder to Colorado Springs, where Bill would be having surgery, to pick up Mercy and Goodness and care for them during our stay. The night before surgery, my anxiety was so intense I thought I was having a heart attack. I needed Mercy to put my hand on and help me calm down. The day of the surgery was the same. Ostracized from Bill, my dogs, and the hospital, I did my best to breathe deeply while waiting for the surgeon to call. Once she did, her news sent my blood pressure soaring: Bill would be intubated and kept on a ventilator longer than anticipated due to concerns about blood clots. Seeing my beloved unconscious with a machine breathing for him was a difficult sight.

Two days later, Bill was checked out amidst an intense blizzard that had hit Colorado Springs the day before. Not a confident driver in the best of circumstances, I agonized about driving Bill through snow and ice over La Veta Mountain Pass. Annie and Patty made the long trek back to deliver Goodness and Mercy, then I loaded up Bill, the dogs, and a bedraggled me and headed home through blowing snow. Mercy never lay down during the three-hour drive.

Mercy Mercy Me

Although Mercy wasn't allowed in bed with Bill, she checked on him often. I thought of how she had been after both my knee surgeries and decided some dogs are natural emotional support dogs. She was now on double duty: tiptoeing into the room often to look at Bill, then coming to my side and bopping my hand on her head.

Calm down, Mom. I'm right here. Over the next few days, my heart rate and blood pressure returned to normal with her and Goodness by my side and Bill alive and safe at home.

Come summer, a new neighbor moved into the rented house next to us with his blue nose pit bull named Lexi. Any calm in our lives went out our windows, perpetually open in the Alamosa summers since air conditioners are rare here with forty-to-fifty-degree nights that cool our homes. Mercy and Lexi clawed at the fence and barked like they would kill each other. And I thought the leash aggression had been fierce! Mercy was a screamer—a barker with a hysterical edge to her rant. Lexi threatened with her bulk and a low, ferocious growl. After a bout of histrionics, Mercy would seem immensely proud of her guard-dogging as if she were a dog doing her job, and as far as she was concerned, we'd hired her fair and square. Goodness might toss out her seal-like bark to back up Mercy, but she wasn't really interested in a squall.

I started covering the dog doors and staking out our backyard so that my dogs went out when Lexi wasn't in her backyard. Because Lexi's owner had a predictable work schedule, we could gauge when he would let her out in the morning, at lunch, and in the evenings. Sadly, our dogs were used to going out whenever they wished, then suddenly their freedom was severely restricted.

"At least you get daily walks, girls. Lexi doesn't, so it's important she get outside when her dad is home."

But she wants me out there, Mercy insisted, *so we can bark at each other!*

Dog Love Stories

"Well, Mercy, it's a little scary for me. What if Lexi hauls herself over the fence or pushes a board off and squeezes through? You can't protect me by barking like a maniac!"

There had to be another solution. Bill and I got black roofing paper and covered our fence where the dogs peered through the half-inch spaces between boards and gnawed at each other. Then I ordered metal fencing panels that we set about four feet from the wooden fence, keeping Mercy from jumping on and tearing up the fence covering. Oddly, without being able to see each other and claw at one another with only an inch-thick board between them, Mercy started getting bored. She'd still bark for a few minutes, then saunter inside. Bill and I were able to feel the cool air coming through our open windows again, and I could relax having made my dogs safer.

The Lexi problem I could solve, but the new resident coyote around the levee was an entirely different matter. We had coyotes at Graceland and occasionally saw one cross our path when on a hike. We heard them almost every night, along with the wolf dogs howling at dusk. Mercy never tried to chase a coyote, but instead she would stop and look wary. I'd reach around to my hiking vest's back pocket, grab her leash, and snap it onto her collar.

At first, I noticed the coyote sunning itself in the field west of the levee, watching us watch it. Mercy would poke her nose in the air before I saw it, fixing her gaze and tucking her tail. Lifting my binoculars, I found the coyote quickly and leashed both dogs out of caution until we were a safe distance from that area.

Soon, however, the coyote began venturing up onto the levee. It would scamper down to the eastern side when we got closer and watch us from a safe distance. I wondered if it would run at us and grab a leashed dog. On the other hand, the coyote looked healthy, like it had plenty of rabbits to eat, so maybe not.

Mercy Mercy Me

One day, the coyote remained sitting on the levee as if daring us to walk closer. Of course, we didn't. People from the nearby dog park were pointing at it. I turned the dogs around, and we walked northwest, looking back frequently. The coyote started moving along in our direction on the eastern side of the levee. I kept both dogs leashed. Mercy continued looking back, whining. When the coyote seemed to get bored, it moved farther away into the field. I still didn't feel safe. A friend came walking from the opposite direction with her two dogs, and I pointed out the coyote, who had now moved ahead of us, beside the levee.

I pulled out my cell phone and called Alamosa Animal Control, who arrived within fifteen minutes. Unfortunately, this coyote did not appear afraid of people or dogs and was a little too brazen for an area close to the dog park and walking trails. The coyote had since scampered into hiding, but the officer said he would contact Wildlife Control for help.

Just like the peace and safety I felt at Graceland and in my backyard had disappeared, now the calm of my daily walks on the levee was in jeopardy. I quit taking Goodness on our walks, since at twenty pounds she was assuredly coyote bait. One late winter morning while out walking Mercy, I was in a reverie, thinking about the eighth dog's death (Amber's) I had just written about for this book. That would be the last one I'd be writing about for this project started two years prior. The experience of each dog's death had been so difficult to relive and put into words. I felt relieved to be done writing about these losses. As I walked, I let out long sighs of relief and found my mind wandering as to how I would start the next dog's story—Mercy's.

Mercy. Where was she? She had been right here! "Mercy!"

I whipped around on the trail beneath the levee where I was walking. Empty space. Then, looking up, I saw Mercy on my slope side of the levee, stock-still, tail tucked, eyes locked on something.

"Mercy! Come!" I hobbled toward her, cursing my painful knee under my breath. But she ran to me before I had gone too far, and I quickly leashed her. We crept up the levee's slope, and sure enough, there was Coyote—with a capital *C*—glaring at us.

"Get out! G'on!" I screamed and waved my free arm, wishing I had my gun to fire off to its side to scare it away, making it associate us with gunfire so it would never come close again. Of course, I would never do that since I was just on the edge of town. But right then I was feeling mighty protective of my dog.

Coyote slinked away. "Oh my God, Mercy, that was too close. What a good girl you are. All because I was lost in my thoughts!" I rubbed her ears, her neck, her sides and lavished more praise on her.

Yeah, Mom, Coyote surprised me too. I was being careful and even a little afraid. But I didn't bark.

"You were perfect, girl. You did everything right. I'm the one at fault. You were paying attention, but I wasn't. I'm so glad you are okay, my brave girl."

Although I haven't seen Coyote since that day, my walks on the levee have not been the same. Maybe Wildlife Control took care of Coyote. But now my backyard, my land, and the levee all present the constant challenge of staying alert. Mercy wears her beeper collar in case she is hunting and I need to alert her because I see Coyote. I carry bear spray in my pocket in the event Coyote gets too close. I am constantly scanning the fields 360 degrees, looking for movement. My goal is to never let Coyote sneak up on us again.

Bill and I were turning seventy—together thirty-two years with a decade divorced in the middle of our two marriages to each other—and we wanted to celebrate. After all, it felt like after two heart attacks and an aortic valve replacement, Bill could have missed this opportunity. His health was better, but his energy still wasn't up to par. Although it was 2022 and COVID still wasn't over, vaccinations and COVID tests had people taking off masks and no longer adhering to keeping three to six feet apart. We threw around the idea of a celebratory gathering at Graceland to some outdoorsy friends who might like to camp out a few nights. Before we knew it, plans began churning. We chose June when the valley is just waking to summer's beauty. Our delight at being able to spend time with friends at our favorite place opened us to how the promise of fun, friendship, and the sacredness of place could carry us into our eighth decade.

Two weeks before the date, Bill started coughing.

"You better take a COVID test, darlin'," I encouraged. He tested positive. We stared at each other with dismay. He quarantined in his room, and I left his meals out for him to eat alone. We washed our hands and wiped down surfaces. Maybe I could avoid getting it, but I felt worse every day despite negative tests. Six days later, I tested positive.

We contacted the people who had expressed interest in spending our birthdays with us and warned them of the possibility of canceling. Then we waited. Friend Lindsey had driven out in May from Houston to build a structure to house a compost toilet, something long overdue at Graceland. As one of Houston's epidemiologists, Lindsey did the math on our days with and without symptoms and the timing of negative testing, and speculated that if we had the energy, guests in an outdoor setting would be safe.

Our friends joined us at Graceland, and we gathered under the piñon tree, much more spacious now with Gavy's headstone moved into the dog cemetery that Bill and I had built that past fall. Bill had even dug a hole in the cemetery in case one of our dogs died in the winter. I had put a cover over the empty grave, then moved some dirt onto that. I didn't want anyone to fall into the hole while walking among the gravestones.

We set out long tables and covered them in white tablecloths with battery-operated candles arranged down the middle. Spanish Rioja wine, one of Bill's and my favorites, was poured. We dined, we laughed, we gazed at the beauty in the faces and the views around us. Becky and Patty, along with songwriter and recording artist Annie, all sang. Mercy rested at my feet, one paw on my foot. Goodness was curled up beneath Bill's chair. Bill and I squeezed one another's hands, feeling grateful for our years together and this opportunity to be with people we loved.

As darkness fell, Becky suggested we all move to the Prayer Circle. Once there, we filled the outer path, walking the circle quietly several times, Mercy keeping the same pace right behind me as I did behind Bill. When we stopped, barely seeing one another in dusk's light, people spoke about their experience of sharing life with us. Bill and I listened, our hearts tender and receptive, feeling prayers full of gratitude for the kind and sensitive souls in our circle.

Coming into seventy was worth all we had each been through in our lives.

Bill and I often comment to one another how we never thought when we were in our twenties, thirties, forties, or even fifties that we would be spending so much time with one other person in our sixties and seventies. Our lives were once about working eight-to-twelve-hour days, commuting, hustling to get food in the fridge and on the stove, cleaning the house, nursing gardens, emptying laundry baskets, moving from one home, city, or state to another, tending to Shawn's care, maintaining cars, getting exercise, pursuing another degree, and, of course, nurturing dogs. Suddenly, it seemed we were eating breakfast and dinner together every day, and often lunch. With home offices back-to-back, we now know when the other is on the phone or working quietly. We are connected to each other's schedule: he knows when I am writing or off on a walk, and I know when he is going to the grocery store

Mercy Mercy Me

or on a country drive. We make a weekly meal plan and know when the other will cook. Our out-of-town doctor appointments are scheduled on the same days for ease. We travel together, two humans and two dogs, to go stay with friends Annie and Patty or with Becky and Maggie.

We are rarely apart.

Mercy and I are even closer. She makes sure of it. She warms my feet at night and is in the curve of my back or curl of my arms in the morning. Our breathing synchronizes. She follows me from room to room once I get up, biting at my feet—practically pulling me over—pushy for her walk. I never go for a walk, a hike, or snowshoe without her. When I work in the greenhouse, she waits at its entrance, or when I'm in my flower garden outside, she peers through the gate, happy when invited in so she can lie on the sun-warmed circular path. She rests under my desk in my studio as I write, just like Amber used to do. Friend Carolyn on one visit exclaimed, "Does Mercy always go in the bathroom with you?" It's one of the best times for her to get a focused head rub.

I never imagined I would be spending this much time with a dog either.

Not having either Bill or Mercy or Goodness with me is an excruciating thought. My days are filled with their presence, their energies. The human can be more challenging at times when we get on each other's nerves or fail to meet one another's expectations. The canine molds more easily to my life and moods without expecting the same of me. Theirs is an effortless devotion. Dogs watch our patterns, cue into our routines, come to understand our tones of voice and sounds. After all, smart dogs get smarter.

"Mercy, you may be the smartest dog I've ever had! But maybe I've felt that way with all my dogs. Goodness is mighty smart too!"

I am really smart, Mom. Probably the smartest dog in your life.

Dog Love Stories

Like you always say, I'm an honor student, Mercy jumped in to claim the title after Goodness gave an it-doesn't-matter-to-me snort.

In the evenings, Bill and I meet in our living room, often in front of the fire, for a happy hour of either a virgin cocktail or red wine— our "connecting time," we call this. Bill slips on his glasses, takes out the current book we are reading, and begins to read out loud, his Arkansas-Texas accent warm and resonant. I listen as Mercy leans on my left leg while Goodness is curled in the opposite corner of the love seat. Our family of four. Mercy places her right leg over mine in that possessive manner, but I take it to mean more. In two months, I'll have the third surgery on that still-painful knee, hopefully correcting it with a full revision. I remember how Mercy lay beside me for the original surgery and later the partial revision, her leg protectively draped over my healing leg.

I'm here for you, Mom. I hope you get better so we can take more walks.

"I hear ya, girl. There's a lotta life for us to live out there. More mice for you to hunt, more birds for me to see."

Mercy continues to gift me with this opportunity to experience the world through her eyes and ears. Maybe it really is true that what we see in our dogs is the kind of person we want to be. Mercy lives in the present moment and asks that I do the same, which, for me, is setting aside my to-dos, my worries, and my anxieties, and paying close attention to what or who is around me. Attention, after all, is a form of love, isn't it? Whether being attentive to nature, my spouse, or my dog.

TEN

Goodness Gracious

(met her in 2019 while I had Mercy)

"Oh my God, he's so cute! Look at that face!" gushed an admirer, assuming Goodness was male as many people do with dogs. It was another on the street ga-ga at my little gal, who waited patiently as if wondering what all the fuss was about. People claim some dog owners look like their dogs. Most of my dogs have looked so different, I'm not sure which dog I may have resembled or resemble now. I sure hope I don't look like Goodness, although never have the looks of one of my dogs attracted so much attention.

Soon after getting her, I learned that the broad face of a pug mix, the short nose, and those big eyes are features that get people acting like they do with babies, using baby talk and lots of goochy-goochy-goos. The broad forehead does allow ample space for a kiss, certainly a better prospect for my lips than on that short, scrunched-up nose. I am, however, able to affectionately fit my nose into the little divot between her schnozzle and the upslope of her forehead. While doing that, even I find myself talking to Goodness like she is a puppy or a baby.

One morning while walking Goodness around our neighborhood, a woman started yelling at me from across the street. I couldn't tell what she was saying, so I slowed down. She ran toward us hollering, "Wiggles!" Goodness watched, then looked away, tail not wagging, absolutely zero display of recognition or affection. "Where did you find her?" she asked, out of breath. "I left her at someone's house when I went into the homeless shelter with my daughter, and Wiggles got out of their yard!"

My grip on the leash tightened. Wiggles hadn't even wiggled her tail with this unexpected rendezvous. Bill and I had had Goodness a month by this point, and she was a solid part of our family. It never takes me long to get attached to a dog. I explained that I had adopted her from the Alamosa shelter. I skipped the part about the shelter calling the number on Wiggles's chip, and the guy who answered never showing up like he said he would. Just then a man called for the woman to hurry up from where he was waiting outside the parole office.

I quickly asked a few questions about Wiggles's background. The young woman shared that she got her from a backyard breeder of pug mixes in Oklahoma who claimed Wiggles was about five years old. She had had multiple litters and been kept in a confined area. I imagined her pups being whisked away, leaving Wiggles alone repeatedly. This woman and her toddler daughter brought Wiggles to live with them in Texas. "But things got real bad with me and my boyfriend after that, and we had to leave." She picked at chewed nails, and I noticed she was rail thin.

Goodness Gracious

The guy across the street called out louder, and the woman obediently crossed back, glancing several times as Goodness and I continued our walk. Although I felt some sadness for the woman, I was relieved she appeared to accept that her dog was settled in a stable home. I guessed that Wiggles may have been in an abusive household and, before that, suffered abuse from being bred repeatedly and isolated in a breeder's backyard.

A dog's identity is imprinted by what she has endured in her life—something I can also say about myself. When I met Goodness in the shelter, her demeanor of vulnerability jumped out at me, perhaps because of how often I have felt my own. Author Ken Foster writes, "There's a strange intimacy between a lost animal and the person who finds him . . . the moment is a vital pivot in the animal's life, the line between his old life and a better, new one."[6]

Not all my dogs were adopted, but those who were came with a past I usually knew nothing or little about. Bandi-Lune's spirit was almost destroyed by isolation. Well-cared-for Dancer appeared confused about her possible abandonment. Solitary Zorro exuded an earnest independence. Gavroche's feisty reputation and snarl kept the dogcatcher at a distance. Amber's reticence with humans signaled possible abuse and seclusion. Mercy's frequent escapes to Sonic were well-known, prompting her older owner to relinquish her. On the day I walked through the Alamosa shelter, Goodness looked like a dog who was close to giving up. She turned those big, brown, vacant eyes on me, and I felt her yearning as if communicating, *I'll try to be whoever you want me to be. Will you give me a chance?*

I wanted Mercy to have a more vibrant playmate than me since I wasn't feeling so spry with my painful knee. I imagined Mercy having daily tugs-of-war and chases that would tire her out.

But Goodness is an unreliable player, preferring to suck on

a worn-out cloth-stuffed bone, a hand-me-down from a friend whose dog died. Mercy tries, sneaking in and grabbing the suck-bone from Goodness and zipping off. That is reason enough for Goodness to dive in, not so much for play as to get her suck-toy back. A brief tug-of-war might ensue, with Goodness always winning upon delivering a no-nonsense snarl to force Mercy to let go. I stitch up that stuffing-filled suck-bone often from those matches. Goodness loves that bone, holding it carefully with her front two paws as she cleans it like a puppy. Then she sucks on it and nods off, just like Gavroche used to do with his monkey. At some point along Goodness's journey, she must have learned self-soothing as a survival tool.

Goodness found a spot on my bed—her ascent aided by an ottoman I leave there for her—and she snoozes for hours. I learned that pugs like to eat, sleep, and sniff. I soon replaced her walks around two blocks to morning walks with Mercy and me, four to five times the distance she had been covering, in hopes of preventing her from pudging out from lack of exercise. Gavroche's stint as a football taught me not to let a little dog pack on the pounds. I started referring to Goodness's walks as "trudging," since that's what it looks like as she plods along.

As soon as Goodness had been with us for six months, I let her off-leash. She responds to "Come!" unless her nose gets stuck in a powerful sniff, then nothing will lure her away from what she has stopped to smell. I soon started saying we were going out for a sniff instead of a walk. Still, my need for exercise usurped Goodness's desire to poke a pug nose in a clump of grass and sniff herself into oblivion, so before long, she was on the leash again.

On Goodness's first night with us, friend Carolyn was visiting. Goodness was in the dining room in her crate and Carolyn in the adjacent guest room. I woke to noisy snoring during the night and thought how in all my years of knowing Carolyn, I had never noticed she snored. The next night when Carolyn was

Goodness Gracious

gone and the noise resumed, I got up and stood in front of Goodness's crate. She snored as loudly as Bill! How could a big sound come out of such a small dog? "My goodness, Goodness! You sure make yourself heard, girl." I had already noticed that she snorted, too, usually when I bend over for some baby talk while kissing that wide forehead. It is like an affectionate response. I snort back in solidarity.

The best part is when I come home and Goodness greets me with a wide upturned pug smile, her wonky left ear giving her a lopsided look. She runs in a few circles before racing to the kitchen for a drink of water; she drinks when excited, that wide mouth slinging water across our constantly wet kitchen floor. There's no wandering around our house in sock feet.

Dog people know that dogs have an extraordinary sense of timing, especially when it comes to mealtimes. Although Goodness has never turned up her scrunched-up nose at anything, we had better serve her food on time, or those big pug eyes will burn a hole right through us. Then, after dinner, she takes a post-prandial chew. Once Bill and I are settled in the living room for our read-aloud time, we hear the thunder of pug paws on our wooden floors. She runs to the back of the house and then tears back with a Nylabone hanging out the side of her mouth like a cigar. She peels around the corner, hops up on the couch, settles in, and chews until she gets sleepy. It's the same thing every day, making us laugh. Every. Single. Time. I am reminded of how two dogs are double the pleasure.

This is a dog who loves her bones—whether the old deer bones she finds at Graceland, bones Bill gives her after making bone broth soup, or that Nylabone. But her greatest pleasure is sucking on the old cloth bone until her eyes close and her sleepy body twitches. She appears to revel in being unworried, calm, quiet, and simply sinking into the moment, displaying a penchant for taking it easy, characteristics I strive to emulate.

Dog Love Stories

I do my best to cultivate a sense of wonder around each dog that comes into my life, observing them carefully and learning who they are and what they like and don't like. Sometimes it helps to understand their breed's characteristics: Lab Pookie loved chasing balls, Mercy is a mouser, and Amber stayed glued to my heels. People often notice Goodness isn't a full pug and ask about her mix, so I decided to test her DNA. Because I'd heard Goodness had been used for breeding cute pups, I was curious what the results would be. What a surprise to learn she is a pug-pit-huahua: 60 percent pug, 13 percent pit, and 8 percent Chihuahua, with the remaining percentage a mix of Boston terrier, boxer, and bulldog.

None of these are breeds familiar to me. However, knowing my dogs' breeds hasn't helped me understand them as much as daily observation of all their little habits. For example, after spending time in bed with me in the mornings while I sip coffee and journal—Mercy on one side and Goodness on the other—Goodness promptly heads to Bill's office to say good morning with a wag and a lick. Then she begins bringing her toys into his room, leaving his floor littered with her suck-bone, the Nylabone, a real bone, and her little stuffed piggy. Bill believes that the way she gathers her toys, cleans them, and holds them could come from a habit of nurturing puppies. As the day progresses, she returns to his room to retrieve her things and bring them to wherever I am. Back and forth she goes, immersed in her maternal duties.

After a little more than three years with us, in many ways Goodness feels more like Bill's dog than mine, the dog tolerator in him having morphed into a veritable dog daddy. They are oddly similar; both move at a slow pace and prefer ease rather than busyness in their days. When Goodness greets Bill, he affectionately starts rattling off a handful of nicknames he has made up for her: Pootifer, Pooter, Poofer, Pooty, Poot-a-toot. A

Goodness Gracious

blank look comes over his face when I quiz him about where these names come from. "They just pop out of my mouth," he answers, dumbfounded by the question. I understand, as I've experienced that myself with a few nicknames I've added to this collection: Pee-barrel (since Goodness chooses to hold her pee from about eight at night until seven in the morning), Pugwug, Puggy, Lil' Pig Lil' Pig, and my personal favorite, Pugworts.

The adage that God is Dog spelled backward is well-known, particularly among dog people. My God is a dog lover whom I believe knew that my having a dog as a child buffered confusing and traumatic experiences. Along with the comfort I have received and still receive from having dogs, prayer also helps. I have a regular practice of prayer, walking them near my home on the levee or in the Prayer Circle at Graceland.

Lately, I've been wearing out these paths hoping the Dog-God is listening.

I was almost finished with this book and in the middle of writing Goodness's story when she became ill. Although Goodness had peed on Bill's bed at Graceland, we attributed this incident to her being mad when we didn't let her sit around the fire with us. She's not much of a lap dog and, when kept on a leash in the dark, wound herself tightly around our chair legs. We decided it was best if she stayed inside the trailer that evening, later finding the wet spot. Then we started noticing she could no longer hear us unless we said her name exceptionally loud. There is something incongruent about hollering the word "Goodness!" when trying to get your dog to hear you. Soon she began drinking more—*slurp, slurp, slurp, slurp*—prompting us to shake our heads and again yell, "Goodness!" in our attempts to curtail her water intake.

One afternoon, Mercy was trying to get Goodness to play tug-of-war with her treasured suck-bone, and Goodness wasn't going to have it. She gave a fierce growl, grabbed the bone away, then flopped on her side, her legs stiff, and her neck arching. A horrible keening sound spilled out of her grimaced mouth, and her bladder released. I kneeled and petted her, talking calmly while Bill cleaned up. Gradually she was able to stand.

"Was that a seizure?" I asked, pushing on the outside of a cheek while giving the inside a good chomp. I noticed a sinking sensation in my gut. We chalked it up to overexcitement and started discouraging Mercy's efforts at getting Goodness to play.

A few days later, when I came home after being gone for only a few hours, Goodness ran into the kitchen to get a drink and plopped over with another seizure. I resumed my cheek chomping and forced a deep breath.

After two more seizures, I took her to the vet.

Our vet did an exam and then recommended a full chemistry panel and complete blood count that could reveal more information on Goodness's health status. "All looks normal on these tests," the vet announced. "No diabetes, so I'm wondering why she's drinking so much, as you mentioned. That and seizures are reasons to check for a brain tumor with an MRI or CT scan, which would involve some travel for you since those aren't done here in the valley."

Brain tumor? I ran my hand over Goodness's forehead as I sat upright and furrowed my brow. "And if a brain tumor is found, what happens after that?" I felt a hitch in my breath.

"Surgery, radiation, chemotherapy. It would depend on what the scan reveals. Again, not treatment offered here." The vet tilted her head, her lips stretched in a flat line, her eyes sad. "The costs are considerable. Several thousand for the testing and much more than that for surgery and follow-up treatment. Survival rate after all that might only be months to a year."

I've read about people mortgaging their homes to cover such expenses for their beloved animals. Although I understand that screaming desire to do whatever it takes, I've chosen the path

Goodness Gracious

of fewer extreme measures with my dogs. This has been both for financial as well as emotional and logistical reasons. These are not expenditures of money, time, and travel that Bill and I can comfortably make. Extending a dog's life beyond her comfort level when there is minimal hope for prolonged survival doesn't feel like the best choice for us.

Bringing a hand to my mouth, I looked down, not wanting to cry in the office, chewing the inside of my mouth instead. The vet noticed. "Seizures are bursts of electrical activity in the brain that sometimes occur because of a brain tumor. There are medications that slow these electrical signals down to help control seizures. Let's try that and see how she does, and if one doesn't work, we can try another." Then more softly she added, "Meanwhile, consider that putting your little pug to sleep could be what's best for her eventually."

I came to the vet that day thinking Goodness might have a mild form of epilepsy and would just need medication. "Yes, let's try the medication," I replied in a shaky voice, my facial muscles tightening in a painful grimace.

It's such a challenge to now write about this experience in real time and certainly not how I imagined bringing my last dog's story in this book to a close. Despite trying two different medications over four months, Goodness's seizures have increased in frequency and intensity. We can usually tell when one is about to happen. She stops, stares into space, wobbles, then plops over. We gently move her off a rug, the couch, or the bed. Her neck arches, her feet splay and go stiff, and she makes that horrible sound, sometimes foaming at her mouth. Her bladder releases. We grab one of the towels we've placed in every room in the house and stick it underneath her bottom.

"Everything's okay, sweetie," I comfort. "You're going to be all right. I'm right here."

Dog Love Stories

I find myself telling Goodness things are okay these days when, clearly, they aren't. When I took her to the second vet three months after seeing the first vet, he also encouraged me to consider euthanasia. Does making the decision to put her to sleep mean "everything is okay"? When I say, "I'm right here," am I assuring her that right here, right now, I will make decisions that will make everything okay? This is one of the biggest challenges for me as a dog parent: knowing when to let one of my dogs go and recognizing when I may be keeping my dog alive for me more than for her.

Several nights ago, after repeatedly hearing the *flap-flap* of the dog door and knowing it wasn't Mercy, I forced myself out of my warm bed, donned my robe, and headed out. Goodness was in a daze, pacing in snow up to her belly and limping due to snow freezing in her paws at temps barely above zero. I waved my hand in front of the motion light so it would flash, and she looked my way. She came toward me, and I opened the back door.

She walked slowly, paused, and carefully made her way up the two steps to the laundry room and then into our kitchen. Once in, I reached down and felt how cold she was. I carried her into the bedroom and put her in my bed, wrapping us in warm blankets as I lay with her, massaging her forehead. Maybe a brain tumor makes her have headaches? Head rubs seem to calm her.

Her behavior worsened for two more days. Had she gone into the bitter cold night on purpose, like Pookie did that night in Denver? Were those behaviors indicating they were ready to die?

It had been four and a half years since I scheduled an appointment for euthanasia for one of my dogs. First, Bill and I discussed this decision. Next, we let these thoughts be there between Goodness and us as her symptoms got worse. Her symptoms and behavior continued to communicate that we needed to make the call. The Call. There is such responsibility in taking that step. I scheduled an appointment.

Goodness Gracious

Bill drove up to Graceland to find out whether the steep, rocky roads were passable after the latest snow. "We can back up to the dog cemetery. We'll need to shovel around the grave, then see if we can lift and pull the cover off. The dirt on top of it is frozen solid." When we dug that hole last fall, we didn't expect to be using it so soon, but we knew if a dog died during the winter, we'd never be able to break ground. Goodness would be the first dog buried in the dog cemetery, which held eight gravestones representing the dogs I'd had before her.

Bill and I look at one another with pained expressions, sighing heavily, postures slumping. Our bodies are already sore from kneeling down to be with Goodness during seizures and from lifting and carrying her so often in the last few weeks. But most of all, it's the heaviness of our aching hearts that is weighing us down.

Goodness has begun suffering from an insatiable thirst and bloating so big she looks like the pregnant cows ready to deliver in the field beside the levee. She walks slowly and can't jump up on the couch or bed anymore. She is only minimally interested in sucking on her bone. Mostly, she wants to drink and drink and drink—big, slurpy gulps. We watch while her belly grows even rounder. We periodically cover her and Mercy's water dish with a plate, a plastic bowl topper, and a large bowl. She pushes every one of them aside and dunks her little pug nose into the water. She can't stop. Pugs and other short-nosed breeds, we have learned, are more likely to develop certain types of tumors that can cause these symptoms: insatiable thirst, fatigue, disorientation, panting, and bloating.

Sometimes on her way to another room in the house, she must stop and lie down. She is out of breath, maybe from lugging that distended belly around. When I lift her onto the bed or couch, then bend down to kiss that wide forehead, I hear short little breaths. Then she starts licking my hand. *Thank you, thank you, thank you,* she communicates with big-eyed pug love.

In the past, each time I've gotten a dog, I've realized I would most likely outlive her or him. Yet this has never hindered me from opening my heart and hearth to another pooch, even recognizing how a dog comes with this guarantee of heartbreak at some point. But by now, I know that experiencing heartbreak over an animal only opens my heart wider. Right now, however, I need to focus on how to best hold this dread, this hurt of letting go while providing palliative care for my dying dog.

I pull out my meditation cushion and flop onto it. "Help, please." I light a candle and drop into efforts to breathe through my pain. When I seek guidance in prayer, answers often come with images. "Look!" and I suddenly feel my attention directed to my mind's eye.

There they are: Dabb, Bandi, Dancer, Bebe, Pookie, Zorro, Gavroche, and Amber! Lined up like they are ready for a race, but really, they are all just waiting. Tails wagging. Grins on every face.

"Oh, you're waiting for Goodness!! What a lovely sight!"

We'll take care of her, Mom, I hear in unison.

She looks like she could be my puppy—blonde like me! Pookie answers. *Dancer and I will show her around. Don't worry!*

My eyes move over every dog, feeling the presence of each one, remembering how it felt to run my hands over that dog, how his or her ears and coat felt. How lucky I've been. How lucky I am! Even when I'm letting another one go.

I think of the quality of Goodness's life. It's not as though she has anything to finish in her life, some kind of project to complete. She isn't dreading death. She is making it through each day, still spreading dog love. Bill and I make her comfortable in whatever room one of us is in so she can be close to us. I put her to bed at night over and over until she doesn't get up to wander again. We uncover the water bowl regularly. She still eats. We lead her outside to pee and poop. When I walk her down the

Goodness Gracious

alley and back, moving at a snail's pace, she sniffs a little here and there, although without much interest anymore. I take frequent opportunities to sit with her, massage her head, and tell her about my pack, who is waiting to welcome her.

Bill goes inside and tells the woman behind the desk that we'll be waiting for the vet in our car. I've packed Chux Pads, towels, and a plastic bag to handle any mess. No telling what that belly is holding. I spread everything out under Goodness in the back of the Blazer where we sit together. This is the third time in almost five years I've been back here with a dog to do this. I squeeze my eyes shut and struggle for a deep breath. Goodness leans into my arms.

"You ready for an adventure, Pugworts?" I force a cheery voice. She is looking out the window at a woman walking by and makes a little whine, something she has always done when she sees someone outside the car. It's a soft, caring cry Bill and I have interpreted in the past to mean: *That person might need my help!*

The vet comes out and I gesture for him to open the back door. Then, after a kind explanation of the process, he asks if we are ready for the tranquilizing shot, adding that after the first shot, he'll be back in fifteen minutes to complete the procedure.

Bill and I are ready, and Goodness as well. I hold her close as the vet pricks her and leaves. Then I lean toward her wonky ear and begin singing her special song, watching her eyes close and open, reluctant to give in and let them stay closed:

Puggy Pug Pugworts
Puggy Pug Pugworts
She my little puggy dog.
Goodness Gracious, she's so fine!
She is a mighty good doggy!
Goodness Gracious, she's so fine!
She is a mighty good dog! Oh!

Dog Love Stories

I believe she can hear me as she drifts off to a familiar voice and tune. I keep singing her happy dog song despite every fiber in my body dissolving into sadness, like Bill in the front seat.

Later, the vet returns and does the final injection. Goodness becomes lifeless in my arms. I stroke her head, sides, and her silky chest, then close my eyes and place my nose in that little divot below her forehead and above her nose. My favorite spot. It is still warm.

"My sweet girl."

On arriving home, Bill and I carry her body inside. I want Mercy to see and smell Goodness. We lay her on a soft yellow blanket on the rug. The blanket is the same color as her fur. Mercy watches, then steps over and cautiously smells her.

"She's traveled on, Mercy, probably sniffing around her new hood by now, hanging out with Dancer and Pookie and the others. You'll see her someday, Merce, but not too soon, ya hear?"

Mercy circles, sits down, and looks at me like she doesn't understand.

I can't say I understand either. Later there is a piercing emptiness in our house with one of four of its creatures gone. I realize that although I've spent nights away, I've not spent one night in our home without either one or both of these dogs. No pitter-patter of pug paws running to get her suck-bone. How could one little dog's energy make our home feel so alive and full?

Bill and I sit together in the living room. Mercy jumps up on the couch, too roomy with just her and me. When Bill or I start to say something, before any sound escapes our throats, our words fall apart letter by letter into a pile of what's-already-been-said on the floor. Nothing we can say would help. My doubts about putting her to sleep niggle me. Did we do the right thing? Would she have frozen in the snow that night while she was out there pacing? Should I have let her?

Goodness Gracious

We have been keeping Goodness cool in an ice chest overnight after arriving home from the vet yesterday evening. Today we are driving up the mountain to Graceland, despite freezing twenty-five-to-forty-mile-per-hour February winds. Mercy is with us.

Bill tries breaking the frozen soil on top of the cover that's spread over the empty grave. Impossible. Besides grunting and moaning, we work quietly. He gets wood to use as leverage, and we eventually heave the hard block of soil over onto one side of the grave.

While Bill shovels more dirt out of the hole, I go to get Goodness ready. I lift her stiff body out of the ice chest and place her on the tailgate. As I unfold the blanket, I notice how comfortable she looks, her legs in positions they were often in as she slept. I stroke her forehead, then kiss my index finger, and tenderly place it in that groove between her eyes and forehead. "Have you met Pookie and Dancer yet, Pugworts?"

Bill comes over to pet her, then provides a wind shield as I sprinkle sage, rosemary, and dried pink bougainvillea petals over her body. We fold the blanket in a way to lift and carry her to the open hole. Bill bends over and I kneel so we can lower Goodness into her grave. I step down, pull the blanket away from her face, and with utmost tenderness, tuck her suck-bone between her paws. There is something else I want to add, something I thought of last night when I remembered burying my first memoir's manuscript with Amber, who had supported me throughout its creation.

"I have something for you to deliver, Goodness. The almost completed manuscript of *Dog Love Stories*. You've been with me the entire time I've been writing it, giving me joy-breaks. Now, will you please show these stories to my pup pack?"

I take the printed manuscript I tied with a sheer green bow and gently place it on top of her. My chest cramps when I notice how she looks like a baby swaddled in its crib. I reach over and pull the blanket over her precious pug face.

Dog Love Stories

Bill and I return soil to her grave, packing it down and placing rocks around as a coyote deterrent. I've chosen a gravestone for her that I will write on in warmer days, possibly "Loving Presence," because that's what she was in our home and lives.

Bill leaves to walk the Prayer Circle, giving me some time alone. Mercy continues to watch from outside the cemetery's fence. I reach into my pocket and take out the bright orange collar with GOODNESS GRACIOUS and my phone number printed on it and tug it over the top of her headstone, just like I did with Gavroche's almost five years earlier. The wind whips tears off my face.

I pass Bill coming back when I head to the circle. I stop at the entrance, breathe deeply, then step forward. At each direction, I pause, noticing the beauty and abundance of goodness surrounding me—snowy peaks, piñons, junipers, dried grasses bending in the wind, yuccas, a blue sky, ravens, the valley below spreading horizon to horizon. I look up and see Bill gazing at Pooter's grave, his chin tucked.

"Goodness," I utter with a long, tired sigh, then turn to keep walking the Prayer Circle, Mercy at my heels.

Goodness Gracious
LOVING PRESENCE
2013(?)–2023

Epilogue

I once asked a beloved mentor of mine if life ever gets any easier. Not easier, she answered, but we do get better at it. Perhaps I'm getting better at life, although sometimes I wonder—how many more deaths can I go through and keep my heart intact? While all aspects of a death experience can be devastating, with dogs—after the deaths of nine—I believe I can bear one more. I know what's at risk. I know I'll weep. I know I'll grieve. And gradually, I know I will want another dog because, after healing from the last dog's death, I'll realize I am stronger than I thought.

Shortly after this book's final edits were submitted, my husband Bill died after a cancer diagnosis. The deaths of my dogs in no way prepared me for the profound grief of losing the person I've been closest to in this world. While I doubt I could bear this again, I do know that the depth of pain I feel around life and death has been helped by all the dogs I have had and, without a doubt, by the companionship and comfort from the tenth, Mercy, who walks beside me now.

Notes

1. Mark Doty, *Dog Years: A Memoir* (New York: HarperCollins, 2007), 8.
2. Hal Borland, *The Dog Who Came to Stay* (Philadelphia: J. B. Lippincott, 1962), XXX.
3. Doty, *Dog Years*, 12.
4. Anna Quindlen, *Good Dog. Stay.* (New York: Random House, 2007), 66.
5. Suzanne Clothier, *Bones Would Rain from the Sky: Deepening Our Relationships with Dogs* (New York: Warner Books, 2002), 79.
6. Ken Foster, *The Dogs Who Found Me: What I've Learned from Pets Who Were Left Behind* (Guilford, CT: Lyons Press, 2016), 26.

Gratitudes

Writing a book is an endeavor I couldn't navigate without an immense amount of help.

The talented folks at She Writes Press are skilled at shepherding authors, and this author is very grateful for every one of them.

My dear friend, writing companion, and editor Sharon Fabriz walked this entire book's journey with me, through every chapter, and then again as a whole and beyond. Whether we are sitting on the breezy porch at Goliad or in front of a warm fire at Graceland, one constant topic of conversation is our writing, and I am such a stronger writer because of all we share.

My gratitude also goes to Jean Alger, who provided a complete edit of the full book and ongoing professional help I continue to request. I thank Elsa Lantz for her editing as well.

I thank the talented Tom Laetz for accepting the challenge of sketching my dogs from old and new photographs.

My beta readers were extraordinary in their commitment to giving me helpful feedback: Pamela Alexander, Sarah Bainbridge, Talli Delaney, Annie Garretson, Cecilia Green (who went far and beyond being a beta reader), Patti Iles, Carolyn Laetz, Lisa Martin, Patty Petersen, and Lindsey Wiginton.

Other people also provided valuable help and/or feedback along the way: Barrett Briske, Christa Hillhouse, Andy Packard, Becky Reardon, Matt Struck, Marty Webb, and Peggy Weiss.

Dog Love Stories

Of course, this book wouldn't exist were it not for my dog companions. Each dog contributed toward making me a better human. And now, here on this unfathomable journey after Bill's death—and barely a year after Goodness died—I could not make it day to day without Mercy's gentle presence.

My beloved, who parented seven of these dogs with me, consistently championed me as a writer, whether buying me a sit/stand desk or listening to me read each of these stories as I completed them, predictably responding: "That's nice, darlin'." Bill, I'm unsure what life will be from here forward, but I know it will be better because of what I learned from loving you and from all we shared in our long journey together.

About the Author

Photo credit: Matt Struck

Patricia Eagle composed her first dog love story at age ten and published her first book, *Being Mean: A Memoir of Sexual Abuse and Survival*, in her sixties. As a writer, speaker, and memorial and wedding celebrant, Eagle weaves meaning into stories that acknowledge and honor our lives' paths. After the death of her spouse just prior to publication of *Dog Love Stories*, Eagle and their dog Mercy have been left to blaze a new trail—life after deep sorrow. She and Mercy live among the wonders of the San Luis Valley in South-Central Colorado.

Looking for your next great read?

We can help!

Visit www.shewritespress.com/next-read
or scan the QR code below for a list
of our recommended titles.

She Writes Press is an award-winning
independent publishing company founded to
serve women writers everywhere.